Ancient Roman Gardens

LINDA FARRAR

SUTTON PUBLISHING

First published in 1998 by
Sutton Publishing Limited · Phoenix Mill
Thrupp · Stroud · Gloucestershire · GL5 2BU

British Library Cataloguing in Publication Data
A catalogue record for this book is available from the British Library

ISBN 0 7509 1725 3

For my husband Jim

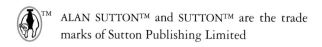 ALAN SUTTON™ and SUTTON™ are the trade marks of Sutton Publishing Limited

Typeset in 10.5/13pt Garamond.
Typesetting and origination by
Sutton Publishing Limited.
Printed in Great Britain by
Butler & Tanner, Frome, Somerset.

Contents

Chapter Five

Chapter Six

Chapter Seven

Chapter Eight

Chapter Nine

Chapter Ten

Colour Plates

Picture Credits

Acknowledgements

There are numerous people whom I would like to thank for their kindness and help in my research. Members of staff and colleagues at Warwick University have been especially kind, and have provided great support, and I would like to give special thanks to Dr Stanley Ireland.

Many thanks are also due to Dr Martin Henig for reading the typescript and for his helpful suggestions. I would also like to thank the following institutions and individuals for providing information and assistance: Professor Barry Cunliffe; Dr Adília Alarcão, Director of the Museum at Conimbriga; Dr Francesco Buranelli of the Vatican Museum; Dr Stefano De Caro, Soprintendente of the Province of Naples and Caserta; Yoko Chikira of the Miho Museum, Japan; B. Conticello, Soprintendente scavi di Pompei, for permission to view gardens not open to the public; Alessandra Corti from Fratelli Alinari; Christian Dewez (from the Villa at La Malagne), who kindly gave an impromptu detailed tour of the villa and its valley setting in the pouring rain, also for giving details of the research programme that is being undertaken; Dr Rosanna Friggeri of the Museo Nazional Romano, Rome; Dr Kathryn Gleason; B. Younes Habib from the Bardo Museum, Tunis; the photographic section of the Deutsches Archaeologisches Institut, Rome; Professor W.F. Jashemski; Vincent Jolivet and Catherine Virlouvet from the French School at Rome, for information on their excavations there; Professor Eugenio La Rocca of the Museo della Civiltà Romana; Professor Philippe Leveau for information on a water basin from Cherchel; Lisa Moffett from Birmingham University, for material on plant remains at Alcester; Eddie Price, excavator of the Villa at Frocester Court; Claire Ryley, Education Officer at Fishbourne Palace, for information regarding flowerpots found on site, and of a survey in progress on the Roman flora of Britain; Dr Stefanie Schips of the Rheinisches Landesmuseum Trier; Dr Christopher Tuplin from Liverpool University, for information on Persian gardens; Professor W.J.H. Willems, excavator of the villa at Voerendaal, for information on the pathway and Jupiter column; Dr Stephen Hill and Dr Dominic Montserrat of Warwick University, also Janet Amos, Maureen Bourne and Marion from Print Services; Margery Dunlevy; Graham Hoddinott; Michael Townsend; the late Hilde Smith, who translated some passages from the German; Gillian Carmichael for producing a collection of drawings commissioned for this work; Eric

Knight and R.L. Dalladay for supplying several photographs; and the John Paul Getty Museum, Los Angeles.

For permission to quote two lengthy extracts from Pliny, reprinted by permission of the publishers and the Loeb Classical Library from *Pliny the Younger: Letters and Panegyricus*, translated by Betty Radice, Cambridge, MA: Harvard University Press, 1969. Also for an extract from *The Odyssey of Homer*, translated by Richard Lattimore, 1975, © R. Lattimore, HarperCollins Publishers Inc.

I would like to express my gratitude to staff at Sutton Publishing for their help in preparing this book.

List of Abbreviations

AJA	American Journal of Archaeology
Ant. J	Antiquaries Journal
ARA	Bulletin of Association for Roman Archaeology
BAR	British Archaeological Reports
BCH	Bulletin de Correspondance Hellénique
CBA	Council for British Archaeology
CIL	Corpus Inscriptionum Latinarum
JHS	Journal of Hellenic Studies
JRA	Journal of Roman Archaeology
JRS	Journal of Roman Studies
L	C. Linnaeus (1707–78)
MEFRA	Mélanges de l'Ecole française de Rome, Antiquité
NSc	Notizie degli scavi di Antichità
PACT	Journal of the European Study Group on Physical, Chemical, Biological and Mathematical Techniques Applied to Archaeology
PBSR	Papers of the British School at Rome
RA	Revue Archéologique
RICA	Researches in Campanian Archaeology
RM	Römische Mitteilungen des Deutschen Archäologischen Instituts
SHA	Scriptores Historiae Augustae

Chronology

Relevant dates concerning Roman gardens

4th century BC to 27 BC

	The Republican Period
55 BC	The construction of Pompey's Portico, the first public park in Rome.
44 BC	Death of Caesar, and the opening of his gardens to the public.
AD 75	Construction of the palace and gardens at Fishbourne in Britain.
AD 79	Eruption of Vesuvius and the ash fall burying Pompeii and Herculaneum.
AD 92	The architect Rabirius completes the building of the Imperial Palace on the Palatine, Rome (for Domitian).
AD 103–7	Date of Pliny the Younger's villas at Tusculum and Laurentum.
AD 118	Work begins on Hadrian's villa at Tivoli.

Notable Emperors of Rome

27 BC-AD14	Augustus
AD 14-37	Tiberius
AD 41-54	Claudius
AD 54-68	Nero
AD 69-79	Vespasian
AD 79-81	Titus
AD 81-96	Domitian
AD 98-117	Trajan
AD 117-38	Hadrian
AD 138-61	Antoninus Pius
AD 161-80	Marcus Aurelius
AD 180-92	Commodus
AD 193-211	Septimus Severus
AD 211-17	Caracalla
AD 218-22	Elagabulus
AD 236-44	Gordian
AD 284-305	Diocletian
AD 306-37	Constantine
AD 360-63	Julian
AD 527-65	Justinian

Ancient authors and notable individuals with an indication of dates of birth/death, if known, or period of floruit

Eighth century BC Homer

Fourth century BC Xenophon (c. 428-359 BC)
Aristotle (384-322 BC)

c. 370–288 BC	Theophrastus
Second century BC	Cato (234-149 BC)
	Hero of Alexandria (c. 150 BC)
Republican Period	Catulus (84-54 BC)
	Cicero (106-43 BC)
	Diodorus Siculus (c. 60-30 BC)
	Horace (65-8 BC)
	Lucullus (c. 114-57 BC)
	Maecenas (died 8 BC)
	Ovid (43 BC-AD 17)
	Pompey 'the Great' (106-48 BC)
	Propertius (c. 50-16 BC)
	Sallust (86-35 BC)
	Strabo (64 BC-AD 25)
	Tibullus (c. 55-19 BC)
	Varro (116-27 BC)
	Virgil (70-19 BC)
	Vitruvius (c. 50-26 BC)
Early Empire First to Second century AD	Arrian (AD 85-90)
	Calpernius Siculus (c. AD 50–60)
	Columella (c. AD 60-65)
	Dioscorides (mid-1st century AD)
	Juvenal (c. AD 110-27)
	Martial (c. AD40-104)
	Petronius (c. AD 65)
	Pliny the Elder (AD 23-79)
	Pliny the Younger (AD 61-113)
	Plutarch (AD 46-120)
	Quintus Curtius Rufus (1st century AD)
	Seneca (c. 4 BC-AD 65)
	Statius (c. AD 45-96)
	Suetonius (c. AD 70-c. AD 122)
	Tacitus (AD 56-c. AD117)
Third century AD	Athenaeus (c. AD 200)
	Cassius Dio (c. AD 150-235)
	Philostratus (c. AD 244)
Fourth century AD	Palladius
Fifth century AD	Macrobius (c. AD 400)
	Sidonius Apollinaris (c. AD 430-80)
Sixth century AD	Cassiodorus (c. AD 490-583)
	Luxorius (early 6th century AD)
	Procopius (c. AD 500-62)

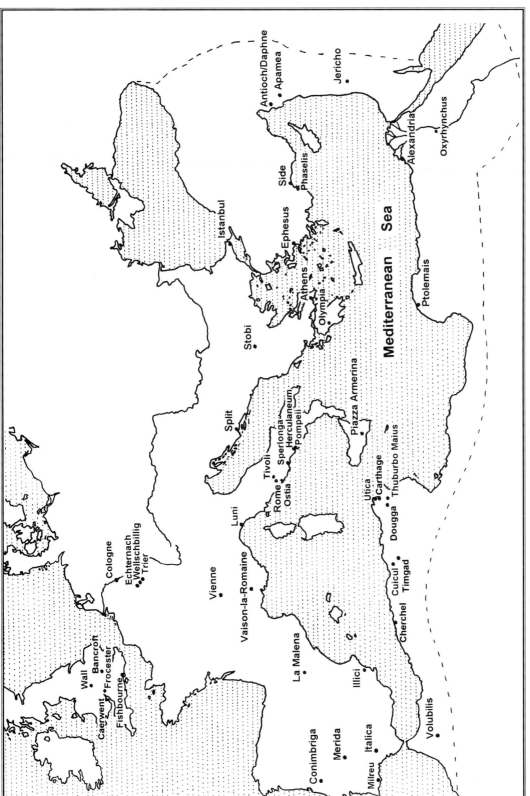

Map of the Roman Empire locating some of the most important sites mentioned in the text.

Introduction

The garden in the Roman period was called a *hortus*. This word, just like its English counterpart, has many shades of meaning for there are and were many different forms of garden. A *hortus* could imply a small or large garden, in town or country, a rustic vegetable garden, market garden or the landscaped gardens of a palatial estate. Often we assume that a Roman garden was intrinsically of a domestic nature, but as we shall see they could also be found in public areas. The word *hortus* (plural *horti*) was also used when referring to gardens or parks open to the public, and it has been found that a number of public buildings were provided with a garden as an amenity for the townspeople. Several inns were furnished with a garden to attract customers and at times gardens were even attached to some of the larger funerary monuments.

The study of these Roman gardens can be likened to a giant jigsaw puzzle; little pieces of information are gathered from far and wide to bring the whole picture together. The appearance of their gardens is drawn from the wealth of wonderful frescos and mosaics of the period and from the remains discovered by archaeologists. Ancient literary sources have been used throughout and evidence shows that the Romans made good use of their gardens, with these areas being enjoyed by all members of the family: in good weather much time would have been spent out in the fresh air. Large gardens were often equipped with a promenade and seats were provided so that people could rest under the shade of a tree to read, write poetry or discuss the state of the Empire. The larger gardens were well landscaped and contained a number of architectural features and sculpture which were used to great effect. There were also small shrines, pools, fountains, exotic trees and flowers. Splendid arbours were created, and trellis-covered walkways provided

Miniature fresco with garden features, Pompeii.

yet more shady promenades and private corners. After a gentle stroll around the garden you could perhaps rest in a garden pavilion put there expressly for that purpose. Alfresco dining was quite popular in the summer months and areas were found to place couches and a table, then friends could be invited to dine under a vine-covered canopy. There they would be protected from the sun but could still enjoy the delights of a life out of doors. The garden around them was full of scent from flowers and aromatic foliage and the setting was enhanced by the pleasant sound of birds singing in the trees. As frescos show, birds were encouraged to come into the garden and would enjoy the many fountains playing throughout.

The Romans were sensitive to beauty and form and the open areas in a garden were also ideal places to show off their culture and wealth to the world. A garden was an admirable setting to display a collection of sculpture, placed not in a haphazard fashion but to a loose plan which could be appreciated from all important reception rooms. Gardens were indispensable for many reasons and perhaps the most fundamental one for their existence was the fact that in an urban setting they provided a source of good light for nearby rooms and a necessary breath of fresh air. The scented flowers and aromatic foliage of plants would give off a subtle perfume that could mask any lingering and unpleasant odours.

Mosaic of Lord Julius showing life on a country estate. From Carthage, now in the Bardo Museum, Tunis.

Small gardens could also enjoy many of the luxury items mentioned above, if reproduced on a reduced scale to suit a more restricted area. However, if space was limited, one could enjoy the illusion of an extensive area by painting a fresco of one on the rear wall of a small courtyard, turning it into a beautiful verdant garden. Some or all of the above mentioned features were the ideal and can be found on many archaeological sites throughout the Roman Empire. This book is a comprehensive study of such gardens, tracing the development from their humble origins to the highly ornamented forms seen during the height of the Roman Empire.

The word *hortus* has left its legacy in our own language, for gardeners participate in or practise horticulture, a term derived from the culture of *horti*. Some Latin names for certain garden items are included in the text in the belief that they are evocative of the period and help to immerse the reader in the life and society of Rome. These words are immediately recognizable and in some cases are more definitive than the roughly equivalent modern word. A glossary for the Latin words used in the text can be found at the back of this book.

SOURCES

Many interesting facts about Roman gardens have come from surviving works of ancient literature. One of our most informative sources is Pliny the Elder, a man of great industry who, among other things, wrote thirty-seven books on natural history. Of these several contain details on trees, flowers and vegetables, which are discussed for their medicinal or culinary properties, and at times Pliny mentions plants used for decorative purposes. His own wide-ranging source material covers the cultivation and distribution of numerous plants with, in some cases, notes on their origins. Pliny also gives details of notable examples of flora and fauna and in the process provides snippets of information on private and public gardens. In his collected letters his nephew Pliny the Younger has also provided two lengthy descriptions of gardens surrounding his country properties that are an extremely important insight in the design of large gardens and, like the letters of Cicero, they shed light on the affluent society in Rome. Some of the garden features they describe are thought to be typical of their kind.

Cicero's correspondence is very important: in his letters we see the evolution of Roman garden art during the Republican Era. Seneca, a stoic philosopher and former tutor to the Emperor Nero, decried the lack of morals in Roman society and he believed that some garden innovations were yet another sign of a general decadence. Some of his complaints reveal the extravagances of that time, which appear to have included this indulgence in garden art. References are also found in the numerous works of Ovid, who was exiled after the publication of his *Ars*

Amatoria, a racy work that included places where you could expect to meet the opposite sex (such as public gardens). During exile Ovid wrote of his misery and his longing to return home, his letters including brief descriptions of some of his favourite haunts, in the course of which he sheds light on some of the famous gardens of Rome. Martial is notable for his *Epigrams*, observations full of sharp and sometimes sarcastic wit, and he provides further snippets of information on gardens. Horace was a master of satire and is quite candid about some of the new fashions in Rome. The satirical books written by Petronius and Juvenal are immensely revealing, if a little cruel, and give a humorous insight into Roman life. Other horticultural references can be found in the poetical works of Statius and Luxorius, but as there are quite a number of sources in ancient literature those consulted are included with a date list at the beginning of this book. The majority of ancient authors were writing during the Late Republican period and the Early Empire, and were therefore witnesses to the evolution and flowering of the 'Roman' garden. Often just brief comments are found – and not all are flattering. In general they comment on urban parks in Rome or large estates rather than the small private garden of a town house. This omission is understandable though, for the small and ordinary were less remarkable, and in overlooking them they reflect attitudes of their circle in society, and especially that of their patrons.

We are also fortunate that the works of four major agriculturalists have survived almost complete, the earliest of whom is Cato (second century BC), then Varro (*c.* 36 BC), Columella (*c.* AD 60) and Palladius (fourth century AD). They wrote manuals primarily on farm management and husbandry but sections are included on the culture of the *hortus* as part of the farm or villa estate. Their works contain a great deal of practical advice and are very informative on the skills necessary to maintain such gardens. These agriculturalists acknowledge their debt to earlier writers such as the Carthaginian Mago, whose works were considered so useful that all of his twenty-eight books were translated from Punic into Latin; unfortunately they have not survived. They also cite Greek authors but these wrote on individual aspects of agriculture rather than a combined manual, which was the Latin aim. All of these may, however, have been influential in the development of the science of agriculture and horticulture in Rome.

Cato 'the Censor', as he was known in Rome, fought to promote the ancient *mores* of Rome that had originated in a simple agricultural society. He wrote a number of books on the early history of Rome and neighbouring cities but his manual *De Agri Cultura* is of especial note here. Being a landowner himself he decided to impart his experience for the benefit of his son and the state. His work is brief and succinct but nevertheless worthwhile, for he is quite informative on early practices. Varro was celebrated as a man of great learning and was a prodigious writer on many subjects. Out of his large output only one volume survives in its entirety, the *Rerum Rusticarum*, a title meaning 'on rustic matters'. This manual, written in his eightieth year, contains less horticulture than Cato's but gives advice on profit-making occupations, such as bee-keeping, and the management of fish stocks, aviaries and game preserves. Varro provides a number of examples where these features were incorporated into large domains and shows how they could be turned into decorative elements in a garden. Columella, a farmer from Gades (Cadiz) in Spain, was concerned about the growing neglect of farming practices and was prompted to write a thorough manual on all aspects of agriculture and horticulture. His important work was cited by many contemporary and later writers, such as Pliny the Elder, and was used extensively by Palladius in the fourth century.

In the first century AD Dioscorides wrote a herbal, primarily concerned with medicinal plants, but his description and illustration of the numerous plants growing during the Roman period are a very good source for exploring the ancient flora of the Mediterranean area. Not all of these were used in gardens, however, for many plants Dioscorides describes were gathered from the wild, and the search for garden plants needs to encompass evidence from frescos and works such as those of Pliny the Elder, who at times actually states if they were included in a *hortus*. Some of the Mediterranean plants may be unfamiliar, for several are too delicate to grow well in northerly latitudes, and it is helpful to consult modern reference works devoted to Mediterranean flora. Many tend to produce separate volumes for wild flowers, shrubs and trees but one of the most useful is *Mediterranean Wild Flowers* by Blamey & Grey-Wilson which combines the two. Baumann's *Greek Wild Flowers*, although confined to one region, includes many interesting examples of ancient plant lore, and many of the species mentioned could also be found in Italy and other Mediterranean countries within the Roman Empire.

Unlike other aspects of ancient history and archaeology, there are relatively few modern authors writing on the subject of Roman gardens. Numerous works have been used to explore certain aspects of gardens, such as sculpture or the water supply, but there are few reference books devoted solely to this genre. The most prominent authors in this field are Pierre Grimal and Wilhelmina F. Jashemski. *Les Jardins Romaines* by Grimal was first published in 1943 and concerns the period up to AD 138, aiming to illustrate Roman gardens at the peak of their perfection. Material from the area of Pompeii was used but the larger proportion of evidence was sought from the gardens of the city of Rome itself. Grimal includes a lengthy philosophical survey of Ancient Roman literary attitudes to gardens, and gives many instances where Rome's love of nature relates to the garden. *The Gardens of Pompeii, Herculaneum and the Villas destroyed by Vesuvius*, by Wilhelmina F. Jashemski (1979) contains a significant amount of information on various aspects of Roman gardens, and is an important source of comparable data. Her second volume (printed in 1993), being an appendix of the first, is a source book for all the details of gardens excavated under the area covered by Vesuvius. She pioneered the use of scientific archaeology in gardens at Pompeii and carried out a detailed study of a number of them. This book also includes illustrations of a large number of Pompeian frescos depicting scenes from a Roman garden.

Ancient illustrations in the medium of fresco and mosaic from Pompeii and elsewhere are a rich source of information on Roman gardens. Rustic scenes and landscapes were a popular genre and in the latter category there are several depicting plants of the period in a setting resembling a form of garden. These paintings are often of a large size and may include ornamental items such as garden sculpture. Similar garden furnishings are also documented archaeologically and the painted versions give an impression of a real garden. Smaller frescos or miniature landscape scenes are sometimes painted in a more impressionistic manner but their details can reveal further elements used in garden landscape design; in many cases we see parterres, terracing or trellis-work enclosures arranged to form one or more 'garden rooms'. The frescos are brought to life by the inclusion of all manner of birds and they illustrate the Romans' intrinsic love of nature. In some cases the naturalistic rendition of this apparently abundant flora and fauna has allowed botanists to identify the species shown. For all of these reasons the frescos are illustrative of the actual appearance of elements in a Roman garden.

Unfortunately frescos are fragile and it needs to be borne in mind that most are at least 1,900 years old. Today, many surviving examples are quite faded from their constant exposure to sunlight and winter rains, for not all garden scenes have been protected from the elements since excavation. Over the years several have just disappeared or the painted plaster has fallen away from the wall; this genre was until recently not considered as fine art and so few were recorded. The surviving frescos that do illustrate a garden scene are therefore often found to have areas where paint is missing, having simply flaked away. One interesting result of this sad destruction is that we can see there were a number of hands at work in these paintings. The birds, for instance, were painted on top of the foliage and evidence points to the fact that there must have been specialist painters for these very detailed ornithological studies. Likewise some of the artefacts discovered in actual Roman gardens have suffered over the years. Many have eroded features and pieces missing, for they were, after all, left out in all weathers during the Roman period, have suffered from years of burial, and sometimes have been subjected to a further number of years in an open museum courtyard.

Many of the garden areas on archaeological sites are left unattended and are now covered by grass or weeds and it is sometimes difficult to visualize their former appearance. In these cases we need to resort to the wide range of sources available. Many of the features described in ancient literature have their existence proven by archaeology, and archaeological investigations have in fact furthered our knowledge on numerous aspects of gardens from this period. Often excavations have provided a great deal of new evidence not normally touched upon by ancient sources; for example, out of the wide range of ornamental pools and fountains that can be found on many archaeological sites only one form is mentioned in literature and that is the *euripus*.

For many years, however, the archaeology of ancient gardens has been overlooked. There had been a natural tendency for excavators to concentrate on the more spectacular public buildings rather than on housing, and gardens have often been regarded as an open space which would not justify the cost and time needed for detailed examination. As a consequence these areas appear simply as a blank space on site plans. Large-scale excavations are expensive and garden features can vary from one part of a garden to another; they may also leave little trace behind, therefore excavations need to be meticulous to produce satisfactory results.

Archaeological evidence for gardens is of course complicated by the passage of time. Where a site was in use over a long period the garden area, like the house itself, could be redesigned a number of times and this would have the effect of complicating its later interpretation. Also, when a house or villa falls into decay, the garden would soon become overgrown, weeds and seedlings of wild trees would colonize the space and confuse any remaining traces. Later if the site reverted to agriculture deep ploughing could then inflict further damage, as at Frocester Court in Britain where half of the garden details were lost in this way. Therefore on many sites preservation is slight, ephemeral and a matter of chance survival. At Pompeii, however, the catastrophic eruption of Vesuvius that engulfed the city with a thick layer of ash and lapilli sealed the surface of AD 79. This has protected traces of cultivation and many of the gardens' furnishings. Although a catastrophe for the residents, it has at least been fortunate for archaeologists since a date can now be allocated for the style of garden art found in that city. Because of the large number of garden areas here (there are approximately 450),[1] they provide a major source of comparative material, whereas elsewhere garden evidence is less obvious and more fragmentary.

Many of the best known Roman archaeological sites were excavated a long time ago, when standards of archaeology were not so stringent as they are today, and the limited nature of some of the records kept at that time has hampered this study. When the soil is removed from site vital information is lost for ever. Where a garden area was examined all that now remains are the structural elements, which would possibly include the position of shrines, altars, *nymphaea*, pools, drains and sometimes even pathways. However, with the increasing use of scientific methods of archaeology, more details can be uncovered than were even looked for in the past. Recording techniques have greatly improved in the last fifty years and modern excavations often include an environmental archaeologist, who is able to examine the plant and animal materials and investigates questions such as land use and its effect on the economy of the area. When such methods are applied to the garden, its flora and fauna can sometimes be revealed. The more specific and relatively new science of garden archaeology has primarily been used in Britain to uncover lost parterres and garden features of sixteenth to nineteenth century AD country houses but it can also be applied to the Roman period. This new field is interdisciplinary, for it includes a study of paleobotany, palynology, geology, Classical art and architecture, garden design, ancient literature, ancient religious practices, the Roman diet, culinary and ornamental plants grown, and those for medicinal purposes, and aspects of Roman domestic life and society. The information that can be accumulated is therefore extremely diverse.

In spite of the difficulties in tracing archaeological garden remains, more and more evidence is becoming available today, so that we are able to reconstruct the atmosphere of these places which were such an attractive and important feature of Ancient Rome.

CHAPTER ONE

Historical Background

N ature has been respected and worshipped from the earliest times, and numerous special places were believed to be inhabited by spirits or guarded by a superhuman figure or demi-god. In the Babylonian story of Gilgamesh, already an ancient legend when it was recorded on cuneiform clay tablets in the second millennium BC, we hear of a sacred wood where there was a 'cedar mount, the dwelling of gods, the sanctuary of the Irini'. The Greek gods dwelt specifically on Mount Olympus but sacred places could also be found in dark mysterious caves and grottos, natural springs and rivers, groves of trees, or a single interestingly shaped or contorted tree. In many parts of the world such places became associated with a deity of one kind or another, often linked exclusively to that location. Offerings could be made to appease the spirits who dwelt there, particularly if there was any intention to carry out some work that might disturb them.

We all know of the creation myth set in the Garden of Eden, which has an apple tree at its centre, and a serpent that is wise and perhaps also evil. This creature is portrayed as living in the tree, so the setting has similarities with other groves that were inhabited by a deity. However, in this case the area is a cultivated garden, possibly an orchard of fruit trees rather than a natural wood. Other cultures look back to a mystic garden or tree of life, such as Yygdrasil of the Norse legends, although some may have a common origin. The earliest known myths originate in the East, partly because the advanced cultures in this part of the world used a form of writing that has preserved some of their beliefs and ideals. They show that the art of gardening does in fact go back to time immemorial, and this is where we need to go to look for the germ of inspiration that led to the flowering of Roman gardens.

GARDENS IN ANCIENT EGYPT

Egypt is a land that receives almost no rain but water from the Nile was used to irrigate a narrow strip of cultivable soil on either side of the great river. The important annual flooding of the valley brought rich silt to fertilize the soil. In such conditions water was all important and was

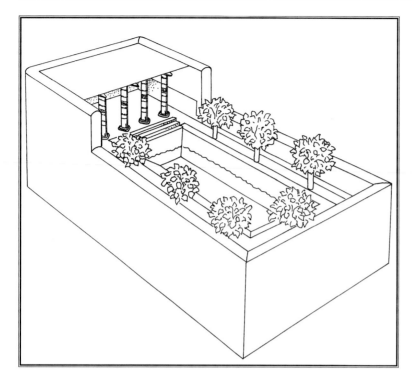

Ancient Egyptian funerary model of a house and garden. A portico opens on to a small walled garden in which there are seven trees around a rectangular fish pond (New York, Metropolitan Museum).

carefully channelled to any garden area. The possession of a garden of pleasure appears to have been confined to the wealthy and was in the main found either in a palace or temple complex. In the temples priests tended plants and experimented with the art of horticulture, as did later Christian monks in their monastery gardens. There were few trees native to Egypt but over the centuries others were brought to temple and palace gardens to acclimatize. One such expedition was reputedly sent to acquire incense trees from the land of Punt (thought to be Yemen). These valuable trees were planted to form a grove around the elaborate temple tomb of Queen Hatshepsut. In front of a temple associated with Mentuhotep II, sycamore and tamarisk trees were placed into rows of large ready prepared planting holes. Archaeologists have uncovered a number of these pits and they show that each tree root had been provided with a good quantity of fertile soil to encourage growth in otherwise poor ground; they also reveal that there had been quite an extensive grove.[1]

Many of the Ancient Egyptian tomb paintings provide a great deal of evidence on everyday life in Egypt. They depict lifelike objects and scenes meant to re-create the present, enabling the deceased to live a similar and full life after death. One of the scenes painted on tomb walls shows an Ancient Egyptian garden. On occasion they include a view of the owner sitting inside his house with attendants to serve him and his family, and through an open door he views a garden. Often a few gardeners are shown so that throughout eternity there will be staff to draw water to irrigate and tend plants in the owner's garden. There is usually a centrally placed pond, often painted in such a way as to emphasize that it is well stocked with fish. Trees are more commonly shown surrounding the pool but lines of low-growing plants in full flower are also represented at times. It appears that plants tended to be planted in groups, by species rather than being mixed together. Offerings were also placed in tombs and some of these were in the form of models of everyday objects, one from the Metropolitan Museum, New York, is a model of a house which shows a delightful example of a small domestic Egyptian garden. The house is only represented by a colonnade but this opens on to a walled area, in the middle of which is a deep rectangular fish pond surrounded by seven large trees in full leaf. These items are very evocative of life in Ancient Egypt.

The rich nature of the irrigated land in Egypt enabled many species to flourish and with care the Nile valley was able to produce almost any crop of fruit or flower. Egyptian gardeners continued through the ages to impart their knowledge to later generations and they perhaps influenced other cultures, such as the Assyrians and possibly at a later date the Greeks, who established a trading colony at Naucratis in the Delta.

ANCIENT MESOPOTAMIA

In Ancient Mesopotamia, the cradle of civilization, the two large rivers in that region, the Euphrates and Tigris, were from an early date used to irrigate the land and to encourage crops to grow in areas with an otherwise hostile, hot, dry climate. The earliest reference to gardening practices came from this region, from the ancient city of Sumer. Fragments of a poem written in a cuneiform script suggested the planting of shade-giving trees so that plants could grow below their canopy and be partly protected from wind damage and the fierce rays of the sun.[2] Wells are also mentioned in this text but otherwise gardens, whether vegetable plots or otherwise, would have been placed close to a river from which water could be drawn. Unfortunately no depictions survive to indicate their possible appearance. However, the war-like Assyrians, who later conquered this large region, left for posterity a number of stone carved reliefs, some of which include, in the background, a collection of trees in an irrigated area. This landscaping detail is perhaps suggestive of a large park rather than a domestic garden. The trees are somewhat stylized but appear either with branches pointing upwards like a lance blade, and may be coniferous, or others are a fan shape suggestive of fruit-bearing varieties. Sometimes the stone reliefs show an Assyrian god in the act of fertilizing the flowers of fruit trees so there was evidently a respect for arboriculture. Writing preserved on cuneiform tablets reveals that the ruling nobility had an interest in gardens. Trees were in fact so highly praised that they were sometimes listed as plunder after battles with rival powers. These were then replanted in palace gardens. Records show that Sennacherib had 'brought plants from the land of the Hittites' (modern

Turkey) to create gardens 'in the upper and the lower town'.[3] Turkey is today a source for a great number of wild plants, many now to be found in our gardens. Tiglath Pilesar I (*c.* 1100 BC) records that 'Cedars and Box, Alkanu-wood have I carried off from the lands I conquered, trees that none of my forefathers have possessed'. Also a long list of plants, dating from the time of Ashurbanipal (*c.* 876 BC), suggests a great interest in botanical specimens, of both unusual fruiting trees and scented plants: 'From lands I travelled and hills I traversed the trees and seeds I noticed and collected.'[4]

During the later civilization of Babylon, King Nebuchadnezzar (604-562 BC) built the fabulous spectacle of the Hanging Gardens of Babylon. These gardens were such a beautiful sight that they were recognized in antiquity as a great feat of construction, especially in an otherwise flat landscape. Their fame grew over the centuries and they were justifiably included in a list commemorating the Seven Wonders of the World. Only their memory survives today but they are thought to have resembled the tall stepped ziggurats found throughout the territory of Ancient Mesopotamia. These were mainly constructed to raise a temple as close to the sky as possible, to find and make a high place for their god. A number of terraces, decreasing in size as the structure rose, were made to form a man-made mountain. The Greek geographer Strabo, in all probability using an earlier source, states that 'the uppermost floor had step-like entrances close to which lay screw-pumps, by means of which people employed for the job continually lifted water from the Euphrates up to the garden'.[5] This implies that the terraces did indeed contain earth-retaining modules and a large number of irrigation and drainage channels to keep the plants well watered. A later description of the gardens survives in the works of Diodorus Siculus, he mentions that:

> since the approach to the garden sloped like a hillside and the several parts of the structure rose from one another tier on tier, the appearance of the whole resembled that of a theatre. When the ascending terraces had been built, there had been constructed beneath them galleries which carried the entire weight of the planted garden and rose little by little one above the other.[6]

Such feats of engineering were admired by the Romans and some of their gardens were also grown on terraces, although not in the form of a mountain. It is possible that such gardens may have provided a fanciful allusion to the fabled garden at Babylon.

ANCIENT GREECE

Little is known of garden areas in Greece during the Bronze Age (Minoan and Mycenaean cultures) but engraved seal stones of that period indicate the existence of a sacred tree, usually depicted next to or within a shrine.

Floral motifs were widely used, especially the crocus and lily, and ancient frescos illustrate these flowers in what appears to be a landscape rather than a garden. However, one fragmentary fresco shows red martagon lilies in a tall banded terracotta vessel. These could be interpreted as either picked flowers for indoor decoration, or that they had been planted. A few flower pots have been discovered at Knossos, but there is still insufficient evidence to suggest the cultivation of gardens.

The ancient epics of Homer tell of deeds long ago but also provide pieces of information about gardens in Ancient Greece. Some sections look back to the relatively prosperous Bronze Age of Mycenaean culture, but the type of garden described in the course of these long narratives is more representative of the later period of the Greek Dark Ages, when these oral poems were brought together and finally written down. The gardens, however, appear to be of a rustic nature. We learn that they were walled and the species mentioned consisted mainly of fruit-bearing trees. In the *Odyssey* Laertes, the father of Odysseus, is found in his orchard digging around a plant under a pear tree. Odysseus speaks to him and in doing so reveals the plants that could be found in such a place, 'there is never a plant, neither fig tree nor yet grapevine nor olive nor pear tree nor leek bed uncared for in your garden'.[7] The longer description of the garden of Alkinoös, the king of the mythical Phaiakians, became famous in antiquity as the ideal; this was the proverbial garden that was fertile and well watered, was abundantly fruitful and where you could guarantee a never-ending supply of produce. This, however, was still essentially a rustic orchard garden, and no flowers as such are mentioned.

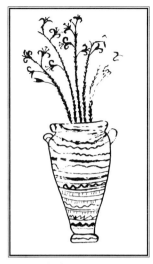

Detail of a fragmentary Minoan fresco depicting red martagon lilies in a tall vase, Thera.

On the outside of the courtyard and next to the doors is his orchard, a great one, four land measures, with a fence driven all around it, and there is the place where his fruit trees are grown tall and flourishing, pear trees and pomegranate trees and apple trees with their shining fruit, and the sweet fig trees and the flourishing olive. Never is the fruit spoiled on these, never does it give out, neither in winter time nor summer, but always the West Wind blowing on the fruits brings some to ripeness while he starts others. Pear matures on pear in that place, apple on apple, grape cluster on grape cluster, fig upon fig. There also he has a vineyard planted that gives abundant produce, some of it a warm area on level ground where the grapes are left to dry in the sun, but elsewhere they are gathering others and trampling out yet others, and in front of these are unripe grapes that have cast off their bloom while others are darkening. And there at the bottom strip of the field are growing orderly rows of greens, all kinds, and these are lush through the seasons; and there two springs distribute water, one through all the garden space, and one on the other side jets out by the courtyard door, and the lofty house, where townspeople come for their water. Such are the glorious gifts of the gods at the house of Alkinoös.[8]

As can be seen, this productive garden is more reminiscent of those associated with a farm or smallholding and is far removed from the decorative forms found in palaces further to the east, or those to be found in Egypt.

There may have been garden areas in the country in the Archaic and later Classical Greek periods but there is little archaeological or literary evidence to support this. The Greeks seem to have had a love of flowers and the rose is mentioned; it was also adopted as the symbol of Rhodes, but at that time flowers were mostly those picked from the wild. References tend to show an agricultural society with plantations of olive trees and vineyards, and it is possible that a beautiful fruitful vineyard with its Dionysiac or Bacchic connotations may have been seen as the ideal form of garden.

The archaeological remains of Archaic and Classical Greece are usually found on city sites, typically an acropolis that could readily be fortified and defended. It can easily be assumed that all Greeks lived in a citadel of this type and while some may have been traders in the cities most made a living from agriculture and would have cultivated nearby fields and market gardens situated outside the city walls. A tradition had become established where citizen and slave would go out to tend the fields by day and return at night, or when alerted to danger. However, there was also a large population who lived on the land in the countryside who, if they were citizens, would journey to their city for civic or social purposes. Many would have resorted to the city for security during their frequent wars. The cities were largely built on rocky heights with little soil and the densely packed housing left little space for gardens within the city. The water supply was limited to springs, communal wells and cisterns, leaving only a small amount to spare for plants that could not grow on rocky ground without moisture.

Excavations show that there do not appear to be gardens in Greek town houses, even in later housing built on lower ground. The entrance of a Greek home opened directly on to an open court that was either paved or of beaten earth[9] and as a rule the rooms were irregularly placed around the yard. Even the planned towns such as at Olynthos or Priene, built on a grid system devised by Hippodamus (a famous town planner), were not provided with house gardens. Again this was partly because of lack of space; even here urban housing was built to a high density. With no direct water supply the townspeople still relied on water from cisterns, wells and fountain houses. At least one law from Pergamon, but this may have applied elsewhere, specifically forbade the planting of trees close to walls.[10] There was always a threat of undermining and if house walls were of mudbrick they could easily be damaged by roots. Interestingly a law recorded by Aristotle[11] shows that provision was made for all household refuse to be carried out of the city by civic dung collectors and used as manure on extramural market gardens. Again no mention is given to any gardens within the town.

The democratic nature of the Greeks in all probability contributed to the fact that there was no garden in their houses. Greek life was lived in public, at least where men were concerned, for they needed to be involved in politics and other public activities, and so there was a tendency to favour buildings for the good of the *demos*, the community as a whole, rather than for the individual. The movements of women were largely restricted to the house and when male visitors came they would be entertained in the *andron*, the men's dining room, while the womenfolk would keep to their own quarters. In general Greek houses were smaller than their Roman counterparts and the courtyards were really used as work areas, so the part of the house that was more often decorated tended to be the *andron* rather than the yard. It does appear, however, that plants in pots may have been grown in courtyards, four have been found in different houses at Olynthos,[12] but there is little evidence to suggest whether these were used for pot herbs or flowers. Ancient Greek literature does mention the practice in connection with the rituals of the cult of Adonis, which was mainly followed by women. This is illustrated in a Greek red-figure vase painting, now in the Karlsruhe museum. In this cult quick-growing seeds were sown in old pots or broken amphorae and then the pots were lifted on to roofs, after which the plants were left to die in memory of the death of Adonis. One of the versions of this vegetation myth relates how Venus had fallen in love with Adonis and after he was mortally wounded by a wild boar her tears fell to the earth and turned into the anemone flower. He was later restored to life but only for six months of the year. Therefore the celebrations of his cult involved a day of lamentation following his death and then the planting of the flowers which, like his rebirth, would last but a short time. The Karlsruhe vase shows Venus climbing halfway up a ladder while her son Cupid passes to her the 'Adonis gardens' that are destined to be left on the roof. Another painted Greek vase depicts twigs in a tall vase, but whether these were picked to bring into the house or were grown in the pot it is difficult to say without further evidence. There are some references to branches of sweet-smelling foliage or blossoms that were gathered to scent the room for a bride at a wedding, and conversely to counter the odours at funerals, but again these may have been gathered outside the city.

Adonis gardens. Cupid offers a bowl of seedlings to his mother Venus who will place the 'gardens' on the house roof (detail from the Karlsruhe Greek vase painting).

However, within the *polis* (town), public areas were sometimes provided with shade trees, such as the planes in the Agora at Athens planted by Cimon in the fifth century BC. In this case water may have been available from the overflow of nearby fountain houses. There are several references to plantations or groves around shrines, and excavations in an area just above the Agora, around the temple of Hephaistos, have revealed evidence that would support this. Here two rows of holes had been excavated into the hard rock around its perimeter in a design that was symmetrically aligned with the columns of the temple. The pits were then filled with soil sufficient to support bushes; these have been replanted today with myrtle and pomegranate and they are effective in enhancing the scene.[13] These small trees and bushes are perhaps ideal here, for they will never grow too large and obscure the temple from view. Other sacred groves were usually located near a spring or stream and were therefore often located in a valley outside the town.

Pomegranate tree, mosaic detail, from Umm Al-Rasas, Jordan.

Cimon is also given credit for bringing water to an area just outside the city of Athens for a plantation of trees that became a celebrated public park, the Academy. The walks under the canopy of trees were frequented by philosophers such as Plato and his followers. From ancient Greek plays we learn that some of the philosophers would engage in discussions with the male citizens and athletes who came here regularly to train – they were obliged to keep fit in readiness for war. In these green spaces, however, no mention is made of plant beds or ornamental flowers or shrubs but there may have been an altar and perhaps one or two statues, which would suggest that the area somehow still retained the aspect of a sacred grove. Such promenades situated under trees were the lungs of these ancient cities and were clearly appreciated by the citizen and visitor alike.

The unsettled nature of Greece may also have contributed to the focusing of attention on unusual natural sites in the landscape that could be venerated by all parties. Natural caves with springs were often thought to be the home of a nymph or other deity and these sacred sites were adorned with much statuary and flowers. Groves surrounding sanctuaries in the countryside were universally protected from the woodsman with a penalty of death, and these areas of beauty greatly impressed later visitors, such as Pausanias on his 'grand tour' (*c.* AD 160).

HELLENISTIC GARDENS

It appears that ornamental gardens (if they existed in Greece) were the result of influences from the East. The earliest occurrence was possibly when Xenophon returned from battles in the heartland of Persia in the fourth century BC, after which he described some of the features he saw. Through the works of Theophrastus and his pupils we learn of people making a study of a wide range of plants later in the same century. In his *Enquiry into Plants* Theophrastus mentions several garden plant species, the majority are vegetables or herbs but he does list a few cultivated flowers, which he says 'are not numerous' and consist almost entirely of plants to make crowns and garlands. These were: 'rose, gilliflower, carnation, sweet marjoram, martagon lily, thyme, bergamot, calamint and southernwood.'[14] Theophrastus himself was known to have a garden but its whereabouts in or out of town is not certain. We are informed, however, that Epicurus (*c.* 250 BC) was the first person to introduce a house garden in a Greek city,[15] but unfortunately its form is not mentioned either.

After the conquests of Alexander the Great the ensuing Hellenistic period saw many changes. We hear how the army was greatly impressed by the wealth and beauty of the land, and the sight of Persian paradise gardens and game parks had a great impact on Alexander and his Macedonian colleagues. After Alexander's death the conquered lands were divided into several large kingdoms ruled by his closest friends and, like Alexander, these Hellenistic rulers and their followers adopted many of the trappings of the East. A form of the Persian garden is believed to have been re-created in Greek lands by the ruling class and possibly by a number of wealthy landowners as well. At Pergamon, Aigai, Pella and Demetrias the royal abodes are thought to have reflected the Persian pillared halls and incorporated a large open area surrounded by the colonnades of various wings of the palace. Unfortunately these gardens have not been studied in detail and therefore we lack knowledge of any internal features.

Urban housing of the same period shows that a veranda or porticos were placed around courts but as before these were still paved in some way, rather than being transformed into a garden. Excavations at Glanum in Gaul have shown this to be the case in an early dwelling dating back to the Hellenistic phase of the town. Only part of the house survives but sufficient to show that it had been provided with a small peristyle and the centre had been paved with medium-sized slabs of limestone.

PERSIAN GARDENS OR *PARADEISOS*

The Persians took over the legacy of plant collection and gardening from the Assyrian and Babylonian cultures before them but almost all the evidence for these important gardens comes from ancient literary sources. There appears to have been two distinct forms of *paradeisos*: a reserve containing wild animals to hunt and a garden for produce or ornamental species of plants. These would have been walled gardens and they are known to have varied greatly in size. The name was used variously to imply an orchard or a vegetable-growing area and yet they could also include flowering and fruiting trees together with a variety of botanical specimens. These were undeniably beautiful places, so much so that the Hellenes emulated the idea and continued to use their Persian name *paradeisos*, which has come down to us as a paradise. Xenophon recalls the 'beauty of the trees';[16] he also mentions how they were well spaced in straight rows and notes that fruiting and non-fruiting trees were planted separately. He was also impressed by 'the multitude of sweet scents that clung round them as they walked'. Plutarch adds that these places were supplied with water and could be furnished with some

A *Paradeisios* garden, in this case a hunting park. An example of the type visualized by the Romans in frescos.

buildings or pavilions so that you would be able to rest and be entertained surrounded by lush vegetation and no doubt bird song.[17]

Little has been discovered archaeologically but at Pasargadae (in Iran) Stronach has revealed the orderly plan of the royal park or *paradeisos* of Cyrus, constructed some time after 546 BC. This shows a well laid out enclosure with rows of trees and columned pavilions opening on to a symmetrically planned irrigated garden at its heart. The Persian garden appears to have been enclosed by bands of trees and ultimately the boundary wall. The palace was set inside this forested garden landscape.

THE ETRUSCANS

The Etruscans at one time ruled a large area of northern and central Italy and had quite an advanced culture. Unfortunately there are few written records and therefore most of the evidence for their life and society has been gleaned from their richly decorated tombs. Their artefacts and tomb frescos reveal a community that took great pleasure in life. The Etruscans were to some extent influenced by their Greek trading partners and like them they appear to have preferred to live in fortified sites on well-defended hilltops. As yet no garden areas have been identified.

Plants are shown in their frescos but are subsidiary to the main design, for they are mainly used to separate different human figures and do not really represent a garden. One exception is in the tomb of the Bulls, which depicts a scene from Greek myth, the slaying of the young Trojan prince by Achilles. Several trees are included in this panel and the one below; as this myth was originally set in a grove with a spring, however, it is probable that we are viewing a representation of a wooded landscape rather than a garden. There was apparently an Etruscan agronomist in the second century BC named Saserna whose works survive only in references made by later writers. It is not known if he included any information on horticulture.

At one time Early Rome had an Etruscan ruler, and over the years of living in close proximity to Etruria there were inevitably cultural exchanges. The Etruscans and the Romans would have both influenced each other but by the time we find gardens being developed the

Etruscans had effectively been absorbed into Rome, and perhaps had little influence on the evolution of the Roman garden.

As the Roman sphere of influence grew it came into contact with the Etruscans, the Samnites (another group of people in Italy) and the Greek colonists of southern Italy and Sicily, and later, after the expansion of their Empire in the East, they were brought into contact with many other new ideas. The Romans were to some extent influenced by the rich way of life enjoyed by the fabulously wealthy Hellenistic rulers of the East (the successors of Alexander), and some of their habits filtered down into Roman society.

CHAPTER TWO

Roman Housing and the Growth of the Garden

From the earliest of times a garden was considered an important part of a Roman family home, although it was originally more of a vegetable garden than a decorative one. During the time of the Roman Republic, before this developed into the Empire under Augustus, most of the population was agrarian, living on farms or smallholdings. The garden could be made in an enclosed area to prevent entry by livestock, and this enclosure would be set apart from the open fields devoted to agriculture and could be reserved for producing salads and vegetables for the family table. This plot would play an important role in the effort towards the goal of self-sufficiency. In this 'garden' Columella and others show that a distinction is made between the name given to beds for plants within the garden, which are referred to by the Latin word *area*, and the word *ager*, which is used for the cultivated fields on a farm, hence *agri*-culture. The potager or vegetable garden of old was enveloped in tradition and ancient lore because it was so central to the needs of the family; so much so that Pliny refers to 'a certain sense of sanctity attached to a garden'.[1] For almost every task performed there was a relevant spirit or deity that needed to be invoked and placated, for the fear of a failed harvest was ever present.

The garden was generally placed next to the farmhouse so that the womenfolk could conveniently work there between dealing with chores inside the house. Pliny[2] shows that the *matrona*, the mistress of the house, had the responsibility for provisioning the household with produce from the *hortus*. In Britain, at the Frocester Court villa site, women's hairpins found in garden areas support the view that women worked there.[3] On the other hand agriculture was usually practised by the stronger male population, although hoeing was sometimes carried out by women, and Seneca refers to women who brought their children out with them while working. An example of this is seen in a mosaic

Drawing of a rustic mosaic from Zliten, Libya, showing women working in a *hortus*. Young children play under the shade of a large tree growing in the ruins of a venerable shrine. In the middle ground their mothers keep a watchful eye as they work. The fifth woman, leaning heavily on a stick, could be the *matrona* of the farm/villa which appears in the top left. The badly damaged upper section is occupied by grazing animals and trees.

from Zliten in Libya,[4] where there are five women, three of whom are shown in action, apparently hoeing – a fourth straightens her back for a moment – while another woman standing upright might be their supervisor or mistress. Two babies are placed below, in the shade of a small shrine overhung by a large tree, while in the background you can see the proximity of the farmhouse or villa to the area where the women are working. On large farms, however, there may also have been a number of servants or slaves of either sex working in field or garden. The mixed nature of the work staff is illustrated throughout this book with a number of vignettes based on small details found in Roman mosaics showing what might be either agricultural or horticultural scenes.

One of the earliest references to gardens is found in the ancient laws of Early Rome, the Twelve Tables, which date to the fifth century BC. Of these Table VII concerned land rights and the ancient *heredium*, the inheritable portion of the property. The term appears to have been used when referring to the vegetable garden and it was much later that the word *hortus* came into use. The appellation *hortus* then applied to an enclosure but paradoxically it could also mean the farm as a whole. A Greek source for this change of nomenclature can perhaps be found with the name χόρτος, or *hortos*, which had been used in Ancient Greece when referring to an enclosure of cultivated greens. Certainly by the second century BC, in our earliest surviving Latin agricultural treatise, Cato names the garden as a *hortus* and lists the subdivisions of a rustic farm. Here he places the watered *hortus* (meaning the vegetable garden) as the second most important area, first place being reserved for a vineyard.[5]

Several Latin authors who wrote on bucolic themes, among them Virgil (*Eclogues and Georgics*) and the rustic works of Tibullus and Calpurnius Siculus, can also be used to throw light on the forms of early Roman gardens. Their books are full of vivid descriptions of a simple but idealized life in the country, where pastoral and agricultural/ horticultural work are performed against a background of religious piety. However, when a garden is described they tend to show what appears to be a potager, an area arranged as a vegetable garden or orchard. This type of garden, especially those with orchards, features in several ancient myths, such as the Garden of the Hesperides, and one is reminded of the fabulous gardens of Alkinoös, the king of the immortal Phaiakians. The latter became a model for the ideal qualities in a garden, that of being ever fruitful and plentiful, on land that was fertile and well watered. Pliny records 'that antiquity gave its highest admiration' to these gardens.[6]

Throughout the Roman period the rustic type of garden remained in use for humble properties and in places solely committed to farming. This simple and wholesome way of life in later ages was admired for its closeness to nature and the virtues of old Rome. The contemplative idea of a back-to-basics routine, seen through the eyes of a peasant farmer, is skilfully evoked in the Virgilian tale of the 'Old Man of Tarentum':

> I saw an old man, a Corycian, who owned a few poor acres of land once derelict, useless for arable, no good for grazing, unfit for the cultivation of vines. But he laid out a kitchen garden in rows amid the brushwood, bordering it with white lilies, verbena, small-seeded poppy. He was happy there as a king. He could go indoors at night to a table heaped with dainties he never had to buy. His the first rose of spring, the earliest apples in autumn: and when grim winter still was splitting the rocks with cold and holding the watercourses with curb of ice, already that man would be cutting his soft-haired hyacinths, complaining of summer's backwardness and the west winds slow to come . . .[7]

VILLAE RUSTICAE

The living accommodation of a large country farm, or *fundus*, was often called a *villa rustica* and like humble cottage-type smallholdings they also possessed a *hortus*. Several rustic villas have been excavated in Campania but garden areas were not looked for. It is only more recently, at the Villa Regina at Boscoreale, that modern scientific archaeological methods have been applied on a larger scale to include the land surrounding the villa, revealing details of a field system chiefly planted with vines. Importantly it also revealed an area identified as a *hortus*.[8] It is notable that the *hortus* is right next to the living quarters of the villa. Raised edges marked *areas* or individual vegetable plots within the garden and a circular well-head marked the site of a cistern placed off-centre, which would have enabled the gardener to 'quench the garden's ceaseless thirst'.[9] Outside the region engulfed by Vesuvius it is difficult to distinguish a rustic form of *hortus* from an agricultural field by archaeological means, even if it has a clear boundary such as a wall. Such a delineated area could have been used in a number of ways: as an orchard, for vegetables, as a vineyard or to contain livestock. In England, at the villa at Bancroft (Milton Keynes, Bucks.), such a situation existed. To find out which of these applied, pollen samples were taken from inside the walled area and on examination the plant species identified were sufficient to suggest that this enclosure could have been a place where vegetables had been cultivated, perhaps indicating the existence of a kitchen garden or *hortus rusticus*.

GARDENS IN THE ROMAN *DOMUS* OR TOWN HOUSE

Houses and shops in cities or towns were required to fit into a restricted network of streets that were ideally based on a grid-like pattern. The closely built houses each had a doorway facing the street and this part of the house would lead straight on to the pavement. Often the street frontage was converted into small shops which could be let and therefore provide a modest income for the owner. These houses would have been fairly uniform in the first instance and the ensuing design of the *domus* most often encountered in early times appears to be that with an *atrium tuscanicum*, which was thought to have derived from Etruscan prototypes.[10] These were generally axial in plan and comprised three main elements, *atrium*, *tablinium* and *hortus*, in that order one behind the other. This arrangement is sometimes described as an 'Italic house'. From the street an entrance passage led to the *atrium*, a wide hall with a open roofed central section, the *compluvium*, which let in light for a number of rooms arranged around the *atrium* below. The *tablinium*, traditionally the master's bedroom or official reception room, was placed on the opposite side of the *atrium*, facing the street entrance. The *tablinium*, which also had a rear window or door, therefore looked into both the *atrium* and *hortus*. The *hortus* as a rule was sited to the rear of the dwelling and was as large as space would allow. This type of house can be detected in the early phase of housing at Pompeii and Cosa, and dates to the end of the fourth or the beginning of the third century BC.[11]

In towns an adequate supply of water was often difficult to obtain and this type of house helped in many ways to overcome the problem by

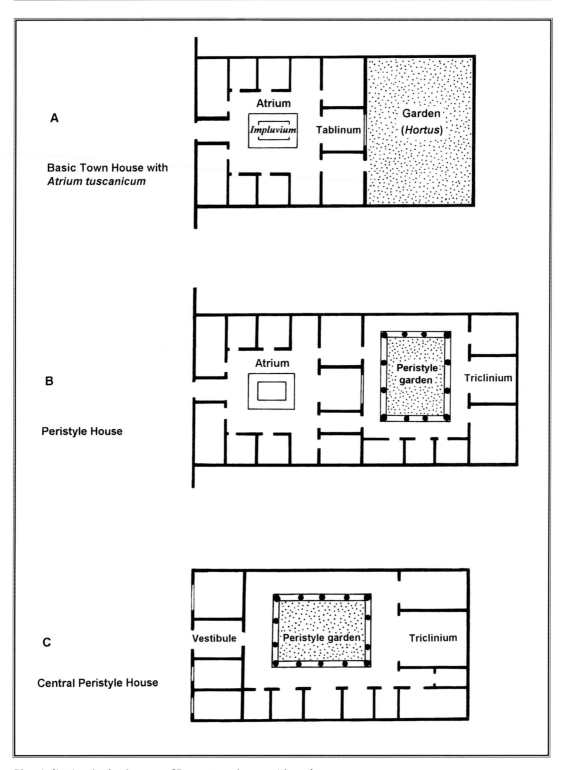

Plans indicating the development of Roman town houses with gardens.

allowing water to be collected from the roof. The houses were of necessity inward facing and properties tended to have a party wall between one another. Therefore the roofs of this type of house were given an inward slope over the *atrium* to direct falling rainwater through the opening of the *compluvium* down into the *impluvium* water catchment basin below. From here water was channelled into a cistern, usually located to the side of the *impluvium*. Water could then be drawn up for the use of the household and to water plants in the garden.

The style of Roman domestic housing changed with the introduction of a peristyle garden. In general these were also placed to the rear of the *tablinium* in the area of the old *hortus*, which was converted in line with the new tastes in fashion. Ideally, the garden was surrounded by four covered walkways but where space was more restricted there might only be room for two or three colonnades or porticos. The earliest of those at Pompeii date to the second century BC.[12] The peristyle garden is believed by some to have been adopted from the Greeks, or perhaps even the Etruscans, for Diodorus Siculus[13] does associate the Etruscans with its invention. The Etruscans were believed to have influenced the Romans on a number of points, and were considered responsible for the introduction of the early form of *atrium*, so perhaps Diodorus's authority can be trusted here also. Current thought now suggests that the Roman peristyle garden was not borrowed directly from the Greeks but was more likely to have been a mixture of Hellenistic/Persian and Etruscan ideas. The Roman peristyle was imprinted on to the old *hortus* at the rear of the house and did not replace the *atrium*, which for many centuries held the sanctity of tradition. In accordance with this we find that rooms associated with the *atrium* retain their Latin names but paradoxically those facing on to the new garden area were given Greek names, the *exedra* and *oecus,* as was the *peristylium* itself. These might suggest an origin in the Greek world but might equally refer to the increasing Hellenization of the Roman world. Where possible the axiality of the Roman *domus* was preserved and through their love of nature we find that the Romans preferred to include, even on a small scale, a living tableau of plants in their colonnaded courts.

A house with *atrium* and peristyle became highly popular, and this style is found in numerous dwellings at Pompeii and other Roman cities in the western provinces. A detailed study of just one area in Pompeii illustrates how many houses had a garden and which, before additions, had as their nucleus the basic features of the 'Italic house'. At Rome three appear on a fragment of the Severan *Forma Urbis*, a map of the city inscribed on marble commissioned under the Emperor Septimius Severus (*c.* AD 200), and this is a testament to the longevity of the type. Its popularity was partly because it was a means of enlarging the house and the open area was used as a means to gain light for surrounding rooms, but in addition the garden and its shady porticos provided an extra living space where there would be fresh air. The Augustan

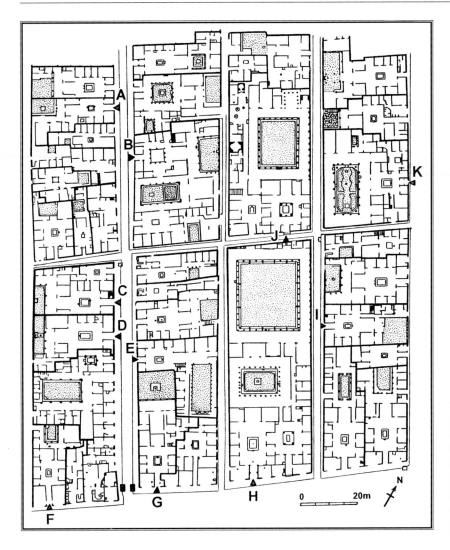

A map showing a small area of Pompeii, part of Region VI, indicating that the majority of houses have a garden, here stippled. House boundaries are outlined with a thicker black line.

A: House of Apollo. The small garden surrounded by two porticos is partly enclosed by a low wall. This barrier and the north wall is adorned by garden frescos.

B: House of the Dioscuri. The first garden has a pseudo-peristyle; a row of engaged columns were placed against the rear wall. There is also a small shrine and altar to the rear of the garden. The second garden has a large fishpond.

C: House of the Small Fountain. A mosaic-covered *nymphaeum* is sited to the rear of the garden. There are remains of garden and landscape frescos on the west and south walls.

D: House of the Large Fountain. A decorative *nymphaeum* and small pool were sited on the rear wall of the garden so that it could be seen from the street.

E: House of Ancora Nera. This house was provided with a sunken garden, which had decorative niches in the south wall.

F: House of the Tragic Poet. There is a shrine in the north-west corner of this small garden.

G: House of the Ship. There was a portico on the south side of this garden, and in the centre a summer *triclinium* with table.

H: House of the Faun. This large house occupies a whole block. It has two gardens.

I: House of Sextus Pompeius Axiochus. The rear wall of this garden was decorated with a row of six small niches.

J: House of the Labyrinth. In this large garden the conservators have planted a maze to reflect the subject of a mosaic found within the house.

K: House of the Vettii. The layout of plant beds and paths were preserved and are re-created in this garden. Garden furnishings included fountain basins, herms, and statuary.

architectural writer Vitruvius shows to what extent these qualities were valued: 'the air from greenery is rarefied and removes the thick humor from the eyes, thus improving vision, as well as removing other humors from the body.'[14] Vitruvius[15] also mentions that *vestibula* courtyards and peristyles were areas of the house that were open to the view of others. Therefore the proportionally larger area occupied by the peristyle could be developed in a number of ways to show how fashion conscious the owners were, and this area would become an ideal location in which Romans could display their wealth and love of ostentation.

Gardens became an integral part of the Roman lifestyle and the possession of a garden became another status symbol. Therefore when opportunity allowed garden areas were enlarged; this can be seen at the House of Obellius Firmus, Pompeii, where there is an L-shaped peristyle and an extra garden area beyond. Other alterations or additions could involve the installation of a second garden, as at the House of the Faun, where an even larger peristyle garden was placed behind the first. The increasing importance attached to gardens is shown by a later development where even the *atrium* is altered to allow plants to be grown there too. Garden elements invade the home and the light-well of the atrium becomes a little *viridarium*, or interior garden. The open space in the roof, the *compluvium*, is widened and the area below becomes almost another peristyle. The *impluvium* was then often converted into a water basin surrounded by in-built planting troughs. Examples can be seen in the *atrium* of the House of the Relief of Telephus at Herculaneum, and at the House of Loreius Tiburtinus at Pompeii, which today has been replanted with roses.

In a further development the *atrium* all but disappears. The entrance from the street now leads into a *vestibulum*, which provides a reception area for visitors or clients. This was variable in size and was sometimes provided with benches. A doorway from here led into a central peristyle garden. At many sites a view of the garden was still possible through an open street door. A number of houses in southern Spain and North Africa incorporate a *vestibulum*, for example the Casa de los Pájaros at Italica (of the second century AD). At Ostia, in the House of Fortuna Annonaria (dating from first century AD), on the other hand, the vestibule is little more than a narrow passage leading directly on to a peristyle garden. Variations of earlier and later peristyle houses are found throughout the Roman Empire; in North Africa, the Iberian peninsula, Gaul and at the Roman town of Venta Silurum (Caerwent in South Wales). At Volubilis in modern Morocco, rows of the later central peristyle house were constructed, showing how standardized this later form had become by the third century AD. Even in dry hot countries with limited water supplies, small peristyle courts that were paved (or covered in mosaics) could be lined with in-built stone plant containers or long troughs, as in the Maison aux Jardinières at Timgad and the House of '*Omnia tibi Felicia*' at Dougga. In this way green foliage and

Cistem

PLAN

Plant containers adorn a small court. House of '*Omnia tibi Felicia*' at Dougga, Tunisia.

flowers would add life to the area and brighten the scene as a whole. In the Romanized Greek East, however, evidence is less well defined, for occupation on most sites continued well into the Byzantine period, and in many cases still overlays the earlier phases which we are seeking. It appears that large palatial properties possessed gardens but many of the more modest town dwellings, such as the terraced houses at Ephesus, or at Apamea in Syria, Daphne near Antioch, or Side, retain the Greek preference of having a paved court. Nevertheless a number of owners had decided to admit certain garden elements, such as a Roman-style *nymphaeum*, although here only the box-like water basin below the fountain remains. Plants may have grown in pots in these courts, although none are recorded archaeologically. Local traditions as well as the climate were influential in determining the design of housing.

Some cities had to cope with a rapidly increasing population, sometimes the result of people seeking their fortune in town, and to provide the necessary housing for the masses apartment blocks or *insulae* were built. In general these were arranged around a court or light-well which contained little more than a cistern and a *dolium*, a large earthenware pot for the night soil. In Ostia there are a number of *insulae*, which clearly show the restrictions in space and comfort especially on the upper floors. Literary references indicate that even here Romans could bring nature into their confined living area by having plants in pots either on balconies or on window ledges. Martial[16] describes his efforts at growing plants on his window ledge and Juvenal[17] reminds us of the dangers of walking in streets beside these blocks – you needed to beware of projectiles (perhaps also the occasional flowerpot) falling from above. Wall paintings of street scenes from Boscoreale show balconies with pots but as these appear to be broken ones they may have contained Adonis gardens rather than permanent plantings. However, gardens on upper levels are difficult to find archaeologically as in most cases only the foundations of houses or the lower storey survives. Pliny records how plants in window boxes were felt to be an expression of a longing for a view of the country but the rise in burglaries now sadly 'compelled them to bar out all the view with shutters'.[18] There are also references by Seneca to roof gardens but again these cannot be found archaeologically. He mentions that there were groves of trees and fishponds[19] but we must bear in mind that these may be an exaggeration. Due to the problems of weight, a garden grown on a raised terrace is a more logical interpretation than a true roof garden.

A particularly interesting example of *insulae* is seen in the so-called garden houses at Ostia (dating to *c.* AD 128) which were the most spacious apartments in this town. During their design and construction extra space had been allocated for a communal garden with decorative fountains. Tenants would have no doubt paid a higher rent for the amenity of the gardens but these would have made their outlook more pleasant.

VILLAE URBANAE AND SUBURBANAE

With the advent of a more luxurious lifestyle the rustic farm or *villa rustica* became more and more inappropriate and many were modernized to conform to new fashions. Many villas were simply given a new wing, thereby separating the owner's accommodation from work areas, such as at the villa of Sette Finestre in Italy. Varro (*c.* 36 BC) tells of changes in country life, and how some of the new fashions could be made to turn a profit for the owner instead of being merely classed as decorative, a trend of which he disapproved but which was clearly becoming prevalent.[20]

A passage in Cicero may be used to indicate when the construction of villas designed for comfort and luxury rather than farming started to become popular. He indirectly informs us that alterations to his family home commenced in the space of time after his grandfather's lifetime, 'when the homestead according to old custom, was small', for during his father's occupancy, when he 'rebuilt and extended' the family home,[21] the *villa rustica* was transformed into a *villa urbana*. This period saw the introduction of well-appointed and desirable properties with gardens and suggests a date of late second to first century BC. Varro shows that the term *villa* was then used when speaking of a farmhouse, country mansion or luxurious town house.[22]

The term *villa suburbana* referred more often to a building, usually a very large property, in or close to the city. However, the property as a whole was usually still referred to as the *hortus* of a particular person; as such sixty-seven at Rome have been recorded.[23] These gardens became landmarks in the city and were sufficiently well known to be useful when locating a person's address – houses then did not have a numbering system. Vitruvius states that the homes of men of substance both in town and country should be suitable to their station, they should contain 'princely vestibules, lofty halls, and very spacious peristyles, plantations and broad avenues finished in a majestic manner'.[24]

Pleasant and attractive gardens became desirable and land associated with *villae urbanae* was remodelled into extensive gardens. We hear of colonnades opening on to ornamental terraces called *xysti*; those of Pliny's Laurentine villa were 'scented by violets'.[25] He, however, retained a *hortus rusticus*, showing that perhaps there was still a place somewhere for the needs of the table. Promenades and shady groves were popular and are thought to have been a re-creation of the famous walks in the Academy at Athens that were so admired by Roman visitors. Many of the new elements in gardens were given Greek names, such as Academy, Lyceum, *gymnasium*, *xystos* and *hippodromos*, and again this points to a growing philhellenism, but in many cases the Roman meaning of the word changes. For instance the Roman meaning of *xystos* (in Latin *xystus*) is discussed by Vitruvius; he relates how the Greek term signified a wide colonnade where athletes trained in winter, whereas the Romans translated this into a new concept which was in effect an open area with promenades.[26] This was usually found close to a building so that a colonnade would open on to the *xystus*. Varro deplores the fact that 'they' (here he refers to the new fashion-conscious Romans) 'do not think they have a real villa unless it rings with many resounding Greek names'.[27] In general the Greeks appear to have preferred public rather than private gardens and they therefore tended to focus their attention on enhancing religious sites or natural features in the landscape, such as caves with springs, which became the shrines of nymphs in grottos. These places were venerated with the addition of flowers and statuary. As with the Greek appellations the Romans adapted these basic Greek/Hellenistic concepts but the resulting new garden form was their own invention.

More than anything Roman technology, especially where water was concerned, introduced a new element to gardens and revolutionized the art of gardening. The Greeks relied on spring water and therefore in all fairness this development can only be attributed to Roman ingenuity. The introduction of aqueducts and plumbing to private houses and estates enabled a wider range of plants to be grown. Also gardens could now be enlivened by water features. The scope that the new technology allowed was enormous. Many Romans decided to construct fountains and pools, and extravagance was clearly a feature of the day. For instance a conspicuous waste of water, which in the city was chargeable and

Lady carrying a basket of fruit, mosaic detail, Mount Nebo, Jordan.

therefore expensive, would serve to show the unlimited wealth at the owner's disposal. It became fashionable to have fishponds. Pliny noted that by his day an ornamental garden of two acres had become insufficient for some of Nero's ex-slaves, and 'now they like to have fishponds larger than that'.[28] This perhaps may be an exaggeration but it indicates that water features had become commonplace, and therefore they needed to be enlarged or elaborated in some way to make them more noteworthy. However, these and other garden features were also affected by changes in taste and fashion during the long period of the Roman Empire (different forms of water features are discussed in chapter four).

There were many wealthy Romans, such as Cicero and Pliny, who were fortunate enough to possess a number of properties. Even Pliny the Younger's mother-in-law had four properties. However, the growth of large villa estates near Rome was remarked upon by Horace, for he could see that they were becoming so large and numerous that there was little agricultural land left on which to grow food.[29] This 'progress' would eventually lead to shortages in Rome, thereby affecting its economy, but such comments show how important landscaped gardens had become. One rather extravagant example is amply illustrated by Plutarch, who recalls that Pompey had chided Lucullus, whose name became a byword for the excesses of a luxuriant lifestyle, and had pointed out that he had designed his property at Tusculum in such a way that it would be 'uninhabitable in winter. Whereupon Lucullus burst out laughing and said "Do you suppose, then, that I have less sense than cranes and storks, and do not change residences according to the seasons?"'[30]

Literary sources disclose that others vied with Lucullus in the size and quantity of their villa estates.[31] Pliny favoured his estate at Laurentum in winter, as the climate beside the sea was milder,[32] whereas he could avoid the heat of midsummer when he stayed at one of his properties beside Lake Como.[33] He also says that his estate in Tuscany is healthy in summer, for it is 'at the very foot of the Apennines'.[34] Cool air to be found in mountainous districts, by lake shores or beside the sea, encouraged men to favour these localities during the heat of midsummer, so much so that winter and summer resorts soon became well established.

However, the appearance of these villas and gardens may have been different from their counterparts in Rome itself as landowners were to some extent dependent on the local climate and soil conditions. In different regions in the Empire there are variations from the *villae urbanae* mentioned in literary texts. In warm climates the villa opens outwards as well as inwards and porticos face on to garden courts or the extensive landscaped grounds. This can be seen in depictions of villas in frescos and mosaics, and one from the House of Marcus Fronto can be used as an example. The winged villa illustrated in this fresco shows similarities to the partly excavated north-facing façade of the northern

The Villa of Poppaea, Oplontis. The large northern garden and part of the northern façade of the villa. This garden has been faithfully restored following archaeological evidence.

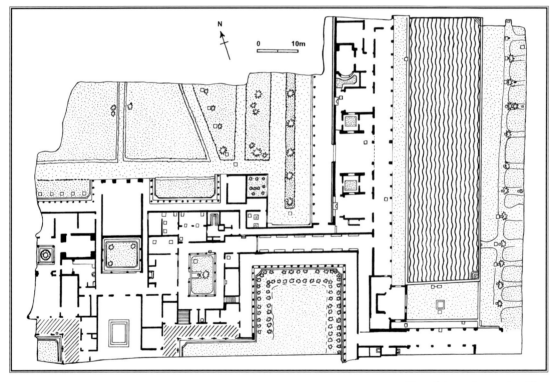

garden at Oplontis, a plan of which is included. The meticulously detailed excavation here has enabled archaeologists to make a reconstruction of the appearance of this garden and it may also be used as a model to assess other gardens associated with *villae urbanae*. Unfortunately no detailed study has been made of the more extensive park-like grounds belonging to country villa estates; this is partly because of the expense of such a project. Often it is really only practicable to carry out detailed archaeological excavations on areas of a limited size. We do, however, have descriptions of Pliny's villa and gardens at Tusculum and Laurentum which give an insight into the wider landscaping of the grounds of such villas.

Plan of the gardens at the *villa urbana* of Poppaea, Oplontis, showing the area excavated. The location of sculpture is marked by a ❑; plant material, such as tree roots are shown by a ☆. W. Jashemski, who excavated the gardens of this villa, found that the large southern garden was planted with two rows of citron trees. The shaded porticos are those partially blocked.

For gardens elsewhere in the Roman Empire the plans of dwellings excavated in Spain bear many similarities to those of Italy. Some were also quite large and contained several open areas, some being peristyles or courts, and evidence suggests they would have been turned into a useful and pleasant area of greenery in many ways comparable with their Italian counterparts. The Hispanic villas have been classified into three different basic types:[35] one was linear and maybe rustic in character but the other two forms contained garden courts. Of these the courtyard villas had a central peristyle and large complex villas had more than one garden area. In the province of Gaul, which included modern-day France, Belgium, Luxembourg and a part of Germany lying to the west of the River Rhine, there are a number of winged and courtyard villas, as we also find in Britain. Few have been excavated sufficiently but the open space in the courtyard or between the two projecting wings of these villas is likely to have once contained garden features, and perhaps these may have included decorative plant beds such as those found at Fishbourne near Chichester (West Sussex) on the southern coast of England. They might also possess a fishpond, sited so that the owners could view the spectacle from facing rooms or corridors, as is the case at Echternach in Luxembourg and Eccles (Kent), where a large rectangular pond was placed in the open area between the two wings. Preliminary surveys have produced evidence that could indicate that a similar arrangement existed at the Roman villa near Tockenham (Wilts). The villas at Echternach and Fishbourne, although in a cooler climate, have a façade that is reminiscent of those illustrated in a number of miniature fresco scenes. An example in colour is of a winged *villa urbana* with three open-sided porticos. In Pannonia (an area that extended across Serbia and western Hungary), where the climate is even colder in winter, there were also a number of courtyard villas, some with a fortified appearance. Porticos here appear to be less open and the colonnades are usually walled to half their height. Many also enclose a central courtyard garden which in many cases was provided with a central water basin, as

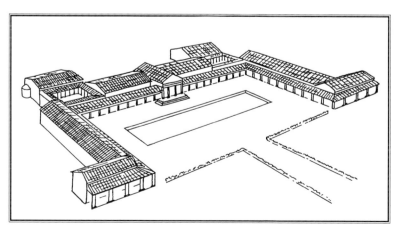

Reconstruction drawing of the *villa urbana* at Echternach. The garden is dominated by a large ornamental pool.

at Gyulafirátót-Pogánytelek.[36]

The partly enclosed corridors are also found in Britain and the Gadebridge Park villa is an example. For many years there has been a tendency to regard the land attached to the majority of Roman villas in Britain as being purely agricultural in function but growing evidence is showing that the existence of gardens in villas can no longer be denied, and that Britain should no longer be seen separately from elsewhere in the Empire. Gardens may have existed but would probably have been on a simpler scale than those found in Rome, owing to differences in climate and taste. Evidence has been found of fishponds and bedding plots: for instance, one recent survey gave the dimensions of eleven fishponds found at different villa sites in Roman Britain,[37] and at Bancroft (Bucks.) there was a pond and possibly a flower bed. At the modestly sized villa at Frocester Court (Glos.) bedding plots have been discovered at both the front and rear of the main block of the villa, which increasingly shows that the area enclosed by the wings of villas may well have been reserved as a pleasant decorative area – perhaps a garden. In fact Varro suggests that when planting on a farm provision should be made for orchards and flower gardens, for they 'are profitable for the pleasure they afford'.[38] Some villas would remain purely rustic but others could be of three parts, as Columella points out; of these the *villa urbana* is the abode of the owner, while a nearby *villa rustica*, the rustic part, was farmed by his manager. The third part was the *villa fructuaria*, or storehouse.[39] Several large well spaced out villa complexes in northern France and Belgium show these distinctions, an example is found in the Ardennes region of Belgium at La Malegne, where a *villa rustica* is roughly 200–300 m distant from the *villa urbana* and its terraced garden.

Where walls with gateways enclosed land close to a *villa urbana* livestock would be kept at bay and the area could then be used for plants or plantations. Owners often lavished great care and expense on decorating the inside and outside appearance of the building. Therefore similar thought and effort would have been expended to provide a satisfactory setting for the building, a pleasant outlook from it, and to demonstrate the social standing of the owner.

CHAPTER THREE

Architectural Features in Roman Garden Design

Many Roman gardens incorporate architectural features and in most cases these follow the same forms found in the architecture of Roman buildings. The scale and character of garden features depend on the nature of their setting, and in the same way that we find a huge variation in the size of Roman buildings we find a similar range in their gardens. In the larger, more fashionable properties architectural features could be set into a landscaped garden that was often entirely ornamental. To achieve a balance the architect would need to work with a landscape gardener. The nature of these developed forms of garden is reflected in the separate Latin name given to a gardener who specifically presided over ornamental gardens – *topiarius*. This occupation derived from a Latin term, *topia*, which the *Oxford Latin Dictionary* translates as 'contrived effects of natural scenery', in other words an ornamental landscape. Therefore a *topiarius* could be seen to create *topia* or landscapes. The Romans believed that a fine landscape was one that had been civilized or improved upon in some way and was enhanced by the addition of buildings. In some cases it appears that architectural elements were sited in a random fashion but many were probably the result of adding new features over the years; yet others can be found to be part of an architectural scheme within an ordered landscape. In several locations in Campania, and also at Fishbourne, we find that plant beds and paths were arranged in a symmetrical manner and in these cases paths invariably led to a special focal point, often of an architectural nature. Therefore the art of a *topiarius*, together with that of the architect, would ensure that the natural surroundings were altered in certain ways (often structurally) to complement and enhance buildings and in turn architecture would provide the frame behind the picture of nature perfected by man.

ARCHITECTURAL COMPONENTS OF A ROMAN GARDEN: THE PERISTYLE

As already mentioned, the design or architecture of house and villa was adapted over time to include gardens. In the earlier town houses the house and garden were sometimes given a veranda or portico which was simply a lean-to roof against the house wall. As the 'Italic' peristyle house developed, however, the preferred form became a garden surrounded by four covered colonnades or porticos. The encircling peristyle can be seen as a border or frame that surrounds a garden; it also forms an ideal backdrop in a view of the house from the garden. The peristyle became so fashionable that householders with insufficient space for a complete peristyle (on all four sides) were driven to imitate this ideal. In such cases a pseudo-peristyle could be built instead. It all depended on the dimensions of the space available, for some owners opted to construct three or just one or two porticos. The remaining solid wall or walls of the garden were then decorated by applying stucco to form a series of engaged columns, or alternatively columns were painted on to the wall to complete a pseudo-peristyle. To break the solidity of these walls, garden scenes were often painted in the intervening spaces, and these would give the effect of a garden beyond; they could also make the garden appear larger than it actually was.

A pseudo-peristyle illustrated in an engraving made by William Gell in his *Pompeiana* of 1835 is a rather Victorian rendition of Roman life around a small garden but illustrates some of the features to be seen there. It shows how a garden, although small, can be made to appear attractive. A highly decorative shrine-like water feature, a *nymphaeum*, has been placed against the rear wall, making a centre of attraction. The

Reconstruction drawing of the House of the Small Fountain, Pompeii. (Gell, *c.* 1835.)

two solid walls to the rear of the house at the edge of the garden have been painted as a pseudo-peristyle with landscape or garden scenes that were meant to be viewed as if appearing through a window. Gell did use a little artistic licence. The columns are taller than in reality, the portico is considerably wider than normal and there is no indication of a rainwater gutter. At the House of the Small Fountain, the actual setting for this drawing, the garden scene behind the *nymphaeum* is somewhat faded today but still shows that below the painted trees there is also a low painted decorative balustrade that does not appear in Gell's drawing. This would have broken his symmetry in the rendition of the frescos but in reality many ancient frescos show a combination of scenes that do not always follow the rules of perspective.

In Pompeii and elsewhere there are examples of both peristyle and pseudo-peristyle. If we examine plans of housing (a detail of only one part of Pompeii is shown here as an example), we see that the majority of dwellings in the town have a garden, small or large. Gardens are of varying sizes and shapes, for house boundaries reflect the fortunes of the various inhabitants. The plans reveal that at some date a number of owners purchased an adjoining property or part of one to create further living accommodation and at the same time enlarge the garden, or make space for a second one. They also highlight the efforts made by inhabitants of diminished dwellings to retain some form of garden or *viridarium*.

Areas of greenery were in the main separated from the rest of the house by an ambulatory covered by a portico and, depending on cost and the availability of materials, the supporting columns were made of marble, stone or brick. In the case of the latter, bricks were manufactured in segments of a circle, then the column was covered with moulded stucco. Many columns were finished to resemble fluted marble but a large number were given a second unfluted pink coating on the lower part only (a third) at some later date. As this coating is both hard and waterproof this was presumably done to protect the more vulnerable lower sections. In some houses holes or slots are visible on the side of columns, these are often a sign that a low barrier fence had been inserted between columns; where they occur at a higher level a curtain pole may have been attached. There are literary references to the latter – Pliny mentions that a red curtain was used to protect moss growing in a peristyle.[1] A curtain could also be used to shade a south-facing colonnade during summer or alternatively to help stop draughts in wintertime. Another method to shade a portico has emerged from the villa at Oplontis. Only part of this villa and its gardens have been excavated but in the small section visible of the south-west garden, and the narrow portion of the large southern garden, the colonnades were partially blocked by inserting a series of panels. These reduced the size of the openings between the columns to a series of doorways. Some had been provided with slit windows above. It is possible that these were a security measure on what may have been an external façade but this feature appears to have only been used on the south-facing porticos that were not shaded by trees. There is ample archaeological evidence to show that two rows of trees would have given sufficient shade to at least three other porticos.

The peristyle of many dwellings was furnished with a low solid masonry wall, a *pluteus*, in place of a fence between the columns. These often appear to have been a later insertion and perhaps relate to a change of fashion, or they may have been installed for comfort, such as a need to deflect low-level draughts from penetrating adjoining rooms in wintertime. In some cases a narrow planting trough had been built into the top part of the wall, as at the House of the Lovers, Pompeii. Here, if trailing plants were allowed to cover the wall, they could create a green hedge-like enclosure to the garden or alternatively the trough provided an additional space in which to grow some herbs for use in the kitchen. A *pluteus* was clearly meant to be a barrier, as in the rustic garden at the Villa of the Mysteries, where the wall was above waist height. However, in a large number of properties the low walls are often about 40–50 cm high; their function was unchanged but they may also have been used as a convenient form of bench seat, where you could sit facing into the portico or on to the garden. A barrier of some kind would certainly save small children in the household from trampling on the plants grown in the garden or knocking over statuary displayed there, and would also stop them from falling into fishponds. However, access into this type of garden was more restricted, and we usually find that a whole intercolumniation of the peristyle is reserved for the entrance. The opening more often than not was made to correspond with that of the main dining room, or *triclinium*, and in a number of houses the space between the pair of columns that framed the entrance to the garden had been widened, so that the diners in the *triclinium* would be able to have a clear view out to the garden. The entrance could even be made to appear more distinguished if it was flanked by a pair of monumental square fluted pillars instead of the columns normally used elsewhere.

Lines of sight appear to be of prime importance and in his book on ritual, space and decoration in Roman housing, Clarke discusses how the architecture of the house was in some cases manipulated to create a through vista.[2] In most cases this was to lead the eye towards a garden, which was often provided with a focal point such as a shrine or *nymphaeum*, as can be seen in several of the houses on the plan of Pompeii. The rear wall of the *tablinium* was often altered to make a large window opening that would have been closed with folding shutters. But when open the splendours of the garden could be revealed, as seen in the House of the Tragic Poet, a view of which has been reconstructed by Gell. When a dwelling was of an irregular plan, corridors and doorways were in many cases placed slightly off centre, and windows were inserted to display a view of the all-important garden. Another example in a larger property is

Reconstruction drawing of the House of Tragic Poet, Pompeii (Gell, *c.* 1835), showing a view of the garden from the atrium. It was actually possible to see the garden from the house entrance.

the House of the Citharist, again at Pompeii. Here the gardens are not in a direct line of sight with the entrance of the house but because the *fauces*, the entrance passageway, was angled and the *tablinium* omitted from the latest design, a partial view could be achieved, even if this was of little more than the columns of the peristyle beyond. It would be, however, enough to show that the owners possessed a garden. Internal rooms that did not directly open on to the garden were often fitted with window openings positioned so that the room could still benefit from a view of the greenery and receive more light and fresh air.

Many gardens with porticos were bordered by stone or brick gutters, designed to collect rainwater dripping off portico roofs. At the villa discovered at Wortley (Glos.) and at Fishbourne (West Sussex) the gutters had been cut out of massive blocks of stone. In some houses, such as the House of Meleager at Pompeii, the corners of gutters are fitted with a concave quarter circle which, during storms, could act as a funnel to direct the precious water down a hole and into the cistern below. Only one or two would lead to a cistern while others would make ideal locations for large plant pots, as at this house. Draw shafts of cisterns are usually placed at the edge of the garden or in the peristyle; they are often in the form of a disc lid placed on to a rebated stone slab. A more decorative version was the *puteal* that resembles a chimney pot. A number of these can be seen in Pompeii and Ostia and were either plain or carved. The more decorative of these items were even considered as fine art, for Cicero, when searching for *objets d'art* to adorn his villa, requested his friend Atticus to purchase two relief-carved *puteal* for him.[3]

PATHS

An essential feature of any garden is the provision of paths to allow a
pleasant walk within the garden. Some of these were laid down to follow
the boundaries of the garden, as at the villa found at Frocester Court
(Glos.); others were circulatory or led to features or plant beds within the
garden. At Voerendaal in the Netherlands the main pathway leading to the
villa widened midway to circle a tall Jupiter column placed in the middle
of its path.[4] At other times paths were used to isolate planted areas, as was
the case at Trier, where the peristyle garden was dissected by two paths to
create four separate plant beds.[5] Paths were of course used for access and
Pliny mentions how gardeners used the ones surrounding bedding plots to
water the plant beds, in this case the beds were delineated by raised edges.[6]
This type of edging is seen on various archaeological plans at Pompeii and
in the *hortus* or produce garden at the Villa Regina, Boscoreale. In the
decorative gardens of Campania the composition of paths is not usually
revealed and any photographs seem to indicate that the narrow paths were
of beaten earth.[7] Paths often become apparent because of a change in soil
texture and colour, from hard-packed earth (being the path) to the more
friable darker enriched soil within bedding areas. Alternatively, where
circumstances allow, the direction of paths can be traced by rows of holes.
The shape of the cavities can indicate that either fencing or hedging was
present. In some cases, as at the *Adonaea* in Rome, paths may be separated
from bedding areas by brick edging.[8]

Where evidence survives elsewhere, materials used to make a walkway
were dependent on available local resources. Vitruvius furnishes details on
how to construct sand-covered walks or *ambulationes* with drains to ensure
that the surface would remain dry.[9] This is practical in hot dry climates but
less so in areas with a higher rainfall, for the sand would remain on one's
feet. It is therefore not surprising to find elsewhere that paths could
alternatively consist of loose or finely broken stones, potsherds of ceramics
and tile, or gravel. In Britain (because of glaciation) gravel is more readily
obtainable, and was therefore used at the Frocester Court villa.[10] Pliny and
Cicero mention long *ambulationes* or promenades in their gardens[11] and the
gestatio, a driveway, where litter-borne outings could be taken. Pliny
possessed a circular *gestatio* in front of his villa at Laurentum, where an
island bed in the middle was planted with mulberry and fig trees; he also
mentions that it was bordered by a hedge of box and rosemary and in the
centre he placed a shady vine-covered pergola.[12]

DECORATIVE FENCING AND TRELLIS-WORK

Recent discoveries at Pompeii at the House of the Chaste Lovers have
found evidence of a simple form of fencing that had been used to
surround plant beds. Two different types of reed had been used to create
an easily made low barrier in the garden. *Arundo donax*, a thicker variety

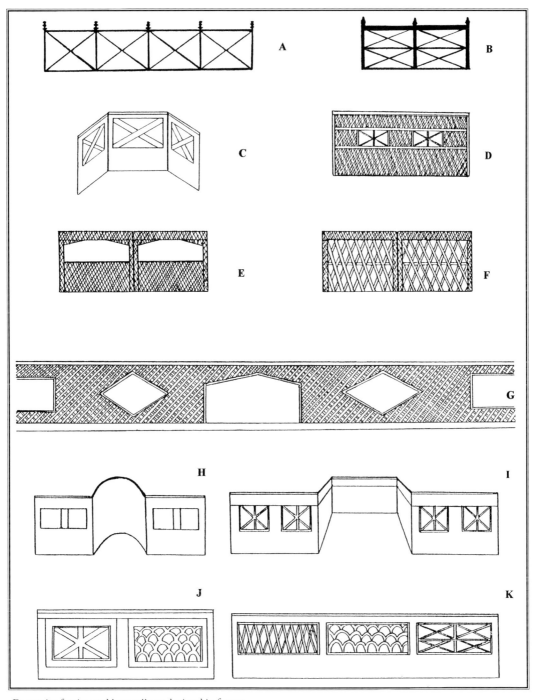

Decorative fencing and low walls, as depicted in frescos.

KEY TO PROVENANCE

Fences:

A: Rudston Villa, Britain.

B: Wortley Villa, Britain.

C: National Museum Naples, Inv. no. 9705.

D & G: House of the Wedding of Alexander, Pompeii.

E & F: Auditorium of Maecenas, Rome.

Walls:

H & I: Auditorium of Maecenas, Rome.

J: House of M.L. Fronto, Pompeii.

K: Livia's Garden Room, Primaporta, Rome.

of reed, was used at intervals for support and *Phragmites australis* for the interwoven main body of the fence.[13] The thinner reed had been inserted into the ground at different angles and when reconstructed a trellis with a diamond pattern was revealed. Unfortunately this type of fence is rather ephemeral and does not usually survive through the centuries to be present in archaeological records; therefore further evidence is needed to identify the forms of garden fencing current during the Roman period. Fortunately these items appear in numerous ancient frescos and they also reveal the many ways in which they were used. There are numerous examples similar to the type mentioned above (see the plan drawn by Ciarallo). This form is illustrated in a miniature fresco of a rustic *hortus* presided over by Priapus (in chapter six), and can also be seen at Oplontis painted on to a half wall below a window opening.

More decorative versions may be seen in a series of frescos painted in niches at the Auditorium of Maecenas in Rome, and also at the House of the Wedding of Alexander, Pompeii (identified in the drawing opposite as e and f, d and g). These have large apertures of different shapes incorporated into their design. This type of fence allowed some foliage to peep through and this helped to soften any straight lines. At the House of the Fruit Orchard in Pompeii a series of frescos in one room illustrates a form that was much taller. Here the trellis-work fence must have had reinforced sections between the lattice panels for they appear to support marble urns and vases. Although these are somewhat hard to credit they are shown on numerous occasions and in sculptural reliefs which would tend to confirm the practice, but perhaps the vessel used was of a lighter weight than appears in the frescos. This kind of fence, although highly decorative, would also be utilized to partition various parts of the garden. Other frescos, mainly miniatures, show how trellis-work was used to make little enclosures, arbours and pavilions, access being through plain or arched doorways. All the above mentioned fences appear somewhat fragile and realistically they would have served to delineate a given area rather than form an effective barrier.

A wooden fence would be more robust but was still of an open nature; an example is found in a fresco in Naples Museum (inv. no. 9705), which has panels in a simple X design above a solid base (c). Simpler versions are shown on frescos at Rudston and Wortley in Britain (a and b), that could have been made out of lengths of cut timber. Metal railings were also used, an example in bronze was found in Lake Nemi.[14] These however were more expensive and are rare finds in archaeology for most would have been melted down in antiquity for reuse elsewhere.

ORNAMENTAL LOW WALLS OR BALUSTRADES

The best examples of low decorative stone or marble walls are those illustrated in the fresco from the House of Livia at Primaporta, Rome (k), which shows that both lattice and wall can exist side by side. The wall has alternating panels of three different designs; one is of overlapping fish scales, another appears to replicate the wooden diamond lattice, while the third is made up of four crossed sections. These three patterns appear to be the most popular forms used for stone decorative walling. A number of frescos depict walls and fences that had been furnished with recesses, either rectangular or semicircular (e.g. h and i). These served to break the severity of otherwise straight lines and the niches also became ideal locations where you could place a fountain, statuary, seat or specimen tree; the important object would then be highlighted and protected by the architectural lines of walling. Hedging, as can be seen at Fishbourne, was often planted along similar architectural patterns.

The fresco from Boscoreale showing a grotto illustrates an ornamental wall at the edge of a cliff and points rather graphically to the fact that decorative stone walling also appears to have been used to stop people from falling from a height or into water. Similar barriers would have protected against the drop at the edge of a garden terrace. Several paintings and carved stone reliefs portray stone balustrades on balconies. In some cases this type might also include a sculptured finial on the post; a large proportion resemble herm heads. A fine example is the series found in decorative walling around the large water basin at Welschbillig in Germany. While protecting people these walls also allowed light through, would not obstruct views and enhanced the landscape.

Decorative low wall from Welschbillig reconstructed in the Rheinisches Landesmuseum, Trier.

PERGOLAS

The grotto scene from Boscoreale may be used once more to show a *pergula* or pergola. This version has stone pillars as supports but many others were of wood or trellis-work. Above, a light open framework provides a support for climbing plants. Vines are shown in this case but they were also used for ivy or gourds, while others would have had roses on top of the trellis. Arbours and pergolas are depicted in a number of frescos, and some of the miniature ones reveal their frequent use. Even in the fourth century AD these were still much admired. One letter mentions what must have been a lengthy pergola covered by roses and vines that 'twist themselves together' creating a wonderfully shaded pathway leading to a pool.[15] These shady canopies made pleasant walkways in summer, and could form an ideal location for seating where one could 'take the air'. An arbour could be used as a shelter and larger ones were even a place for alfresco dining when the weather was pleasant. A large Nilotic mosaic from Praeneste (Palestrina) incorporates a scene in which diners on luxuriously covered couches amuse themselves under an arched vine-covered tunnel of lattice-work. Archaeological evidence for *pergulae* has been found in many gardens in Campania, testifying to the popularity of these features. Generally the upper framework leaves little trace behind but the position of wooden posts or the survival of stone pillar bases used to support it confirm their existence. At the House of Loreius Tiburtinus rows of post holes were found to have cavities of vine roots nearby[16] and vine-covered walkways have recently been reinstated by copying designs seen in wall paintings. The reconstruction of such temporary structures is very effective for it enables the visitor to visualize the effect once on view, and to appreciate how pergolas added to the beauty of a garden.

It is now believed that such features were also used in Roman Britain. Work currently in progress at a villa in the Og valley, near Swindon, has recently found evidence from parch marks to suggest that a pergola led from the villa down to the river below.[17]

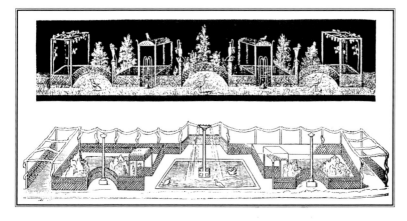

Miniature frescos of gardens depicting lattice-work fences and pergolas.
Top: From Herculaneum, Naples National Museum, Inv. no. 9964.
Bottom: From the Auditorium of Maecenas, Rome.

Reconstructed garden pergola
at the House of Loreius
Tiburtinus, Pompeii.

GARDEN SEATS AND TABLES

Statius reveals that on occasions the Romans made use of portable items
of furniture, such as tables and couches, and placed them in gardens for
the comfort of members of the family and visitors. In this particular
passage he continues to describe the immediate action required to save
these costly items from a sudden storm: 'Helter-skelter we fly, and the
slaves snatch up the festal banquet and wreathed goblets.' They all ran
to the nearest cover, 'Hither all the crowd of us gather, hither throng the
band of slaves with the costly couches and the feast, and all the pleasant
household of elegant Polla. The doors would not contain us . . .'[18] They
had tried to shelter in a half-ruined shrine and this hilarious event made
Statius's friend Polla realize the need of building a better and perhaps
larger shrine or temple in his grounds. Garden furniture appears in
numerous mosaics and one example depicts the villa of Lord Julius. This
large mosaic from Carthage describes life on an extensive estate, in the
centre it shows the villa and the arrival of the *dominus*, the master or
lord. To the right of the villa he goes hunting for hare within his

Stone benches. On the right is
a curved *schola* type bench from
the public garden of the
Triagular Forum at Pompeii.
On the left, from Phaselis, is
one of a pair of seats fitted
around pillars of an archway.

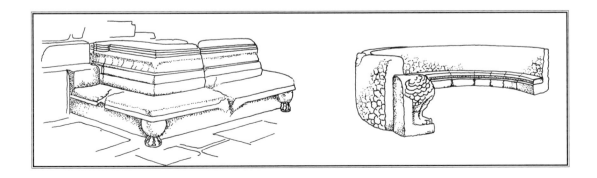

grounds, while above a pastoral scene is shown, and to the left a lady of the house reclines on a couch, fanning herself to keep cool on a sunny day. In the left-hand corner estate workers pick olives while others return from fowling. Below, to the left, a servant has gathered roses from the garden and brings them to his mistress, the *domina* or *matrona*. She stands, leaning nonchalantly, while a maid selects a necklace for her to wear; behind her is a high-backed wicker chair and opposite, a small dog has been placed on a stool.[19] The *dominus* is depicted once more on the lower right-hand side, where he is seated, and servants offer for his inspection the produce of his land. The mosaic contains several garden settings where furnishings had been brought out perhaps only for that day. A brief reference made by Martial implies that his garden couches[20] had been left out in the open and were therefore perhaps a more permanent garden fixture, probably made of wood or wickerwork. Nevertheless he recounts that they were broken, perhaps the elements had taken their toll and rot had set in.

Pliny the Younger mentions garden seats of marble; these would be more durable for outdoor use all year round.[21] Our literary evidence for outdoor seating is strengthened by Cicero, who also informs us that the walks (in the *xystus*) at the Villa of Hortensius were provided with a seat or *sedem*.[22] They are rarely found by archaeology but marble garden seats or benches may resemble an elongated version of Greek thrones seen at theatres, or were an adaptation of *scholae* found beside some tombs or public porticoes. There is a *schola* seat in the triangular forum at Pompeii which has a cantilevered bevel-edged seat with a solid arm rest in the form of a winged griffin. This form was depicted in a garden scene in a fresco at the House of M. Fronto at Pompeii which would confirm its use in garden contexts. It appears in the middle of the dado fresco which illustrates a large decorative enclosure wall of white marble, this curves into a wide

Masonry bench in the museum at Sousse. In the foreground is a demi-lune basin with matching mosaic decoration.

Garden tables.

recess in the centre where an urn fountain is given pride of place. On either side of the fountain a slightly curved white marble bench awaits prospective visitors. Other benches have supports that were carved to resemble a lion's leg, as at Phaselis in southern Turkey, where benches were sited next to one of the town's gateways, and these provide a welcome resting place even to this day. Solid rectangular benches appear to be relatively more frequent on archaeological sites and a number are sited against a wall that could have been used as a convenient back rest. However, even free-standing examples could incorporate a back rest, as seen at Sousse; in this case it had been decorated with a band of mosaic on the seat as well as the back. It is placed fronting on to a similarly decorated semicircular water basin. The cement render and mosaic panels are similar, the seat is the same height and the length matches that of the basin, so they were clearly linked. This form of basin was common to that region and their juxtaposition in the museum courtyard may reflect how they were found on excavation. As can be seen, the provision of wide ledges on this type of water basin (and in *plutei*) would also serve to invite people to sit on the edge and relax for a moment or two.

On excavation, tables found in gardens are often found to have their tops missing, for while the support was usually of marble, stone or masonry, on occasion the top was made of wood. Pliny mentions circular table tops made out of citrus wood, which was highly prized.[23] Of the marble examples a few were shown to have shallow carved depressions marking the positions of individual serving dishes. Tables associated with outdoor *triclinia* were generally fixtures and as such had masonry bases. More decorative versions, mostly of marble, were forms with one, two or three supporting legs. The monopodia form had a single decorative carved leg, which was sometimes fluted, and for stability had a wide splayed foot. The two-footed form was in many ways similar to the *cartibulum*, or ritual table, usually seen in the *atrium*. These were rectangular and had two wide solid supports, the *trapezophori*, which were generally carved with plain rebated panels or an elaborate design with winged griffins or lions. The wings or backs of the beasts were designed to appear to support the weight of the table top. The three-legged forms are often found to have a circular top and slender carved legs, which perhaps recall the more portable wooden or bronze varieties. Many can be seen at Pompeii and Herculaneum; an example of a table with *trapezophori* is in the House of the Dioscuri. This had been placed beside the draw shaft of the cistern in the garden to the rear of the *atrium*. Examples of the three-legged form, with lion-like legs, may be found in the garden at the House of the Stags, Herculaneum, and at the House of the Vettii, Pompeii.

SUMMER DINING COUCHES

The remains of masonry dining couches or traces of wooden ones are frequently found to be shaded by a pergola and testify to the practice of alfresco dining. Examples have been discovered in several urban gardens in Campania and elsewhere, such as at Ostia, Vienne in Gaul, Italica in Spain, and in villas in the countryside of both France and Spain. There was even an example found in Britain, at the Villa of Rockbourne (Hants.). An outdoor dining area is usually called a summer *triclinium* and the most common of the three varieties on archaeological sites comprises three couches (*klini*) forming three sides of a square. Each couch was inclined, the tallest part facing towards the centre, where a small circular or rectangular table was usually placed within reach of all reclining diners. A narrow shelf was often incorporated into the couch and would be ideal for resting drinking cups on. The hard masonry couch was made more comfortable with covers or mattresses. A fine example of a three-sided *triclinium* was found at Vienne. Fifty-one *triclinia*, as opposed to six *biclinia*, have so far been discovered at Pompeii.[24] The less frequent *biclinia*, (in Latin *bi* means two whereas *tri* is three) are usually placed so that diners face each other; a good example survives at the House of the Thunderbolt at Ostia. The curved form, a *stibadium* or *sigma* (the latter word derives from the shape of a Greek letter), is the type of dining couch that is often illustrated in frescos, mosaics and in miniatures found in Byzantine manuscripts; in the latter the sigma couch was used in scenes depicting the Last Supper. The curved shape is no doubt easier to portray but this form may also have been more fashion-able in the period of the later Empire. It is rarely found on excavation and Jashemski states that only one has been found at Pompeii.[25] However, a rather ruinous example has been discovered at Italica; this had been situated right next to a large decorative fishpond and would have been quite pleasant with a large sheet of water nearby. The curved dining couch is well documented in literary sources, Martial, for example, mentions

Summer *triclinium* and water *mensa* from Vienne. This three-sided dining couch and ornamental pool was shaded from the sun by a vine-covered pergola. Coverlets and cushions would have been brought out to make the reclining areas more comfortable.

one that was inlaid with tortoiseshell.[26] Pliny also mentions the use of a water table, or *mensa*, which seems a rather pleasant arrangement of a pool of water in front of the couches.[27] Here trays of food could be floated and kept cool by the refreshing water. This extravagant idea is in reality found in association with the *stibadium* at Italica, the *triclinium* at Vienne and the *biclinium* at the House of Loreius Tiburtinus in Pompeii. A much larger version is seen in the so-called Serapaeum at Hadrian's Villa, Tivoli, where the large curved couch was protected from the sun by a huge half-domed hall. Water *mensae* are often only a small part of interconnected water channels, fountains and pools seen in elaborate water gardens (water features will be fully discussed in the next chapter).

It is rather unfortunate, and a little confusing, that the word *triclinium* has two meanings: it is used to denote a dining couch and also a dining room where these couches were placed. Hence we try to refer to a summer *triclinium* when mentioning those used in the garden. An interesting change in fashion brought about the use of Cyzican *triclinia*, named after the town where they had originated, Cyzicus in Turkey. They are mentioned by Vitruvius, who says that these important large dining rooms were sited so that they could 'command a view of gardens. . . . On the right and the left they have windows which open like folding doors, so that views of the garden may be had from the dining couches through the opened windows'.[28]

Reconstruction drawing of a garden at Italica furnished with a *stibadium* dining couch. This had been placed so that food could be floated on trays in the decorative pool nearby, a fashion described by Pliny the Younger. The owner, his wife and daughter are shown taking a light meal in their garden. Sculpture in this reconstruction drawing is conjectural but is based on items discovered elsewhere in Spain.

Sadly only sporadic excavations have been conducted at Cyzicus itself and to date no details of this special type of *triclinium* have come to light there. We do, however, have a prime example on the Palatine, where the *triclinium* in the Domus Flavia opens on to a large garden, and through windows on either side looks on to a pair of garden fountain courts. This effect is also found elsewhere, in the Casa de los Pájaros at Italica, although restoration has now confused the details. At present a solid wall has been rebuilt in place of the open windows that were indicated in earlier reports of this site. The open nature of these rooms, where they looked out on to three areas of greenery, would mean that they are akin to a loggia or garden pavilion.

AEDICULAE

The small shrines that are seen in gardens often appear similar to *lararia* normally found set against an *atrium* wall. These shrines were dedicated to the gods of the household, the Lares; they were an important feature of the home as all the family members would salute their caring Lares on a daily basis. Also garlands and sacrifices would be laid out for them on feast days and on the occasion of family birthdays. In some cases their shrines were simple but others were often fashioned in the form of an architectural *aedicula*, *aedes* being the Latin term for a shrine.

Aediculae shrines in the garden were usually dedicated to one of the deities associated with gardens (discussed in chapter six) and like those in the *atrium* were usually built out from the wall. A great number of examples seen at Pompeii had a rectangular plinth and a porch-like recess above, where a figurine of the deity could be housed and a space left for offerings. This important area was often fitted with columns to lend a certain *gravitas* to the chamber of the god and to provide a support for the pediment above; this was usually triangular with a pitched roof but some had curved upper sections. The inside was often shaped in the form of a semicircular recess but rectangular examples are also known. In general shrines were constructed of masonry covered with plaster which was then painted.

Because the majority are found in a position against a garden wall we are less likely to find them in a dwelling with a complete peristyle, where there was a portico on all four sides. This decorative yet sacred garden element is therefore more often seen in houses with small gardens, such as at the House of the Tragic Poet and in the first garden at the House of the Dioscuri at Pompeii. It is also seen at Ostia in the House of Fortuna Annonaria. An *aedicula* shrine or *nymphaeum* placed on a rear wall, as in the three examples mentioned, would serve as a focal point to rooms looking on to this space of greenery, and when placed in an axial position in line with the front entrance of the house, the obvious display would be immediately seen when the entrance door from the street was opened. The maximum value for the money spent would therefore be obtained.

AEDICULAE NYMPHAEA

Many of the features of a garden *aedicula* were replicated when creating a small domestic-sized shrine to the nymphs. This version of a similar theme was connected to a water supply and was actually a little fountain house or *nymphaeum*. The *nymphaeum*, however, does not usually stand on a tall plinth. A number of examples are also covered in painted plaster but there are several beautiful versions that have been encrusted with coloured areas of mosaic. The latter were therefore highly decorative and colourful. The mosaic tesserae were placed to form a variety of decorative panels of geometric and figurative design. Shells were also used in *nymphaea* to frame panels and to emphasize the outlines of the exterior and the archway. Although used in a decorative way, shells were also associated with the watery element of Venus, the goddess of gardens, and have therefore a dual symbolic implication.

Where statuary would have obscured the ornamental scheme in the recess, the inner surface of the niche was usually simplified and was often given a rustic coating of applied pumice. This may have been intended to recall the rough rocky surface found in a grotto, which would be the home of a natural spring. In *aediculae nymphaea* water was made to appear from an open mouth of a mask or other outlet and fall down into a water catchment basin below. A number were also furnished with a short flight of steps so that the water could tumble down and make a little cascade to mimic a spring.

The well-preserved examples in Pompeii are useful when making a comparison with the remains of others found elsewhere, and these show that the type was not just regional. Both painted and mosaic versions existed outside of the area covered by Vesuvius; for instance at the House of the Mosaic Niche in Ostia. There was even a mosaic encrusted example in the House of Augustus on the Palatine[29] and at Tivoli.

Façade *nymphaeum* in the House of Cupid and Psyche at Ostia. Water would have poured from statues placed in each of the five niches, originally all clad in marble.

FAÇADE NYMPHAEA

This form was also set against a wall and in many cases a whole wall was utilized. In the House of the Little Bull at Pompeii we can see the transition where the *aedicula* form had been enlarged and replicated three times, but in each niche water cascaded down some steps and fell into a communal basin below. A more elaborate example may be seen at the House of Cupid and Psyche at Ostia. Here the garden is decorated with a series of five niches that are separated by columns. In the lower portion there are semicircular projections and the recesses of the arched upper section are of an alternating semicircular and rectangular form. The whole is reminiscent of a theatre façade and perhaps this type was inspired by the sight of monumental public fountains. Water was introduced into each niche, where presumably it poured from a fountain figure. It fell down a flight of three marble steps, angled in such a way that they form a slope rather than stairs, subsequently falling into a shallow trough. A hole in the side of each trough then directed the water to the projections of the podium, where it would have emerged out of a lion's head or similar outlet. It is believed that a long shallow drainage channel below (now gone) caught the water, as in the *triclinium* dining room at the House of Fortuna Annonaria, also in Ostia.[30]

This type of *nymphaeum* is seen in a number of places and in a variety of adapted forms. For instance, the remains of a *nymphaeum* comprising three niches may be seen in a house at Vienne dated to the early second century AD (to the rear of the summer *triclinium*) and in the villa at Desenzano del Garda, dated to the late fourth century AD,[31] which both appear in a true garden. The Neronian façade *nymphaeum* of the Domus Transitoria on the Palatine is internal,[32] but Terrace House No. 2 at Ephesus[33] and the House of the Psalms at Stobi in Macedonia[34] appear to face on to a paved peristyle courtyard, showing how Roman ingenuity with water could enhance an otherwise plain Greek-style court. Both types indicate the widespread use of this architectural garden element, and that this type of *nymphaeum* continued to be fitted into houses and villas right up to the period of the Late Empire.

WALLING

The enclosing walls around *horti* were usually high. As well as keeping the garden area private they were needed to stop thieves. One method employed can be seen in a rustic kitchen garden at Pompeii (I, xx, 5), where the wall alongside the street was rendered insurmountable by placing jagged fragments of amphora along the top; this would have the same effect as the modern use of broken glass. However, a wall belonging to a more decorative garden would need to be more attractive to look at and could be covered with plaster and embellished by frescos, and *aediculae*, or shrines and *nymphaea*. In many cases these were built on to the wall but alternatively niches could be built into the thickness of it. A small niche could provide a place to rest an oil lamp, to light the garden when dark. Simple versions are found but others were fashioned to imitate a grand architectural portal, albeit in miniature, and were given a correspondingly shortened pair of columns as if to support a pediment, often triangular. A number of other niches were made into a little shrine; some of these were found to contain a small cult figure or a painted version of one. A niche also appears to have been a good place for displaying statuary, as at the House of Pompeius Axiochus in Pompeii. Here two walls had been embellished, on one there was a row of six niches near the top of the garden wall and an *aedicula* shrine against the other.

Another mode of decoration was to include patterned brickwork, although this is normally seen on walls at larger properties. Bands of different coloured stone and brick were employed and made into a lozenge pattern, as in terrace walling at a villa near Tivoli,[35] or as shown by the photograph of the Villa del Pastore at Stabiae[36] where the wall was constructed in *opus reticulatum* of alternate bands of dark and light stone. This wall was also embellished with a decorative crest of semicircular arcs in a wave-like design. Another method was to place little turrets along the line of the wall, as at Sette Finestre.[37] This arrangement may have served as a form of decoration but it could also have made the wall appear more solidly built. Alternatively, because the turrets resembled miniature dovecotes or towers of a city wall, they may have been designed to serve as a false perspective to give the illusion of a bigger garden. As it is quite rare to find walling surviving to its original height, these examples are therefore extremely interesting for they were meant to be seen and not covered. The expenditure incurred in creating decorative walling such as those cited really implies that the area contained within must have been devoted to a pleasure garden rather than being used for husbandry or vegetables. A further method employed in gardens of large estates was to achieve the reverse effect, that of concealing a boundary wall. At Tusculum, Pliny planted hedges of box to be trimmed in tiers.[38] In the right circumstances, as in this case, they would have an effect of incorporating the adjacent landscape as part of the garden. Tiered hedges could be made to mimic a semi-natural-looking belt of shrubbery that would render the boundary almost invisible at a distance. Various landscaping methods were used to create different effects. One option was to construct a sunken garden.

SUNKEN GARDENS

Several gardens were found to have been excavated to some depth below ground level. In the peristyle gardens of the Domus Sollertiana at El-Jem, North Africa, the soil level was only approximately 80 cm below the ambulatory but the lower level would help to conserve moisture for plants grown within the garden. This garden was also provided with a number of terracotta waste water outlets, still visible in the surrounding walls, which would have allowed surplus water to be directed straight to the planted area. These measures would have been a valuable asset, for in such hot and potentially dry countries different techniques or methods were sometimes employed to maintain a garden under difficult conditions. An extreme case is that of Bulla Regia, which is in a very hot, dry, inland region of Tunisia. A number of houses here were

Reconstruction drawing of the sunken garden at the House of Ancora Nera, Pompeii. This is one storey below ground level; the peristyle above is of alternating circular and square pillars. On both side walls of the garden there is a row of statue bases, and at the rear are three decorative niches.

provided with an underground suite of rooms that would have been cooler during the summer. These were arranged around a central light-well and were invariably furnished with garden elements such as decorative water basins.[39] The coolness of the water would have also helped to provide a different temperature from that above ground.

A sunken garden is found in Pompeii at the House of Ancora Nera, where the garden was reached by descending a flight of nine steep steps. The *hortus* was in effect one storey below ground level, slightly less than at Bulla Regia, but here the garden area was much larger. A cryptoporticus ran around all four sides of the garden, in place of a peristyle. On three sides some of the arched openings of the cryptoporticus were partly blocked up to provide niches for statuary yet still let light into the covered passageway behind. The fourth north-facing side was furnished with three rusticated apses, the central one containing an *aedicula*. At upper storey level a colonnade, presumably with a low protective wall, gave the impression of a two-storey dwelling. The height of this structure would certainly help to keep the garden cool and moist and be of especial value in high summer. To the north three dining rooms were placed so that diners could benefit from a view of the verdant scene below, with the *aedicula* as its focal point.

These deep sunken gardens are also seen in palatial abodes, such as in the so-called 'stadium' of the Domus Augustana in Rome. At upper storey level a large *exedra* was constructed, opening on to the enclosed garden below, so that the Emperor and his friends or guests could benefit from a change of air and the scent emanating from the plants nearby. This arrangement of large rooms placed to overlook gardens below is again found in the 'stadium' of Hadrian's Villa at Tivoli, although in this case the garden was not truly sunken but was at a naturally lower level. The architect here made use of the irregular terrain and built on the cliff above; he also cut into the rock to make two large garden-level rooms below.

The most ambitious version, to date, is found in the renovations carried out by Herod the Great to his palace near Jericho (*c.* 15 BC) which included considerable landscaping on both sides of a river bed, or wadi. This Eastern but Romanized client king 'created a landscaped villa in the contemporary Italian manner';[40] by incorporating Roman ideas and building techniques the architect and gardener had used considerable skills to maximize the effect of the terrain. The palace was built right up to the edge of the cliff and porticos opened on to the view of gardens on the opposite bank, with a bridge linking the two sections of the palace complex. A large level area for a garden, approximately 37 m by 113 m, had been excavated out of the hillside opposite. Substantial retaining walls, partly surviving today, enclosed the garden on three sides while the fourth, at the lowest point near the wadi, was left open so that residents in the palace opposite would be able to view the splendour of the decorative semi-sunken garden. Here a portico was placed on each of the two short walls and the long retaining wall was furnished by alternating rectangular and semicircular niches. Traces of mosaic indicate that they would have been highly decorative. The long length of this wall was relieved by a large centrally placed semicircular recess, the interior of which was designed to appear like a theatre seating plan, but the large number of ancient flowerpots discovered in the narrow tiered plant beds show that the intention was to create layers of greenery, as in a hanging garden, or a monumental version of a Victorian auricula theatre (a tiered stand for displaying pots of auricula plants. An example can be seen at Caulke Abbey.) This was the focal point of the spectacle seen from the opposite bank.

TERRACED GARDENS

Terraced gardens are sometimes depicted in miniature frescos and an example is shown here. This particular villa and garden are beside the sea and at the edge of the terrace a row of cypress trees is linked by swags of live ivy that was allowed to grow partially over the trees. The Romans usually preferred to build on level ground and therefore terraces were constructed to provide a flat platform to work on. Ovid, when in exile, wrote to friends and disclosed how he remembered seeing the porticos of Rome 'with its levelled ground'.[41] Rather than have a completely solid foundation the substructures often comprised vaulted cryptoportici. These served to provide extra rooms for storage, or alternatively could be used as cool underground rooms in the hot summer months. When the countryside around Tivoli was surveyed (*c.* 1906) numerous surviving terrace platforms of villas of Roman date were located.[42] Several villas were found to possess more than one

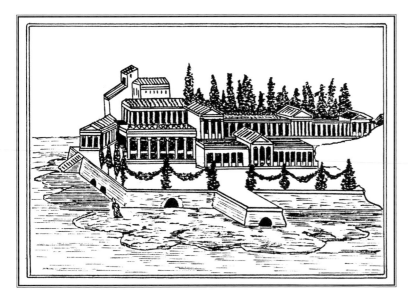

Fresco detail, depicting a villa and its garden on a levelled terrace. The garden is edged by cypress trees linked by ivy. (From Pompeii).

terrace, gardens would perhaps surround buildings, and lower terraces might be devoted solely to gardens and associated pavilions. The terrace above would also provide the necessary height to supply fountains below. As previously mentioned, terraced gardens could create an effect to recall the once-famed Hanging Gardens of Babylon.

Near Pompeii, the Villa of the Mysteries was built on a terrace but only a small part was reserved for a garden. The substructure was provided with a cryptoporticus and we can observe that there is still a sufficient depth of soil above to grow bushes. At the House of the Stags, Herculaneum, the gardens were extended by building up to the town wall. In this way a second garden became a sunny plant-filled terrace from which one could enjoy a marvellous view out to sea. The inhabitants could also now benefit from cooling sea breezes in summer.

Terracing was often used in Rome in the vast landscaping projects carried out by several aristocratic members of society (Lucullus being the first, *c.* 60 BC).[43] Afterwards Maecenas transformed an area on the Esquiline that was once an unsavoury burial ground outside the Servian Wall.[44] Sallust incorporated the valley between the Quirinal and Pincio hills into his gardens, which he enhanced by terracing, and made a feature of a natural spring and brook.[45] An old drawing of about 1828 captures the extent of the valley and some of the surviving buttresses required for the terracing of its sides. The remains of the palace are located on the east side and included a large domed *nymphaeum*, a garden pavilion, parts of which still survive today. Sadly this is now 14 m below street level, for the rest of the valley was filled in and subsequently covered by housing. The gardens of Sallust had been the favourite abode of a number of later emperors, right up to the fall of Rome itself.

Terraced garden at the Villa of the Mysteries near Pompeii. The villa and garden was built on top of a cryptoporticus which incorporated rooms for storage.

The *Horti Luculliani* were constructed in the area of the Pincian Hill, which became known as the *Collis Hortulorum* (the hill of gardens). These were the first large gardens made in Rome and with those of Sallust were among the most renowned. Fortunately, sufficient traces of substructures built to retain soil in terraces remained until up to the sixteenth century for their inclusion in drawings and maps,[46] and are thought to have been more than 13 m high. It is also thought that the '*Muro Torto*' was a continuation of the terrace works carried out at this time. These walls were so massive and strongly built that they were included into the city wall built at the time of the Emperor Aurelian (AD 270-75). This section of the ancient city wall has only recently been hidden from view by reinforcements. Modern excavation in the vicinity has uncovered a long, gently curving *ambulatio* of approximately 180 m, and this in some ways matches plans drawn in about 1553.[47] These show a large semicircular *exedra* that was studded with niches and flanked by a series of ample-sized rooms. They were built on the upper terrace and were linked to lower levels by monumental staircases. The whole building is thought to have been inspired by the earlier imposing structure of the Temple of Fortuna at Praeneste or a theatrical *scenae frons*, the elaborate architectural stage façade found in Roman theatres.[48] With its hillside setting, overlooking the once green and wooded areas of the Campus Martius and the Mausoleum of Augustus, it would have been magnificent. However, one of the dangers in possessing a beautiful garden was that it could invite the envy of the Imperial family. Tacitus reveals how Messalina, the wife of the Emperor Claudius, so coveted the *Horti Luculliani* that its later owner Valerius Asiaticus was finally forced to commit suicide in order that she could take possession.[49] Other gardens were appropriated through the terms of a will, such as the *Hortis Lamiani*, *Maecenatiani* and *Sallustiani*.

Lanciani, the great archaeologist of Rome (*c.* 1893–1901) located all the known remains of these gardens on a map of the city, the *Forma Vrbis Romae*, a relatively modern day equivalent of the Severan Marble Map of Rome. The details include only structures but do reveal a number of terraced walkways and pavilions. For example, within the *Horti Lamiani*, there appears to have been a large semicircular feature, perhaps to rival that in the gardens of Lucullus. There was also a two-sided covered portico for promenades and a long water basin or *euripus*, features that will be discussed later.

Literary sources often like to emphasize Roman ingenuity and the talents of landscape architects. Seneca describes works accomplished at Vattia's villa, such as the labour involved in the construction of two grottos and the novel use of a tidal water course, a *euripus*, running through a grove of plane trees.[50] Elsewhere he comments on the fact that people were building their lordly structures on bays, lakes and on mountain peaks to obtain a fine prospect.[51] Two different types of lakeside properties are briefly mentioned by Pliny, who gives them the names Tragedy and Comedy. 'Tragedy, because it seems to be raised on actor's boots',[52] which evidently stood on an elevated or terraced site above the lake, while Comedy 'wears low shoes' and was made to curve with the shoreline. Another lakeside property has come to light at Sirmione, on Lake Garda. This large courtyard villa had a correspondingly large enclosed garden at its centre and is thought to have belonged to the poet Catullus. It was built on a peninsula and was therefore almost surrounded by the sight and sound of water.

Statius reveals the transformations made by Pollius Felix at Surrentum, on the Bay of Naples, and how the natural scene

> was wild and unlovely, now it is a pleasure to go. . . . Here, where you now see level ground, was a hill . . . where now tall groves appear, there was once not even soil: its owner has tamed the place . . . each window commands a different landscape.[53]

A fine outlook was most desirable and the preferred view needed to be of nature tamed, where architecture enhanced the scene. This is seen in surviving frescos of landscapes, which, according to Pliny, was a genre made famous by Studius, the innovative painter at the time of Augustus.[54] His subjects included country houses with porticos and gardens, groves, woods, hills, fishponds, *euripi*, rivers and coastal scenes. These frescos emphasize the buildings and the works of man, and the role of gardens is to provide a green and pleasant background. Garden elements are in the main used to unite and highlight various architectural groups.

MARITIME VILLAS

The Villa of Lucullus on the Bay of Naples was 'in its day the most famous in this group. Plutarch mentions that here Lucullus had 'built dwellings in the sea'[55] and cut channels through the rock, perhaps to create an island residence that may have looked like a floating palace. Texts indicate that villas beside the sea were popular as a respite from the summer heat of Rome, when a cooling sea breeze would be welcomed. Even the practical Columella advises that 'a villa is always properly placed when it overlooks the sea'.[56] Plants in the gardens, however, could suffer from wind damage and the effects of salt spray. Pliny noted this in the open areas at Laurentum, near Ostia, and therefore placed his kitchen garden behind the protection of a cryptoporticus.[57] Van Buren used Pliny's descriptions to reconstruct a plan of this villa[58] and a model which includes garden areas has been put on display in the Ashmoleum Museum. Other literary quotations are few; we have a passage by Statius, part of which is quoted above, and one by Seneca giving a brief description of Vattia's villa near Baiae. These are exceptions and the few remaining references are mostly concerned with the utilization of sea water for fish ponds.

There were a great number of maritime villas on the shores of the Mediterranean but unfortunately we know very little about their garden areas. For instance, a recent survey identifies and locates around sixty villas lining the Tyrrhenian littoral during the century 50 BC–AD 50, which appears to be the greatest period of their construction,[59] but their gardens are not discussed. At Val Catena[60] on the Adriatic island of Brioni Grande, archaeologists have shown the extent of buildings and gardens around the bay and their relationship to the general landscaping of the whole place. However, details of these garden areas are again left blank. On the other hand, maps locating the partially eroded remains discovered at the sumptuous maritime villas of North Africa, such as at Silin, Zliten and Tagiura,[61] are more informative and show that the villas appear to contain one or more large enclosed gardens or terraces with water features (such as *euripi* at Silin and Zliten, also a demi-lune basin in the latter and a shaped basin at Tagiura), but again further information would be desirable. Villas built on the banks of large rivers and lakes would share many characteristics of maritime villas, in that they would open on to the water's edge; an example is at Wittlich in Germany which overlooked the River Rhine.[62]

There were possibly a few maritime villas in Britain and one was discovered on the cliff tops near Folkestone, but cliff falls over the years have eroded much of the evidence. However, the best example is the palace at Fishbourne. Here the south wing, which is today under modern housing, may have opened on to a landscaped area (with pond) down to the sea and harbour.[63]

GARDENS OF LARGE AND PALATIAL VILLAS

The Golden House of Nero (or Domus Aurea) is perhaps the most infamous of this group for, as Suetonius relates, Nero built without regard to others a grandiose palace set in a vast estate in the middle of the city.[64] His landscaping projects included an artificial lake surrounded by pastures and woodland; in fact he wished to create an atmosphere of *rus in urbe*. Of the buildings that have survived[65] we can see that rooms faced into garden courts or out to a wide terrace from which one would have a view of the lake below. The imposition of so huge an estate which blocked previous arterial routes into the city was too abhorrent for the people and it was broken up after Nero's downfall, with much of the area put aside for buildings that would be used by the public. Such vast areas of land occupied by one man were seen as wrong in the heart of the city but did not cause so much resentment if located in outlying districts or in the countryside.

It is perhaps natural that most of the literary documentation on Roman gardens concerns the large or palatial. As most poets and historians lived within the circles of the wealthy, their work would naturally favour references to the type of properties they were more conversant with, and the average garden was often deemed less worthy of comment. Likewise we see aspects of an affluent society represented in art, for villas in landscape frescos are also normally large. Many owners appear to have decorated their homes and gardens to resemble those of the aristocracy and therefore many features in small gardens reflect those of their larger counterparts. In large gardens, however, there was more space; we still find some enclosed courts or peristyle gardens within the building complex but beyond there may have been areas of greenery linking different buildings within the estate and perhaps even acres devoted to landscaped gardens.

We are fortunate that at the Villa of Hadrian at Tivoli we can see an unusually large area. This enables us to make out the rather loose disposition of groups of buildings and see how the numerous buildings are placed in relation to garden areas. Much in this domain is of a monumental nature and extremely grandiose, but relatively more modest versions would have existed elsewhere. In the plan opposite colonnades, where known, are indicated to show where they open on to garden areas, or to Greek-style open paved courts, such as the 'Doric peristyle'. Hadrian's biographer in the *Historiae Augustae* informs us that Hadrian named parts of his villa after locations of especial interest, such as the Lyceum, Academia, Prytaneum, Canopus, Poikile, Tempe and Hades.[66] With the exception of the Prytaneum these are names that are still in use for what are assumed to be the relevant areas of the villa. It is interesting to note that all are associated with garden features. The appellation Prytaneum could have been given to the so-called Piazza D'Oro area, for the courtyard and associated aristocratic dining facilities found here rather resemble Greek buildings designed to cater for official hospitality.

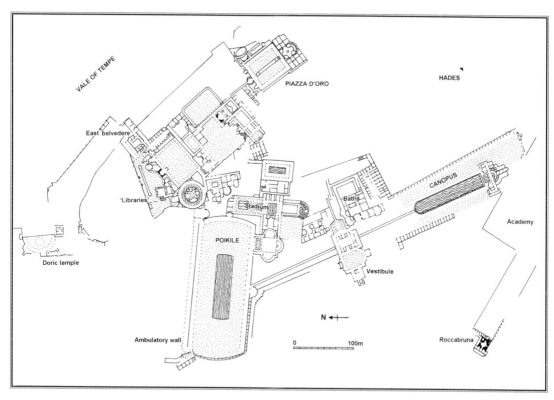

Plan of Hadrian's Villa at Tivoli. The numerous garden areas have been stippled.

At Tivoli the north wall of the Poikile was named after the famous *stoa* at Athens and overlooks a large garden that has been given the same name. The covered portico was used to exercise oneself in walking *in circuitum*, meaning either there and back or a circuit course. This type of portico is usually provided with rounded turning points at one or both ends. Inscriptions, found here and in association with similar features elsewhere,[67] state their distance, often showing that a certain number of turns would make a *stade*. These *ambulationes* are often placed to ensure that one side faces the sun, to provide shelter but warmth on winter walks, while the reverse face would have sufficient shade during hot summer months.

The terrain around Hadrian's villa at Tivoli was used in imaginative ways; to the north of the Piazza D'Oro a pleasant valley was landscaped to recall the idyllic surroundings of the Vale of Tempe in Thessaly, in the foothills of Mount Olympus. A small semi-artificial valley contains the Canopus area and serves to isolate it from other buildings. Here a large water basin and dining facilities re-created that infamous district on the Nile delta. The so-called Greek and Latin libraries that may perhaps have been associated with the Lyceum had an irregularly shaped garden furnished with a thin and shallow *euripus* water basin that had octagonal terminals. The exterior walls of this garden were provided with numerous niches for statuary facing on to what may

Model of Hadrian's Villa, Tivoli, showing the Poikile garden with its long covered walkway.

have been a processional entrance. Literary evidence for such gardens is provided by Plutarch, who reveals that the library of Lucullus and its associated cloister garden were both kept open for public use.[68] Another instance shows that before visiting his friend Varro, Cicero says, 'If you have a garden in your library we will want for nothing.'[69] This would perhaps imply an enclosed garden within or attached to such a building, where texts could be read in good light outdoors. Elsewhere Cicero mentions areas at his various properties that were also named after the Lyceum and Academy at Athens,[70] although they were of a much earlier date. One can imagine that these would also be provided with gardens.

HIPPODROME GARDENS

Some garden areas were of a characteristic shape and in this particular category we see those that were essentially a long but often broad rectangular garden in which one or both of the short ends were rounded; in fact they were meant to re-create the shape of a hippodrome/circus or stadium. These were originally racetracks but the Romans often delighted in such conceit as to have a basic idea or shape and then to adapt or change its usage. There were hippodrome gardens at the large villa of the Quintillii just outside Rome, at Hadrian's villa at Tivoli and on the Palatine; in the last two, however, the excavators have referred to them as stadia. The 'stadium' garden in the Imperial palace on the Palatine was surrounded by colonnades and was furnished with two semicircular water basins for fountains. The architect positioned the arc of these fountain basins to mirror the curve of the short sides of the garden; in doing so he made an analogy with the racecourse, for they could be interpreted as a turning point in the circuit. Also, because the garden lies at a low level, the upper walkways could imitate the viewing area or spectator seating found in a circus or stadium. One rather imaginative reconstruction drawing has been made of this garden which shows a grove of trees on the upper level.[71] At Tivoli the 'stadium' has undergone many alterations in its time and now appears rather cluttered by the number of pavilions and water features that it once contained. The area has been studied in great detail and its complicated arrangements are now clarified.[72] From north to south it featured a narrow pool that was flanked by rectangular plant beds; these were followed by a large semi-open loggia, either side of which were three large tubs for trees or vines which could climb between the series of door openings, up the sides and over the roof. After this there was a large sheet of shallow water which effectively cut the stadium in half. The second half again contained a large pavilion or loggia that opened on to a spectacular curved water feature and *nymphaeum* (see chapter five). The best known 'Hippodrome' garden is found in the grounds of Pliny's Tuscan villa which he describes to a friend. This passage provides many interesting details of Roman garden design and is invaluable in the identification of plants used in such an area. Also it is so descriptive that it does invoke the true spirit of a Roman garden; indeed you almost feel that you are accompanying him in taking a turn around its course.

The design and beauty of the buildings are greatly surpassed by the riding-ground *hippodromus*. The centre is quite open so that the whole extent of the course can be seen as one enters. It is planted round with ivy-clad plane trees, green with their own leaves above, and below with the ivy which climbs over trunk and branch and links tree to tree as it spreads across them. Box shrubs grow between the plane trees, and outside there is a ring of laurel bushes which add their shade to that of the planes. Here the straight part of the course ends, curves round in a semicircle, and changes its appearance, becoming darker and more densely shaded by the cypress trees planted round to shelter it, whereas the inner circuits – for there are several – are in open sunshine; roses grow there and the cool shadow alternates with the pleasant warmth of the sun. At the end of the winding alleys of the rounded end of the course you return to the straight path, or rather paths, for there are several separated by intervening box hedges. Between the grass lawns here and there are box shrubs clipped into innumerable shapes, some being letters which spell the gardener's name or his master's; small obelisks of box alternate with fruit trees, and then suddenly in the midst of this ornamental scene is what looks like a piece of rural country planted there. The open space in the middle is set off by low plane trees planted on each side; farther off are acanthuses with their flexible glossy leaves, then more box figures and names.

At the upper end of the course is a curved dining seat of white marble, shaded by a vine trained over four slender pillars of Carystian marble. Water gushes out through pipes from under the seat as if pressed out by the weight of people sitting there, is caught in a stone cistern and then held in a finely worked marble basin which is regulated by a hidden device so as to remain full without overflowing. The preliminaries and main dishes for dinner are placed on the edge of the basin, while the lighter ones float about in vessels shaped like birds or little boats. A fountain opposite plays and catches its water, throwing it high in the air so that it falls back into the basin, where it is played again at once through a jet connected with the inlet. Facing the seat is a bedroom. . . . Here too a fountain rises and disappears underground, while here and there are marble chairs which anyone tired with walking appreciates as much as the building itself. By every chair is a tiny fountain, and throughout the riding-ground can be heard the sound of the streams directed into it, the flow of which can be controlled by hand to water one part of the garden or another or sometimes the whole at once.[73]

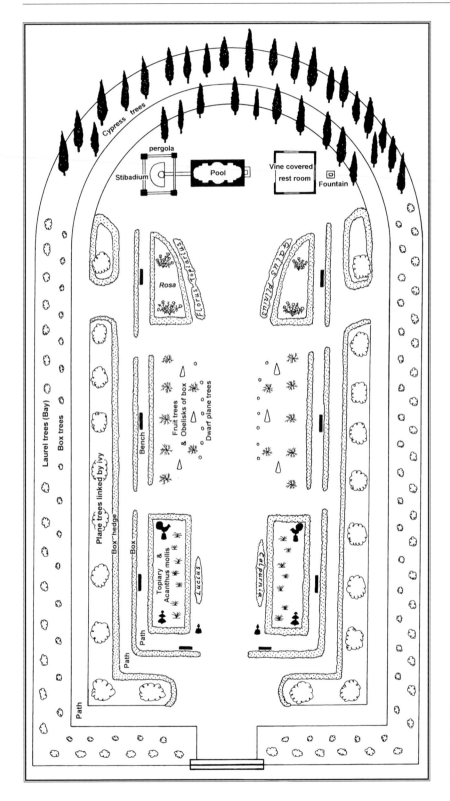

Reconstruction drawing of Pliny's Hippodrome garden, based on details given in his letter.

This vivid description provides sufficient material to attempt a reconstruction of the garden. Several interpretations have been made,[74] and in each case the outer part of their plan has been defined but the interior seems incomplete. In the new reconstruction illustrated here, the alfresco dining area is clarified and a shaped pool is introduced, for this form would have been in vogue at that time. All the plants mentioned have been included, and are placed in a design suggested by the Latin text and its translation. Unfortunately Pliny does not mention statuary in this garden, and therefore we can only assume that there may have been one or two fountain figures at least. A simple mask or lion's head water outlet, for instance, similar to those found in street fountains, could have been used in some of the numerous fountains, but perhaps to Pliny these would not have needed comment.

GARDEN PAVILIONS

Grounds were sometimes laid out with special features such as tree houses. Velletri's was large enough to hold banquets in its canopy and was particularly favoured by Caligula, who called it his 'nest'.[75] One might also find garden pavilions, such as a belvedere or prospect tower described by Luxorius, writing from North Africa. The lofty tower had been furnished with 'a resting place for its owner' and from its height he could see 'On one side a grove and on the other side fountains . . . and a statue of Diana'.[76] Suetonius mentions a belvedere at Rome in an area or *hortus* previously belonging to Maecenas. From here there was a superb prospect of the city of Rome below and this tower became part of legend as the site where Nero took up his lyre and played while Rome burned.[77] Hadrian's villa at Tivoli is believed to have contained at least two belvederes, one to the east of the main residential area where he could enjoy a good view of his beloved Vale of Tempe, and one to the west, the so-called Roccabruna tower, which overlooked another river valley. Being sited on high ground this would have provided a fine panoramic view.

DIAETAE OR REST ROOMS

Another building often found in a garden setting was the *diaeta*. From Pliny's description of his large garden at his Tuscan villa we learn how special outdoor dining areas could be accompanied by a small *cubiculum* or *diaeta* where people could take a siesta after meals. Pliny believed that this building

> contributes as much beauty to the scene as it gains from its position. It is built of shining white marble, extended by folding doors which open straight out into greenery; its upper and lower windows all look out into more greenery above and below. A small alcove which is part

of the room but separated from it contains a bed, and although it has
windows in all its walls, the light inside is dimmed by the dense
shade of a flourishing vine which climbs over the whole building up
to the roof. There you can lie and imagine you are in a wood but
without the risk of rain.[78]

This description gives a good indication that garden pavilions were
functional as well as aesthetic. Rest rooms of this type can be seen at the
House of Lorieus Tiburtinus, Pompeii, and on either side of the terraced
hanging garden at the House of the Stags, Herculaneum.

ORNITHONES OR AVIARIES

Cicero, who supervised the building of his brother's Manilian villa,
mentions that the estate was nearing completion but the outstanding
works to be completed included a promenade and an aviary.[79] Varro also
possessed an *ornithone* on his estate at Casinum; here bridges crossed a
stream, alongside which a path led up to a *museum* (possibly another
form of *nymphaeum* building) and down to his *ornithone*. This ingenious
structure contained nets in the colonnade for 'all manner of birds'[80] and
in the centre ponds for fish and wildfowl. A summer dining area was
also included. Varro remarks that the aviary belonging to Lucullus was
not so hygienic as his own, for there the diners ate among the birds
while in his *ornithone* the birds were confined to the areas in the
colonnade and part of a *tholos*, a round structure where perches were
placed in tiers to mimic a theatre auditorium.

Varro's description is open to a number of interpretations and several
reconstructions have been made.[81] The text refers to a rectangular
enclosure that was lined on three sides by a row of columns, behind
which there was a rivulet and a row of dwarf trees. Netting was hung
between the columns and this formed the framework of the aviary. A
circular *tholos* was placed to the rear but in one reconstruction it appears
as a decorative feature and is quite separate from the dining area, which
Van Buren and Kennedy located in the middle of the open area of the
rectangular enclosure. Three bench seats have been placed so that when
seated, the diners would turn their backs to the spectacle to be seen in
the *tholos*. Another interpretation of the passage describing Varro's
aviary would be to site the dining area under the shade of the *tholos*, for
summer *triclinia* are always shaded in some manner. The Romans
usually arranged their dining rooms/areas in such a way that a fine view
could be enjoyed during the course of the banquet and therefore it
makes sense to place the seating arrangement facing the theatrical
spectacle on the opposite side of the *tholos*. Varro refers to a platform in
this vicinity that could be interpreted as a masonry *stibadium* couch and
this curved form would fit well in the round *tholos*. Directly in front of
this was a narrow path around a pond with a circular island. Here 'a

single manservant' turned a circular table fashioned like the spokes of a wheel. This had a two foot border on which all the varied dishes for the meal could be placed. The wheel could be turned and presumably was within reach of the diners, or items were brought to them by another servant.

TEMPLES AND SHRINES IN LANDSCAPED AREAS

Several estates included a small shrine or temple, often placed to provide a particular focal point, such as in the grounds of both the gardens of Lucullus and Sallust at Rome,[82] where they had been placed on high ground. Statius describes a temple dedicated to Hercules at the villa of Pollius Felix.[83] This appears to have been on a cliff terrace overlooking the sea. Pavilions and shrines would have been included in the landscaping of large domains but unless there is an inscription, literary reference or clear signs for its purpose, identification remains elusive. Pliny reveals the presence of a temple on one of his estates at Laurentum. He mentions that this sacred building, dedicated to the goddess Ceres, needed some restoration work and at the same time he thought that he would build porticos nearby for the convenience of worshippers who could then shelter 'from rain or sun' when visiting this sacred site. Pliny asked advice on the best location for this portico as the terrain would prove challenging. He says that 'they cannot be built round the temple, for the site has a river with steep banks on one side and a road on the other'.[84] It appeared that the porticos would have to be constructed on the other side of a country lane, on the only level land available, but at least they would then lie opposite the temple. The porticos referred to here are in fact a garden feature, more often seen in the public sphere, and will be discussed fully in chapter nine. At Hadrian's villa at Tivoli, our most extensive model for providing comparative material, there were a number of sacred areas inside the main building complex and also in the grounds; a temple below the terrace wall of the Poikile garden and the once-beautiful Doric temple near the present entrance to the archaeological site. This was of course a monumental affair, with a semicircular colonnade behind a *tholos*, a circular shrine itself surrounded by columns.

At Milreu in Portugal there was a modest-sized temple believed to have been dedicated to Neptune. This had been sited near the villa, as at Lullingstone in Britain, where the temple also functioned as a mausoleum. A family tomb, which was also venerated as a shrine, could on occasion be found in the grounds of country villas. A famous example is that of Cicero's daughter Tullia; despairing of ever finding a plot elsewhere he finally decided on placing it in his own garden (for funerary gardens, see chapter nine).

Some details may be taken from the surviving frescos and mosaics depicting landscapes. Many are of a small size, however, and these

A shrine and tree in a Roman landscape scene. Fresco detail, House of the Small Fountain, Pompeii.

vignettes were often painted with quick brushstrokes in what appears to be an impressionistic style, but one can nevertheless make out the main components. They are often termed sacro-idyllic paintings, for their content usually includes buildings of a sacred nature, such as altars, temples and shrines. A temple-like building or shrine may sometimes have had a cult statue placed nearby, perhaps besides the steps leading up to the sacred building. A gnarled old tree often completes this romantic setting, and is usually found to the side of the building where its canopy would shade the building and worshippers who had ventured this distance. Sometimes the tree appears actually to be growing inside the building or a small walled enclosure, implying that the tree itself was sacred. Or perhaps the structure enclosed a site that had become sacred for some reason. On occasion this occurred after a spot had been struck by a thunderbolt (from Jupiter) and subsequently a tree had either been planted or had self-seeded there; such an enclosure was called a *bidental*. The landscape would include old and venerable features as well as new ones. A column or pillar is frequently shown, sometimes with an urn on top; this is always accompanied by a shading tree. The arching branches of the trees remind one of the rural setting and successfully highlight the architectural components in the landscape.

Varro and Cicero mention islands in rivers on their properties. The latter talks of his fondness for this spot and how, whenever possible, he would come to sit there and unwind.[85] Natural phenomena such as waterfalls were, where possible, also incorporated into the landscaping of an estate. We learn of the shrine of the nymphs that was placed close to the much loved Bandusian falls of Horace.[86] At Chedworth in Britain a spring gently flows into a deep stone-lined pool and was incorporated into a fountain house that could be approached from a narrow winding path. Although close to the villa/guest house the feature would have perhaps had an open look, and certainly its setting with trees nearby makes it appear romantic even today. Waterfalls and springs were sometimes enhanced by man but nevertheless they remained beautiful in their setting.

All of these features should not be seen in isolation, for on many estates *nymphaea* in the form of caves or grottos became part of the landscape.

CAVES AND GROTTOS

Grottos feature in a number of large estates and were originally a naturally occurring phenomenon that could be incorporated into the landscape of a Roman villa. Caves were sometimes associated with funerary beliefs such as being the gateway to Hades or the inferno below, and this aspect was used to the full in the subterranean grotto located on the high ground east of the Academy at Hadrian's villa at Tivoli. To affirm its associations a statue of Cerberus, the fierce three-headed guard dog of the underworld, was placed inside. However, caves also had other religious aspects. In Greece water was often derived from a hidden spring and when this occurred in a cave, in the bowels of the earth, it was seen as mystical. Therefore the source was usually linked to a particular divinity, to Pan or in many cases a nymph. Caves were enhanced with the addition of altars and offerings. The mouth of the spring itself was often elaborated upon, so that the spring gushed forth from some form of fountain head and would be caught by a basin below. Several frescos depicting landscape scenes include a cave or grotto where we can see such a spring in its setting, for example, that from Boscoreale. This fresco, originally from the Villa of P. Fannius Sinistor, is now in the Metropolitan Museum in New York. Another fresco with a grotto fountain, the 'paysage Barberini', survives only from drawings made soon after its discovery; a copy is kept in the Windsor Royal Library, no. 19226.[87]

Natural caves were sometimes enlarged and rooms made inside, as in those at Capri, one of which is the famous 'Blue Grotto'. These have been studied recently and a thorough survey was made of the architecture of *nymphaea* and grottos found in Ancient Italy.[88] Further north at Sperlonga the cave also included large fishponds and a dining area. The fact that the owners of this particular cave named their villa *Speluca*, 'the cavern', gives an indication of the attention given to such features in the grounds of a villa. The cave at Sperlonga has been identified as the location of a disaster (*c.* AD 27) recorded by Suetonius and Tacitus, when part of the roof collapsed and fell on the diners below. As the Emperor Tiberius was present on this occasion this event was well recorded – he escaped harm, however.[89] It is believed that the architects of the Sperlonga grotto, with its Hellenistic Odysseus statuary group, came from Rhodes[90] which perhaps reinforces a Greek association with grottos. Seneca mentions that on Vattia's estate two caves had been created, 'one of these does not admit the rays of the sun, while the other keeps them until the sun sets',[91] which would imply that they also contained dining rooms; the former would remain cool for summer use and the latter would be warmed by the sun for the winter months.

Artificial caves could be excavated out of a suitable hillside to make a grotto but elsewhere they needed to be constructed. In gardens with a cryptoporticus the essential elements of a grotto would be fairly simple to re-create; the cryptoporticus of a terrace wall could be made to look like a rock face and an opening could be let into the wall as if it were the bank of a hill; for example, at the villa of Domitian at Castelgandolfo, where there was a series of four grotto *nymphaea* in the cryptoporticus wall of the middle terrace.[92] Terrace walls could be 'ornamented with niches, *nymphaea* and waterfalls'.[93] Pieces of pumice were applied to interior surfaces to create a rustic feel that mimicked the appearance of natural rock. Pliny mentions this process in connection with *musaea*,[94] which were garden structures that were similar, in all but name, to artificial caves or *nymphaea*. Two references show that the appellation was arbitrary: Propertius describes a green (perhaps moss-covered) pumice cave[95] where instruments of the Muses were hung, implying their re-created abode, and Statius refers to nymphs in 'pumice caves'.[96]

In these 'cave-grottos' that quintessential element, the spring, was piped to the site. The outlet of the 'spring' was often placed in a semicircular niche. Side walls were often given subsidiary niches, usually alternating rectangular with semicircular. Ancient models of grottos, such as the one found at Reggio Calabria, give an impression of the appearance of these artificially constructed caves.

NYMPHAEA OF BASILICA FORM

On level ground the basic elements of the artificial cave were translated into masonry structures that often bore little resemblance to the rocky caves of their origin. Such artificial grottos tended to be referred to as a *nymphaeum*, for they were also meant to recall the abode of nymphs. In large properties these often took the form of a garden room or pavilion. Surviving examples, such as at S. Antonio, the so-called Villa of Horace at Tivoli, demonstrate features common to this type of building.[97] They usually consist of a rectangular room with an apse to the rear and therefore resemble a basilica. The roof is mostly barrel vaulted, with a half dome over the recess. 'Spring' water would issue from a centrally located point in the apse and side walls were often furnished with niches, with or without further water outlets. In the Auditorium of Maecenas in Rome the apse incorporated a flight of six semicircular steps. Water issued from a series of points on the uppermost step and tumbled down, like a waterfall, into a basin below which no longer exists. Some of the original painted wall plaster remains, and the subjects depicted in the niches on the upper level of the apse, and those of the main hall, are of a garden, showing birds flying above shrubs and trees in front of which is either a trellis fence or an urn containing a fountain. Although these buildings are wholly artificial, the decor reinforces links with the elements of nature, and their components re-create artificial grottos and caves. Less well-preserved examples have been found as far afield as Welschbillig in Germany[98] and in the Villa of Cardilius at Torres Novas, Portugal.[99]

A fresco from Pompeii illustrates some features of the interior of a basilica *nymphaeum*, although only part of the lateral walls is detailed. These are, however, shown to have a row of columns and fountains, as in the excavated example at Horace's villa. In the fresco each side wall of the fountain house is fitted with five lion's head water spouts pouring water into an elongated decorative basin supported by animal-like legs. Above are niches with frescos depicting garden scenes reminiscent of those in the Auditorium of Maecenas.

Another form of *nymphaeum* was to be found in the large monumental domed or half-domed halls. These pavilions had either a circular area with a number of wide doorways or a semicircular curved apse that opened on to a garden. In some cases they were furnished with a curved façade *nymphaeum*, as in the Piazza D'Oro at Hadrian's villa in Tivoli, or with alternating niches for statuary and fountains, as in the grandiose version seen in the Serapaeum at the head of the Canopus. Multiple niches were also included in the large domed structures found at Rome, such as the *nymphaeum* that served as a pavilion to the Gardens of Sallust, and in the so-called Temple of Minerva Medica, which was a *nymphaeum* belonging to the Licinian Gardens.

Part of the interior of a basilica-style *nymphaeum*. On the side wall water pours from a row of lions' masks into a collective water basin. Above, two niches contain painted garden scenes. Fresco detail from the House of Diomedes, Pompeii.

Many features discussed in this chapter involve the use of water but the main concern here has been to explore the architectural and landscaping aspects. However, in both town and country properties, *nymphaea*, water basins or fishponds also required the excavation of a considerable amount of earth or rock, the construction of the basin itself and the addition of an efficient hydraulic water system. They therefore need to be seen as part of the overall landscaping in the grounds of villas and houses. As these water features are so important to the spirit of a Roman garden they will be discussed in depth in the next chapter.

CHAPTER FOUR

Ornamental Pools

Varro informs us that in the early days there were only natural ponds which were utilized by the Romans to supply a stock of water birds for the table.[1] At that time fish for consumption were mostly taken from the sea but fish from duck ponds could also be harvested when needed and were therefore seen as a useful resource. In general the fish would only be used locally on the estate, for fresh-water fish did not usually command a high price at market. After a time, it was found that some species of salt-water fish could survive in some of the large ponds and these would fetch a good price when taken to sell locally. The landowner who possessed a natural pond was therefore fortunate. There are a number of ancient mosaics and frescos that depict a variety of duck and fish species that must have been common then. Some of the wild fowling scenes in miniature frescos illustrate methods and practices used on rivers, and perhaps also on natural lakes and ponds. Sometimes a lone fisherman with rod and line is shown, or a small number of men working together and hauling in a net. There are several depicting little winged putti fishing or fowling, and humorous make-believe examples where they are seen at play, chasing ducks and even riding harnessed fish or waterbirds as if they were engaged in a race at the circus.

We learn from Pliny that in about 91-88 BC the Elder Licinius Murena invented the use of artificial *piscinas* or fishponds in which he could breed fish.[2] Unfortunately he does not state what type of fishpond this was, but comments made by Pliny and Varro show that they soon proved popular as Murena's example was quickly followed by Philippius, Hortensius and Lucullus. In fact Murena had received his name for his love of a particular type of fish, the *murena*, which is believed to have been an eel, probably the moray eel. As this is a marine creature this would perhaps imply that a salt-water pond may have been created. Varro mentions the existence, at that time, of two sorts of fishpond: the *dulcium*, or fresh water, which were supplied by nymphs (meaning spring water) and the *salsarum*, or salt water, which, he implies, were owned by the nobility.[3]

The second category was mostly confined to the wealthy few who had the resources to construct a commercial salt-water pond and had the land available for such a venture; in some cases this involved making different compartments for non-compatible fish species or alternatively several interconnecting basins. In the early experimental stages, we learn from Varro that some of the fishponds belonging to Marcus Lucullus became stagnant. However, his brother Lucius, who had a maritime villa near Naples, spent huge sums of money on excavating channels or tunnels to connect his water basin to the sea, so that tides or currents could freshen the water of his fishpond.[4] Columella provides us with all the details of how tidal fishponds were constructed, and from this we can see that the Romans had learned to appreciate the importance of a renewal of water. Although of a later date, Cassiodorus describes a rock-cut pool he had excavated at Squillace on the Adriatic coast of Calabria, where the fish were fed by hand. He adds that the sight of the fish 'both refreshes the spirit with pleasure, and charms the eye with wonder'.[5] The number of references to tame fish, or individual 'pet' fish, shows that it was evidently considered fashionable to include a basin for the display of ornamental species, and on occasion a pool could provide an additional form of entertainment for guests who could fish beside it. Or if we believe some of the accounts, which can be somewhat exaggerated at times, diners could even fish from their dining couches. This example is probably a reference to well-stocked water basins that were sometimes sited close to dining areas such as summer *triclinia* (mentioned in chapter three).

Emperor Nero was said to enjoy fishing to such an extent that he had a whole valley at Subiaco dammed to produce an artificial lake for his sport. Even in the centre of Rome space was made available to create a large lake in the grounds of Nero's Golden Palace; this was to be one of the central features in his grand scheme to imitate country landscapes. Such was the hatred for this man and his excesses that it was later drained and the Colosseum was constructed in its place. In contrast a more pleasant tale is told by Statius, who describes a *stagnum*, the Latin term for a lake, within the villa owned by Atedius Melior. This lake and a tree of wondrous shape are woven into a rather romantic myth created for the pleasure of its owner. He recounts how this graceful tree had grown in such a way that its boughs leaned down towards the water, where, in a gesture of adoration, it would be able to shade the nymph living in the waters below.[6]

Few references state the species of fish stocked in artificial pools, just the general term *pisces* is used. The only species actually identified that appear to have been suitable as pets were various types of mullet and the sea-eel or *murena*. References suggest that they would recognize their master's voice and come when called. Passages disclose how Antonia, the wife of Drusus, was so fond of her pet *murena* that she adorned it with earrings, and Crassus gave his own a necklace as well. Many of these pet fish were mourned after their demise. Cicero derides the excesses lavished by such people and called them '*piscinarium Tritones*', tritons of the fishponds,[7] for he considered their behaviour unnatural and they dared to play as gods. Pliny (in his work on natural history) and Ausonius, who provides an insight on aspects of fishing along the River Moselle, both identify a large number of fish, some of which may have been used to stock *piscinae*.

WATER SUPPLY

When constructing a new water basin not connected to the sea-shore various precautions were used to ensure that the water would not become stagnant. The simplest method was to tap a nearby spring. Fresh water was fed to the basin through a channel of mortared stone or by laying terracotta or wooden pipes. An outlet point drained away the overflow and maintained the desired water level. Another provision was to install a fountain so that the water jet(s) could aerate the pond and at the same time introduce a change of water. In this way the fountain had a useful function but would also decorate the area (many were works of art, and will be discussed in chapter five).

To provide enough pressure for a fountain there needed to be a supply of water at a higher level. Pliny attests that 'water rises as high as its source'.[8] Therefore, if the property was on a hillside, water from a spring nearby could be stored in a tank or cistern on a terrace above. Several have been discovered in the vicinity of Tivoli.[9] An example from a more northerly latitude is at Welschbillig in Germany, where the large basin was fed from a spring in the Geidberg.[10] A literary reference is provided by Sidonius, who mentions tapping a mountain stream to supply water for a *piscina*.[11] Other means involved the use of a machine of some kind, such as a *tympanum*, which is a type of a water wheel, or alternatively a water screw could be used, or even a bronze water pump of a type invented by Ctesibius. Vitruvius shows that 'in this way water is supplied from below for fountains by pressure'.[12]

An adequate source of water has always been one of the most important features for the well-being of a garden, especially in areas with a hot climate where growing plants need a regular supply. All the Roman agriculturalists acknowledge this. Literary sources, such as Columella and Pliny, mention that the *hortus* of a villa, here referring to a vegetable or orchard type of garden, should be sited conveniently close to a spring or a source of running water, so that water could be channelled from the stream to irrigate the garden. If the property was too far away from such a source, then the gardener would have to rely on water drawn from a well. However, if the garden lacked both of these, then the only recourse would be to install a cistern to collect precious rainwater. Palladius explains how to make a cistern and adds that fish could be stocked there.[13]

The system of water storage in the gardens at Pompeii has been examined in depth in recent years[14] and the provisions made here would surely be relevant to a number of other localities in the Mediterranean area. In the early period the inhabitants relied on water from wells and rainwater collected off roofs into cisterns. With the introduction of the aqueduct in the Augustan period these cisterns do not appear to have been abandoned, for the flow of public water was then mainly directed to baths and street fountains, and in gardens was limited to small jets or trickles of water. Once a pool was filled only a minimal amount of extra water would be needed to top it up and when pools were placed at different levels water would be re-used, if by gravity it was allowed to flow to lower basins, as at the House of Loreius Tiburtinus. Water was no doubt expensive and also in many areas limited; there still needed to be sufficient water in the catchment area to maintain a continual supply by aqueduct. Earthquakes or accidents could also disrupt services, thus making the continued presence of a cistern useful. It is also noticeable that in Pompeii many water features were placed so that the overflow could run into a drainage channel and from there to a cistern; again this was a conservation measure employed to save the precious supply, and can be seen in the House of the Vettii. At the House of the Small Fountain, Jashemski notes that 'lead pipes carried the overflow from the fountain to the cistern'.[15] Elsewhere an alternative was to allow excess water to flow gently on to plant beds; this was the case in the relatively drier climate at Thuburbo Maius in Tunisia. Here water basins were provided with a narrow water outlet just above ground level and many of these lead pipes are still *in situ*. These small pools would have been periodically drained and perhaps a bronze bung similar to the one found at Macherbach in Germany[16] may have also existed there at one time to seal the outlet.

Where properties were sited in proximity to major rivers a constant source of water could be relied upon, and in such places a multiplicity of water features would be possible. Sometimes it might appear that there was a conspicuous and extravagant use of water, as at Hadrian's villa at Tivoli, where there was a large number of water features, for example, twelve multiple fountains, thirty single fountains, six grottos and twelve pools and basins.[17] If the supply was assured there would be no limit to the amount of fountains any one person could enjoy on a particular property but if water was drawn from a state-controlled aqueduct, as opposed to a privately constructed supply, then the owner could be restricted by the expense of the amount of water used. Therefore at times this form of extravagance would be a sign of the apparent wealth of a particular family.

The first aqueduct in Rome, the Aqua Appia, dates to 312 BC, but the first known garden watered by an aqueduct (the Aqua Virgo in 19 BC) was the park associated with the baths of Agrippa. The Portico of Pompey, the first public park in Rome, was built in 55 BC before this aqueduct was built but Propertius mentions seeing fountains here;[18] these may have functioned through a system of holding tanks and perhaps with the help of a *tympanum*. With the introduction of aqueducts there was almost a revolution in the art of gardening. Water could be channelled from distribution points and directed to holding tanks or piped straight to the water features in gardens. In the area around Tivoli there are also many instances where water was brought from aqueducts to be stored in tanks. This was the case at Fishbourne in Britain; here clay pipes then directed water to various parts of the garden.[19] A pair of joined terracotta water pipes are displayed in the museum at Fishbourne, together with a replica of a box-like wooden version. Because the preservation of wood on most archaeological sites is poor, the presence of wooden pipework is usually revealed by a line of darker soil, the change in soil coloration being all that remains after the wood has rotted away. With luck an archaeologist might also discover a row of iron collars that had been used to join the segments of water pipe made from cut timber; these could then confirm the existence of wooden pipework and the direction of the water supply.

Lead piping was also used and may be seen at a number of houses in Pompeii; for example, the House of the Silver Wedding, where although pipework was discreetly concealed, a small section with a stop tap is located beside an amphora placed in a corner of the garden. At Rome, in the Domus Flavia on the Palatine, the excavators of the large ornamental pool have conveniently left a small area open where you may view a section of lead plumbing showing the junction where water was diverted to the basin. At the House of the Vettii the water pipes were placed in the drainage channel of the garden, in the open, and a stop tap (which was turned by a key) is visible in the south-west quadrant of the garden. The tap was used to regulate the flow of water and individual fountains could be switched off or on when required. Roman taps, however, were only designed for use on low pressure water pipes.[20] Stop taps were usually made of bronze.

Lead plumbing to water features in the garden, House of the Vettii, Pompeii. Piping was laid in the gutter of the peristyle garden. A stop tap, to be turned with a key, is located in the south-west corner.

THE CONSTRUCTION OF WATER BASINS

Like many Roman buildings concrete was used in the construction of pools and a form of concrete called *opus signinum* was added as a lining to make them watertight. A cross section of a large basin at Welschbillig is illustrated here, showing that on this occasion wooden piles had been driven into the ground below to give extra support to the structure above. This was perhaps a necessary precaution when constructing very large pools that would contain a considerable weight of water. Stone slabs lined this pool. On other sites such as Eccles and at Bancroft in Britain, stone or tile was used in the first instance, then coats of cement were applied on the inner surfaces. The thickness of the *opus signinum* lining at Eccles was 2.5 cm on the walls and 7.5 cm on the floor of the basin.[21] Details of the various stages of construction can be made out in this instance and the procedure used there may have been used at other Roman sites. The stages follow a pattern: (a) laying the foundations and the basin floor; (b) construction of the walls; (c) rendering the walls with *opus signinum*; (d) coating the floor with *opus signinum*; and (e) sealing the joints with a rounded moulding. This finishing touch to the interior surface can be seen at a number of archaeological sites where the basin is still intact, and shows that this system was widespread in use.

Cross section of part of a water basin from the villa at Welschbillig. This large pool was surrounded by a low wall that was both decorative and a safety measure.

DECORATIVE LINING OF POOLS

The inner surface of ornamental pools was sometimes coated with a painted waterproof plaster. In Pompeii many basins still have an all-blue interior coating *in situ*, for example, in the House of Meleager and the House of the Hunt. The blue painted interior would help to make the water look healthy and would provide a good reflection. Some pools have traces of painted fish and aquatic creatures swimming against a blue background, for example, in one of the gardens of the House of M. Epidius Sabinus at Pompeii,[22] and any rippling of the water in these pools would give the impression that there were indeed fish swimming inside. Pools were presumably cleaned out periodically or the decor would have become too obscured by deposits of silt and slime. At the Bancroft villa the excavator noted a 'lack of silt deposits in the ponds',[23] and he infers that water may have been previously filtered, such as from an outflow of a cold plunge bath. This practice may have been quite widespread, for a number of villa plans include the lines of water channels or drains, and one is sometimes shown leading away from the bath suite and into the garden area (a policy that was in fact recommended by Palladius).[24] Not all garden areas have been excavated, however, but the introduction of water, if directed into a pool, could save it from turning stagnant, or if there was no pool the excess water could irrigate plant beds.

At La Malena in Spain we can see an alternative to painted plaster, for here, and at a few other locations, the inner walls of the pool had been lined with mosaic. The content of the decoration in this large pool was again of an aquatic nature, here dolphins and fish.[25] In North Africa a number of shallow semicircular basins are completely covered by decorative mosaics, usually depicting marine creatures or subjects

related to the sea, as seen *in situ* at Dougga and in examples now
deposited at the Bardo and Sousse Museums which show fishing scenes
and dolphins, as well as the head of Oceanus (a sea god, or more
specifically the personification of Ocean). In most cases these small pools
served as a catchment basin for a fountain and in fact a basin from
ancient Neapolis, Nabeul in Tunisia, actually carries the logo
'*Nympharum Domus*' which would confirm their function.[26] Splashing
water would have kept the colours of mosaic tesserae bright but this
type of basin was largely decorative, for these pools have a minimal
depth of water making them unsuitable for stocking fish in.

The shallow pools may have originated from the *impluvia* usually seen
in *atria*, for it has been noted that the *atrium* in later times became
regarded as another area to adorn with plants and/or garden elements.
The use of such shallow constructions would be to provide a water
collection point from the fountain rather than the draw shaft of a cistern
and they would have provided a focal point in a courtyard or garden. In
very hot weather the cooling and refreshing effect of the water would
have been particularly beneficial, for the moisture would help to
humidify the otherwise dry atmosphere.

Lining a basin with marble was an expensive method of decoration,
and at many sites this material was one of the first items to be removed
by later people searching for building materials. In this case the exposed
substructures remain and we often encounter rough brickwork and
mortar. However, on occasion marble panels have been left behind, for
example, in the House of the Round Temple at Ostia.

DEPTH OF POOLS AND EVIDENCE FOR
THE KEEPING OF FISH

Basins with a minimum depth of roughly 0. 50 m or more are believed
to have been sufficient to contain fish. The maximum depth of the basin
at Bancroft in Britain is 0.80 m deep[27] while those at Pompeii vary
greatly. At a house in insula VII, ii, 16 the pool is 0.52 m deep, at the
House of Meleager it is 1.77 m and at the House of the Dioscuri it is
1.90 m.[28] These examples show that the depth of a pool was variable.
Columella mentions breeding holes for fish[29] and Pliny refers to the
longevity of fish in Tiberius's Campanian villas,[30] which indicates that
fish would have probably been reared there. Such breeding holes have
been found in excavations at Sperlonga and elsewhere; these are often
referred to as fish refuges and are usually found in the side walls of a
pool. In the House of Julia Felix at Pompeii, and at Bancroft in Britain,
there are square holes or recesses lined with stone. At Nea Phaphos in
Cyprus there was a mixture of small niches at the base of the pool and
large deep recesses.[31] In several other instances, however, amphorae,
normally used for the storage of wine, had been incorporated into the
fabric of the side walls of the basin in such a way that only the open

neck of the vessel remained visible. Fish could then swim into these receptacles to breed or to keep cool on hot days and be out of the direct sun. The refuge would also enable the eels and lampreys to lurk in a cave-like opening as they are wont to do in their natural habitat. Examples of basins fitted with amphorae are found at many sites such as Sperlonga, Pompeii, Herculaneum, Vienne in France and Cuicul in North Africa.[32] Environmental evidence of fish remains is provided at the House of the Centenary, Pompeii,[33] and at Ivy Chimney in Essex.[34] Although the latter was associated with a temple site, a garden setting was probable. It must be mentioned, however, that not all ponds were used to stock fish.

ORNAMENTAL POOLS OF DIFFERENT DESIGNS

There are many different types of water basins, yet to date no attempt has been made to classify individual forms. A summary has proved very difficult, for not all garden areas have been excavated fully and in many instances dating evidence is imprecise. In a number of cases a date for a particular house has been given on an assessment of the style of mosaics present, but this does not necessarily mean that garden features were added or restored at that same time. Water basins appear to have such a variety of forms that I have tried here to ascertain a pattern or trend, with the aim of being able to date their types and to see if there are any indications that a particular form became fashionable at a given period. However, one needs to bear in mind that styles would have been slower to reach the provinces. It also appears that a number of forms were popular throughout the period of study. Evidence for a chronology is slight, for there are few cases where excavation has been thoroughly undertaken. But in this area the most unusual are the more informative, and on occasion it has been found that a simple basin was later replaced by a more decorative version.

Given these limitations, a system of classification for water features found in gardens is included, together with some indication of their distribution within the Empire. The vast majority of ornamental pools appear to fall into one of the seven groups listed below.

A SUGGESTED TYPOLOGY, FOLLOWING ARCHAEOLOGICAL EVIDENCE

Type
A   Simple forms: square, rectangular and circular. A subgroup contains *euripus*-like forms.
B   Rectangular basins with one semicircular recess. Also the so-called gutter basins.
C   Rectangular basin with more than one semicircular recess, for example, at either extremity.

D   A basin where the inner outline is shaped, either with semicircular or rectilinear recesses or both, within a rectangular or subrectangular outer framework.

E   Demi-lune basins.

F   A basin containing watertight caissons.

G   Complex designs, in many cases with interconnecting pools.

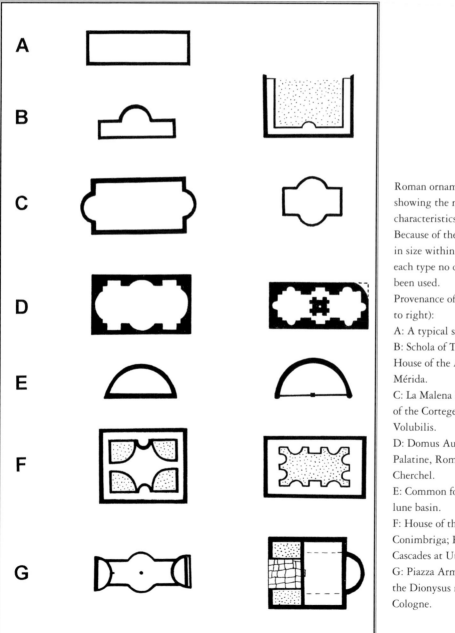

Roman ornamental pools, showing the main characteristics of each group. Because of the great difference in size within and between each type no common scale has been used.

Provenance of pools (from left to right):

A: A typical simple form.

B: Schola of Trajan at Ostia; House of the Amphitheatre at Mérida.

C: La Malena in Spain; House of the Cortege of Venus at Volubilis.

D: Domus Augustana, Palatine, Rome; Cap Tizerine, Cherchel.

E: Common forms of demi-lune basin.

F: House of the Swastikas at Conimbriga; House of the Cascades at Utica.

G: Piazza Armerina; House of the Dionysus mosaic at Cologne.

TYPE A

This form is the most common and perhaps through the simplicity of its design this type was constructed throughout the Roman periods. It can be found in all the provinces of the Empire. The size of these pools varies considerably, and depends to a large extent on the size and shape of the garden. Some large gardens may have more than one pool. However, other factors, such as a lack of water in some areas, could affect an individual's choice but a small basin could still provide enjoyment and not be wasteful of meagre water resources. Conversely, fear of frost damage in winter in more northerly climes would favour a pool that is simple in form and has a sufficient depth so that ice would not crack the exterior or interior lining. Type A is therefore the form most often encountered in Roman Britain. Fish ponds in Britain are shown to vary from those of moderate proportions such as at Bancroft, which is 13 m × 2.6 m, to that at Gadebridge Park, which was 20 m × 13 m.[35] There were large elongated forms at Eccles and Darenth, both in the region of 25 m × 4.45 m, but in other parts of Northern Europe, such as at Echternach and Mersch in Luxembourg, there were very large versions, the latter being 75.6 m × 6.5 m.

Elongated forms that are known as *euripi* are included in type A. These long, narrow, rectangular pools are more often seen in large gardens. They were first named in the letters of Cicero, who reveals that such artificial water basins or canals recalled famous water channels of antiquity, the Nile in Egypt, the Canopus canal in Alexandria, or the Euripus, a narrow tidal channel in Greece.[36] Seneca implies that there were instances where owners of these artificial basins even arranged for a holding tank of water to be discharged further up[37] so that the sudden flow along the basin would re-create a tidal bore. An example of a large *euripus*-type structure may be seen in the famous Canopus at the Villa of Hadrian, where a quantity of Egyptian statuary reaffirms a connection with the Canopus canal itself. Martial mentions that his estate in Spain had a *euripus*,[38] and Seneca informs us that on Vattia's estate there was a *euripus*-like channel 'running through a grove of plane trees';[39] he adds that it was well stocked with fish. There are other literary references to public gardens with *euripi* in the Campus Martius area of Rome; Pliny says that Agrippa supplied water to '*euripis*'[40] among other things. Perhaps these were the famous ones remembered with nostalgia by

A *euripus* basin, House of Loreius Tiburtinus, Pompeii. The whole terrace was shaded by a vine-covered pergola that has recently been restored. A little bridge crosses the canal half way. To the rear is a dining area, a *biclinium*, with a small shrine between the two dining couches.

Ovid.[41] The area has been studied archaeologically and a section drawing of this channel was made.[42] This *euripus* was very long, about 800 m × 3.35 m wide, and the basin had a curved bottom with a maximum depth of 1.70 m. A paved walk ran either side and little bridges were placed where streets traversed its route. In Pompeii the elongated canal-like basins at both the House of Julia Felix and the House of Loreius Tiburtinus were also provided with little bridges, perhaps to recall this famous one in Rome that was constructed in about 19 BC.

TYPE B

Evidence shows that this form dates at least from the first century BC to the second century AD. If we look at Pompeii, for which we have a useful archaeological date where items would be no later than AD 79, we can see that at the time there was a predominance of simple basin forms. Jashemski's plans show that plain rectangular forms are common but there were only eight in the form of a rectangular basin with a recess, type B, indicating that perhaps these were a late feature in Pompeii. Other evidence for dating this type is found at Ostia and Vienne. The type B at Ostia has been dated to the first century BC, and at the House of the Ocean Gods, Vienne, the simple rectangular basin (type A) was altered in about AD 60 into one with a semicircular recess (type B).[43] At the Schola of Trajan in Ostia we can see an alteration that perhaps marks the point where this type of pool gradually goes out of fashion, for the type B was in turn replaced by a much larger pool of type D some time during the Trajanic period (AD 98-117).

Two water basins in the garden of the Schola of Trajan at Ostia. Archaeological excavations have shown that a large type D pool overlies an earlier plan of a smaller garden with a type B water basin.

An interesting feature of a number of rectangular type A and type B basins is that many were placed at the edge of the garden running parallel with a portico, as was the case in the example from Ostia. This is seen at Vaison-la-Romaine, Vienne, and as far afield as Ptolemais in Libya. These may indicate an overlap in forms or a change of use. This alteration, however, would allow rainwater to fall off the roof above into the basin immediately below, thereby eliminating the need to construct an eaves drip-gutter on that side of the garden. A development of this form, dated to the second century AD, may be seen in France and the Iberian peninsula,[44] where a narrow type B pool was converted by extending the basin along three of the four sides of a peristyle garden. The rainwater drainage channel is then transformed into a continuous 'gutter basin'. The portion with a recess, however, remains as a focal point in the garden design.

Type B 'gutter basin', around three sides of the garden, House of the Amphitheatre, Mérida.

Access was now restricted to the uninterrupted fourth side. The channels are wide and deep and now become a feature in their own right. As some of these belong to regions with a higher rainfall, it is possible that continuous basins in replacement of gutters were more efficient in dealing with a larger flow of rainwater; to date, however, this form has not been found in notoriously wet Britain. This scheme exists in a number of houses at Vienne, and is also seen in Frejus and Andance in France, Mérida in Spain and in a secondary garden in the House of Cantaber at Conimbriga.[45] A very large version of this type can be seen in the esplanade area at Bulla Regia. This was, however, in a public portico garden and was on a different scale, but it shows that the form was considered elsewhere in the Empire. At the House of Mithras in Mérida the idea is continued along all four sides of the garden, so that the 'gutter' water channel isolates the garden as an island in the middle of the peristyle court. This version may have influenced the formation of basins of type F.

TYPE C

This type is shown on maps to have existed at the House of the Papyri in Herculaneum but here evidence was gained from records made by tunnelling in the eighteenth and nineteenth centuries, and is therefore speculative. However, this would provide an early date of pre-AD 79 for this type of pool. Only half of a type C water basin has been found in Britain, in the partly excavated Governor's Palace in London, but it does indicate that this form was also used in the northern provinces. Alterations to the basin complicate its dating, which is given as from AD 80 to early second century AD.[46] A more typical and complete example is seen in the portico garden associated with the Library of Hadrian, Athens, which dates to *c.* AD 132.[47] The form is found in a number of villas dated to the third century in Spain and at Volubilis in

North Africa, and appears to have remained popular at least up to the fourth century AD, for example, at La Malena in Spain.[48] The large basin at Welschbillig in Germany might be classified as a variant of type C for the recesses, which are really square; each has a further recess that is semicircular. This huge pool of approximately 60 m × 18 m is a late feature dating to about AD 375. Interestingly, it has a long thin central island that is very akin to the *spina* seen in a Roman circus. The design was perhaps based on the chariot race track but this feature could imply that boat races may have taken place here. This novel idea is found in ancient literature in the late period writings of Sidonius, who recalls events on his lake in Gaul: 'In the middle of the deep part is a small island. Here a turning-post sticks up on top.' This was the scene 'of jolly wrecks of vessels which collide at the sports'.[49]

TYPE D

The earliest to date is that seen in the House of Meleager in Pompeii. This pool was edged in marble but its interior was covered with waterproof plaster painted sky blue. The outline of the interior walls of the basin was designed in a series of alternating rectangular and curved recesses, the curved ones taking central place on each side. At each of the four corners a square plinth intruded into the design, and could have provided more space for a statue or other ornamental item. This particular pool was also furnished with a marble flight of stairs for a fountain, and an additional square water basin located to the side may

Type D pool, House of Meleager, Pompeii. A fountain once cascaded down the short flight of marble stairs on the edge of the basin, and a second fountain was mounted on the pillar in the centre of the pool.

have allowed water to be drawn from the pool without disturbing fish kept in the main pool.

Type D basins are found on the Palatine in Rome and are associated with the phase of construction undertaken in about AD 92 by Rabirius, the architect for the Emperor Domitian. A pool similar in many ways to the example from Pompeii, but minus the extra square basin and steps, appears in a pair of light-wells in the lower levels of the Domus Augustana. One was also discovered in the early layers of an area known as the Adonaea, near to the Imperial palace. The two large gardens on the upper level of the palace each contain a large, fairly shallow pool that has an edging of an unusually complicated design that may also be the work of Rabirius. Here the rectangular and semicircular recesses do not flow smoothly from one to the other but are parted by their own separate frames. Each rectangular recess has a pair of curved projections and each semicircular recess has a squared edge. Occasionally extra projections are added, mainly near the corners of the pool, where there was perhaps insufficient space for the repeated alternating pattern. From a distance this design appears as a serrated edge. Both of these basins have internal features, a maze design in one and a bridge leading to a small *diaeta* or shrine in the other, but these features may have been added at some later date. The rather complicated edging seen in these two large pools is repeated in the lower catchment basin of a pair of boat-shaped *nymphaea* nearby, where it has been used around the edge of the island rather than the edge of the basin itself. However, the outer oval marble-edged basin was indented by four short sections of similar work and would perhaps date to the same period.

Form D is also seen in later periods, for instance at Ostia in the Schola of Trajan and in a house at Italica, which both date to the first half of the second century AD. It is also found in Sicily (at Borgellusa di Avola), at Illici in Spain, and in North Africa, at Cherchel and in a number of houses at Volubilis which may date to the first half of the third century AD.[50] The basin from the establishment at Ostia runs down the centre of the garden and is long and narrow, whereas the latter are similar in size to the example previously mentioned from Pompeii. The pattern of the interior edging of these pools varies, however, from an alternating design of curved and rectangular recesses to versions with a series of semicircular recesses only.

TYPE E

The largest proportion of these small fountain basins is found in North Africa, in particular in Tunisia. One area where they have not been found to date, however, is present-day Morocco (namely at Volubilis), where larger central basins appear to have been more popular. The overall predominance of type E in North Africa could reflect the chances of survival but as most of the occupation sites are within the area of modern Tunisia, which was the most fertile region, type E basins may

Peristyle garden in the House of the Two Fountains, Dougga. The two type E (demi-lune) fountain basins are placed at the edge of the ambulatory.

have originated in this part of the continent. There were two semicircular basins in the garden of the House of the Two Fountains at Dougga and typically they were placed at the edge of the peristyle. This appears to be the normal practice for this type of basin and perhaps the portico gave some degree of shade, which would help to avoid too much evaporation of water in such a hot climate. A series of holes cut into the rim of the demi-lune basin in the House of the Fishes at Bulla Regia suggests that a framework or trellis may have been placed around the garden side of the pool.[51] This would create extra shade yet still appear decorative. A trellis bower in this position would however restrict the view of the rest of the garden beyond, and may not have been used extensively elsewhere. Interestingly, demi-lune basins are often aligned so that they may be seen from important rooms, such as the *triclinium*, so that dinner guests could look outwards across the mosaic floor of the portico to the fountain a short distance away. The straight side of the basin was often sited at the edge of the peristyle so that a statue or fountain figure placed on a plinth beside one of the columns would be close enough to aim a jet of water into the shallow pool, and this fine spectacle would be within full view.

There appear to be two forms: one completely surrounded by a wide ledge, as found in the example from Sousse, while the other has marble or stone slabs slotted into position on the straight side of the basin. These blocks are often missing, presumably lifted by stone robbers in antiquity. However, in a number of cases grooves on the floor of the portico and remaining column bases nearby indicate their original position. A small demi-lune with a stone blocking slab still *in situ* may be found in a small light-well/garden in a modest house near the Anonymous Temple at Dougga. This basin also retains some of the decorative mosaic lining, which on the base shows a lively fishing scene, with men hoisting up the rigging on a fishing boat and catching the plentiful fish that swim below and around the curved side wall of the basin. This small fountain basin is about two-thirds of the size of the example in the Bardo Museum which came from a house at Thuburbo Maius. The latter is an exceptionally fine example of its type.

The earliest date that has been assigned to this type of water basin is late first century AD; an example from the House of the Cascades at Utica has been dated by the excavators to an early phase of house and garden.[52] However, evidence mainly from houses that are dated by the style of their mosaic (for many of these basins are also decorated) indicates that the basins date to either the third or fourth century AD in general. Some houses and villas had more than one of these basins, and so far the prize must go to a house in Porto Magus, Algeria, which had in all five demi-lune basins – these have been dated to about 300 AD.[53] A fine mosaic-covered type E fountain basin, featuring Oceanus, has recently come to light at the Villa of Maternus at Carranque in Spain,[54] and shows that the highly decorated form and motifs common to those of North Africa may also have existed in other provinces. Elsewhere the basins are usually plain and little or no trace of any decoration is left, making it unclear if they had been ornamented to such a high standard. Examples are known in other parts of Spain, Germany and Britain.[55] The two demi-lune basins from Britain, at Letocetum (Wall, Staffs.) and South Shields, were previously identified as either a statue base (the former) or a plunge pool in the garden (the latter). The northern examples could perhaps indicate a link to Mediterranean areas.

TYPE F

This form is typified by those at the Roman town of Conimbriga in Portugal, where a number of houses of the second to third century AD

Mosaic-lined demi-lune type E basin from Thuburbo Maius, now in the Bardo Museum, Tunis. The mosaic shows the head of Oceanus, the personification of Ocean, and mythical sea creatures such as nereids and tritons.

contain basins of this sort, each with differently shaped caissons. The watertight caissons were filled with garden soil, and water surrounded them on all sides making them appear as islands of greenery. The most elaborate was also fitted with a large number of fountains, giving the residence the name of the House of the Water Jets. In this garden around 400 lead water jets are positioned along the outer edge of the basin and along the rim of each caisson. Each water outlet was angled to direct a thin jet of water, in an arc, into the basin below. The effect of so many fountains would have been striking but with such thin jets only a minimal amount of water would have been used. These jets have been restored and the effect can be observed there today.

The evolution of type F basins may be seen as a further development of 'gutter' basins. The House of Mithras in Mérida is perhaps a transitional example where the 'gutter' continues around all four sides of the peristyle and the garden is turned into an island or one giant-sized caisson. At the House of the Swastikas in Conimbriga the gutter-like form of the outer basin together with its small semicircular recess are retained, but the opposite side walls have been opened to allow water into the centre of the garden and around four island plant beds. These watertight caissons were of a simple geometric shape, a quarter circle, but elsewhere the designs were sometimes more complex. On the Palatine, for instance, in the lower storey level of the Domus Augustana at Rome, there is a peristyle garden with caissons which appear in the form of a *pelta*, a popular motif based on the shape of shield used by the Amazons, the famed female warriors of Greco-Roman myth. This design would have been difficult to reproduce in a water-filled context and the planting areas were of necessity confined to the broadest portion of the shield only.

Dating evidence for these pools is somewhat contradictory and is complicated by two gardens where alterations have been made in their design. The earliest occurrence of these pools appears to date from the first century AD, at Luni in northern Italy. Ceramic evidence for alterations in this Roman house and garden has given a date of about AD 50–70.[56] Here the peristyle garden was converted into a large water garden, where water flowed around four octagonal caissons and poured from a number of fountains around its perimeter. This early date is nevertheless surprising, for the form is noticeable by its absence at Pompeii (in AD 79) and is not usually seen until the next century. The *peltae* garden on the Palatine is also generally believed to date to the first century AD but can be seen to overlie a number of marble-edged pathways whose course must have been laid at a previous date. Because of these earlier features, and on stylistic grounds, these two garden pools perhaps should be compared with those in Conimbriga and elsewhere, and might therefore be of a later date. Elsewhere type F is found in Greece in the Roman period guest house, the Leonidaion at Olympia, which the excavator dates to the reign of the Emperor

Hadrian or Antoninus Pius.[57] Examples have also been found in North Africa, at Volubilis,[58] and in the House of the Cascades at Utica. The latter pool was fitted with one large caisson in the centre which was edged in the manner of a theatre façade, with curved and rectangular recesses.[59]

TYPE G

These flamboyant designs appear to be of a later date, ranging from the second half of the second century to the third and fourth century AD, and may have been a parallel development incorporating some of the features from type F; namely the occasional use of caissons. This category includes basins that are multi-lobed, variform or linked in some manner, such as the polylobe basin at Périgueaux in France or the curvaceous pool at the Casa de la Exedra at Italica in Spain. Although the latter may be open to other interpretations, the pool appears to be of two parts and is linked by a circular caisson, with a further caisson in the larger of the two pools. The caissons would have contained plants and perhaps a fountain to play into the pool. In this category we see a desire for elaboration for its own sake but the interconnecting basins are not on different levels, the way we might place them ourselves, as type F basins are invariably constructed on level ground. These basins are found in urban areas and in country villas, as at Piazza Armerina in Sicily, a very large Imperial-sized villa complex dating to about AD 300–30. The main garden contains a large pool of three interconnecting basins and two semicircular ones that have their curved sides facing inwards towards a central rectangular pool; this has curved extensions around a fountain pillar located at the mid-point.

Another form incorporating plant beds or caissons as an extension to the pool is found in the House of the Dionysus Mosaic at Cologne[60] and shows that this developed class also existed in more northerly climes. The garden here was furnished with a second water basin (the earlier one was of type A). This new pool comprised a rectangular basin with a shallow section at either side, to the rear there was a semicircular interconnecting pool and on the opposite side, closer to the portico, there were two square caissons for plants. These were divided by a paved section from which a fountain statue could direct water into the pool. In the much hotter climate of North Africa we can see a more elaborate and highly decorative version in the House of Europa, at Cuicul, in Algeria. The garden contained numerous linked pools of different designs. A multi-lobed demi-lune basin was sited at the edge of the portico in the manner of type E basins; this was connected to a large square pool roughly of type D, and this in turn was linked to a large apse or demi-lune. At either side of the square basin, and set alongside the rear wall of the garden, there were two rectangular boxes for plants. If planted with climbing plants these could have been trained to grow against the rear wall and would have clothed the area with greenery. Two further plant troughs were located by the semicircular connecting basin.

Form F is also encountered in the East but evidence of gardens in this region is relatively incomplete compared with the provinces in the West. However, two large multi-lobed quarter circle pools were placed to fit into the two corners of one side of a peristyle garden at Apamea in Syria.[61]

What is of note is that basins of all types were generally sited so that they would be in view from principal rooms, especially from the *triclinium* or *oecus*. The importance of lines of sight from such rooms is demonstrated by the fact that in general a recess in a pool is placed central to that room. More water would then be visible or alternatively could be the location where a fountain had room to play, although the remains of fountains rarely survive. The design of all seven forms of Roman garden pools appears to be based on geometric principles, using a combination of curves and rectangles, but whatever combination is used they are always symmetrically disposed. There was never a tendency to produce an informal irregularly shaped pond as we see today. The designs in use during the long Roman period tend to reflect forms seen in Roman architecture; for example the apsidal recess and the Roman theatre façade with its numerous projections and re-entrants.

This typology was devised to classify the distinguishing traits between various forms of basins/pools. However, the Romans also used water in other garden features, such as in fountains and *nymphaea*. A large proportion of the gardens at Pompeii had been furnished with a pool or a fountain/*nymphaeum*, which reveals that they were perhaps a characteristic element to be found in 'Italic houses'. Out of the surviving water basins in the area of Pompeii the vast majority were simple forms, such as the rectangular or square. Apart from these, there appears to have been only three semicircular, six circular, two in the form of a cross, eight of type B, two of type C and three of type D. Figures are sporadic elsewhere but the large grouping of 107 plans of peristyle gardens in North Africa collected by Rebuffat (1969) provides a reasonable starting point for a comparison with those of Campania. Rebuffat does not provide any dating evidence, however, but does indicate the range of features present. Out of 107 dwellings, 64 appear to contain a total of 112 water features. Of these there were three square basins; twenty-one rectangular or subrectangular; one of type B; three of type C; six of type D; two appear to be type F; nine of type G; fifteen fountains and fifty-two semicircular basins referred to by Rebuffat as *'abside-fontaine'*[62] which are here classified under type E. This information reinforces the inference that water features were considered an important element in gardens.

In the later Roman Empire some properties, mainly in urban areas with a good water supply, reveal just how important the possession of a pool had become; we increasingly see that a prominent position had been allocated for them. Some pools occupy a considerable proportion of space within a peristyle garden, often amounting to almost half. Several even take up all of the garden space leaving little room for anything else, as seen in the large type D basin at the House of Cantaber in Conimbriga. This form, which is quite literally a water-filled garden, may be dramatic but is really a place to gaze at and admire. The pool itself then becomes the outstanding feature. In these cases plants would have been confined to a mere strip around the pool or plants in containers would have been placed along its perimeter, these at least could add a touch of greenery to the scene and scent to the air. By placing one or two caissons into the pool this would give more scope for a colourful effect. In very hot weather it would be too uncomfortable to work or play in unshaded gardens and therefore life was lived in the peristyle and surrounding rooms. Because of this a view of the garden would be very important and the clear sparkling water seen through the colonnades would also have been refreshing to the spirit and cooling in the heat.

A large sheet of water might restrict passage within a garden but it could have its advantages, for at night lights would create wonderful patterns on the surface. The reflections of the flickering oil flame would dance upon the water and mirrored images of surrounding architecture would also give another dimension to the garden space. The columns of the portico would reflect pleasingly in the water, and statuary placed beside the pool could be angled so that they would appear to be looking down into the water at their own reflections. The effect would be rather sumptuous but the Romans admired display and felt that it was important to show their wealth; and this was a valid consideration when designing a garden.

The beneficial effects of water features in and out of gardens are often referred to in literary texts. Varro proudly describes his creation of a fabulous fish and duck pond associated with an aviary and dining room. Also Varro, Martial, Luxorius and others mention instances where owners became attached to their fish: they would come when called and were fed by hand.[63] Besides beautifying a garden fishponds were also seen as an asset. Cato sold fish from a pond for 40,000 sesterces.[64] However Columella, who recounts this story, later raises the figure to 400,000 and the figure reaches four million in Pliny.[65] Pliny also relates that the estate of Gaius Hirrus was sold for four million sesterces on account of its fishponds.[66] This was partly because of the value of the stock of fish the ponds contained, but also it illustrates the increasing value placed on what were seen as luxury decorative items. Columella hints at the popularity of fishponds, and their rapid introduction throughout the countryside led to Horace declaring that 'On all sides will be seen our fishponds spreading wider than the Lucrine Lake.'[67]

Archaeologically, water features such as *piscinae* are one of the most durable elements of a Roman garden but the loss of features over the centuries is inevitable, the superstructures of the façade *nymphaea,* for example, would leave few traces if robbed out. However, because basins were usually constructed below ground level they had a better chance of survival. When they fell out of use, and were no longer watertight, they were often simply filled in with soil or rubble. In some cases statuary has been preserved because it fell or was thrown into the pool, as at Welschbillig in Germany and Almedinilla in Spain.[68]

Not every garden contained a water basin for, as mentioned, a regular water supply was needed. One must also acknowledge that personal preferences and differing effects of climate may provide reasons for not installing a pool. For instance, in northerly latitudes the cooling effect of a fountain would not be so desirable as in warmer regions, and the effects of frost would have severely limited the use of clay or lead piping to supply water to fountains and basins. However, plans of Roman dwellings often show a blank area that could well be a garden, and perhaps if investigated by modern methods the presence of a greater ratio of water features, and especially ornamental pools, might be revealed.

CHAPTER FIVE

Fountains and Fountain Figures

The gently burbling water trickling out of a rocky fissure has often been seen in the past as a miraculous occurrence, and something to be admired, perhaps with a certain modicum of awe. The site of a natural spring was therefore often revered as a sanctuary, and over time would have been enhanced by visitors who left offerings and perhaps even looked after the site. One particularly beautiful spot that many Romans ventured out into the country to see is mentioned by Pliny the Younger, who encourages his friend to make the worthwhile visit. 'There is a fair sized hill which is densely wooded with ancient cypresses; at the foot of this the spring rises and gushes out through several channels of different size, and when its eddies have subsided it broadens out into a pool as clear as glass. You can count the coins which have been thrown in and the pebbles shining at the bottom.'[1] A temple of great antiquity stood nearby and the spring itself was surrounded by a number of rivulets and little shrines that were also venerated. As can be seen, over time nature was enhanced and when spring water was allowed to flow into a man-made basin, man's intervention created a fountain, or *nymphaeum*.

Where springs were found in the grounds of large villas a shrine and a rustic grotto or a *nymphaeum* could be constructed to honour the spirit presiding over that particular water source. The water could be directed into a building and cajoled to flow gently through a fountain outlet of stone or bronze that would still reproduce the effect of a spring. There was plenty of scope for embellishment and the resulting fountain heads are sometimes found to be quite artistic, but the motifs or themes were generally linked to water divinities and rural rustic contexts. Tufa and pumice were frequently used to line a suitable rocky hollow, and this rough surface created an aspect of rusticity to mask the conceit. These materials were also used when creating a grotto-like niche in an artificially re-created fountain house or *nymphaeum*, literally the abode of nymphs. Because these are really architectural elements in Roman gardens they are discussed in chapter three. Each of the three main forms is discussed separately: the large basilica-hall type, the small *aedicula*, and one that resembled a theatre façade.

A *nymphaeum* or other form of water feature or fountain was an important garden element, and their popularity is shown by the fact that they are also often found in internal light-well courts and even on occasion in garden rooms, a *triclinium*, *exedra* or *oecus* – rooms with an open aspect linked in some way to the garden itself. Garden elements in fact may be said to invade the home. This has been found at Pompeii and in villas in France and Spain.[2]

In urban districts the possession of a fountain was just as desirable, yet before the introduction of aqueducts they required a lot of forethought. As previously mentioned, water rises as high as its source, and a holding tank of water needed to be installed above the intended fountain outlet. The fountain and tank therefore needed to be designed simultaneously so that the water-tank could be concealed from view, perhaps behind a false wall. If the fountain was located in a garden room then a tank could also be placed in an adjoining service room, a room above or in the roof space. A number of slaves would be required to lift up enough water to fill the holding tank in advance of a dinner party, sufficient that the fountain would play during the most important part of the evening's entertainment. The amount of water used would depend on the size of the outlet and the capacity of the tank above. In these cases plumbing to the fountain head was minimal, for the water just trickled down before landing in a decorative setting of some kind. A small aperture would ensure a minimum of water was used but nevertheless the fountain would function satisfactorily, perhaps for at least an hour or two. Slaves would have to remain at hand to top up the water, but as the flow would have been slight this did not necessarily mean too often. But as can be imagined this was laborious work and the effect of the fountain itself would have been limited by the amount of water available, but it was still enough to give pleasure to its owners.

In urban environments this situation changed drastically with the introduction of water supplied by aqueducts, for it was now possible for properties to have a continuous fountain which once installed would require less maintenance. People in towns and cities, if means allowed, could now follow the fashions seen on large estates in the country; no doubt they felt that their own water supply now matched the springs harnessed by those fortunate owners of the luxurious *villae urbanae* in the country.

With a continuous supply of water large fountains become possible. But we must not think of the tall fountain streams seen in Renaissance and more modern times, for these require a large volume of water piped under high pressure to allow the jet to soar into the air. The lead pipework used during the Roman period was only capable of supplying water under low pressure, and plumbing would have leaked if the supply was increased further. There was however great scope in the use and form of water outlets. In general they were left to trickle downwards, giving a gentle calming sound that was much appreciated. When a nozzle was fitted at the end of the pipe a small jet of water could be thrown to produce a pleasing arc of water, and several jets combined could create an imaginative water display. A waterspout could also direct water to land into a basin a short distance away, the reach probably a metre at the most. The water catchment basin no longer needed to be placed directly underneath the water outlet, freeing the fountain figure from close contact with its watery home, and again this would increase the range of fountain figures possible. There was indeed a great leap of the imagination to make the fountain rise. Here the allusion to a natural spring was lost and man's ingenuity became paramount. Some frescos show a jet leaping up from a basin but if one tries to measure the height by the proportions of the basin itself, we could estimate that perhaps at best the jet would reach less than a metre, and more likely half of that. Several frescos depict what we would term a bubbling fountain, where water welled up in the centre and created a low dome of gurgling bubbles. This form is illustrated in the fresco from the House of the Wedding of Alexander in Pompeii, with water issuing from the centrally placed white marble fountain bowl.

URN AND BOWL FOUNTAINS

These ornamental objects are seen in numerous garden frescos where they are often used as the central focal point in a symmetrical composition. Often birds are shown perched on the rim to drink water contained inside the bowl. This scene re-enacts a theme of doves representing souls drinking the water of everlasting life. The model was a Hellenistic one, made in mosaic by Sosus of Pergamon, which was widely acclaimed,[3] and many versions of this original theme survive. The urns and bowls were not mere bird baths, however, and were primarily used as a fountain basin. Pliny the Younger mentions that at Tusculum a small internal courtyard garden or light-well was enlivened by a fountain in a marble basin, 'watering the plane trees round it and the ground beneath them with its light spray'.[4] He does not describe its appearance but it is thought to have been in the form of an urn or bowl, and would therefore be similar to those depicted in several frescos. As a number of these show water bubbling up from the centre of the bowl, this would confirm that many functioned as a fountain basin. A number of examples in museums have been found to have a central hole that runs through the stem and bowl to take plumbing, such as the wide-brimmed dish fountain that stands on a tall slender fluted shaft found in the area of the Horti Lamiani, and is now in the Conservatori Museum, Rome. In general these fountains

Drawing of a fresco depicting an urn fountain from the House of Romulus and Remus, Pompeii. At either side a water nymph holds a shell which was symbolically associated with the source of a spring gently spilling over.

were not provided with a water outlet so the water level would be high, enabling birds to drink easily without the need to overreach and risk falling in. If the rim had a beaded or scalloped edge the water run-off would be directed to the small channels in the design and spill over in a selective pattern rather than an overall flow. The use of this additional feature would ensure certain benefits, for instance the well-spaced droplets of falling water would not conceal any decorative carvings on the urn and its support, whereas a continuous sheet of falling water would. Also if the bowl was not quite level the overflow would tend to spill to one side only, and this additional decoration could compensate for this to a certain degree.

In many cases the fountains appear to have been designed to sit in a shallow water catchment basin which could save the immediate area from getting too waterlogged. In drier areas though, the splashing excess water, which was only a steady trickle really, could be allowed to overflow and would soon be absorbed by large trees and thirsty plants, as is thought to be the case in Pliny's small court.

Garden urns and bowls, for use as a fountain or otherwise, come in all sizes and shapes. There are small-scale ones seen perched on top of walls or fences in frescos, which were more ornamental than practical. At the other end of the scale there are huge versions such as the Warwick Vase found at Hadrian's Villa, Tivoli (now in the Burrell Museum, Glasgow), that is like an urn; and the shallow dish of vast proportions found in the vicinity of the Horti Maecenas in Rome. These were both made of finely carved white marble. The remaining fragments of the latter have been collectively displayed on a wall in the Conversatori Museum in Rome, enabling us to see the richly carved underside which shows four large acanthus leaves radiating outwards from the centre and finally curling at their tip with the turn of the rim. Stems and handles also vary greatly; some handles are placed above the vase, others are tucked under the rim. Some may be plain but many were designed to represent a plant stem or inward-turning leaf. The supporting shaft or stem of these fountains is often fairly plain or fluted. There are however fine, tall, twisted stems, as seen in the fresco at the House of Neptune and Amphitrite at Herculaneum, as well as those which splay outwards at the base. The latter would be more stable and less inclined to break after being used for a number of years.

In the Auditorium of Maecenas the frescos in a series of niches in the apse depict garden scenes and are of alternate designs, one showing a tall narrow urn, the other a wide-brimmed shallow bowl. The variety seen in frescos is reflected in life, confirming the usefulness of frescos for comparative purposes. In a number of frescos we can see that a sculptural figure is used as a support for the bowl above (e.g. centaurs or sphinxes). In museums the range widens. In the Vatican Museum, in the Gallery Candelabri, one finds four crouching

Drawing of a fresco showing a wide-brimmed urn in front of a decorative marble wall, from the Auditorium of Maecenas, Rome.

sileni (who are attendants of Bacchus, see chapter six); each carries a full wineskin on one shoulder, while their other shoulder and spare hand hold aloft a large shallow dished bowl. Occasionally we see fountain bowls in the form of a rectangular table with a shallow water basin on top; one can be seen in the photograph of the peristyle garden at the House of the Vettii.

WATER STAIRS

A number of fountains were designed so that the flow of water would be directed to fall down a short flight of stairs, before reaching a basin below. The pleasing sight and sound of water falling in this way re-created the cascading effect of natural spring water. Water stairs may be found in individual niches in architectural pavilions and in the niches of façade and *aedicula nymphaea*, as seen at the House of Cupid and Psyche in Ostia. In the House of Meleager at Pompeii the marble steps are not in a niche but are placed at the side of the type D pool. Most examples have straight steps like this but on occasion they are curved, although these are usually encountered on large properties where there was ample room to display features on a larger scale. Within the grounds of the Horti Maecenas at Rome the apse of the large basilica *nymphaeum* was fitted with a semicircular flight of six steps. These occupied the whole width of the apse. Water was introduced through a series of openings placed on the underside of each step, and then allowed to tumble down. The catchment basin is unfortunately no longer *in situ*. Another example is found at Tivoli, in the 'stadium garden' of Hadrian's villa. Again a semicircular flight of stairs occupies the curved end of this garden. In this case the design differs and is more directly inspired by theatrical examples. The arrangement comprises tiered plant beds dissected by eight flights of water stairs. This pattern could be seen to mimic areas of seating in the auditorium of a Roman theatre, which was divided by a number of flights of stairs for access to individual rows of seats. This multiple cascade was set at a high level so that the lower part was about shoulder height, and a channel at the bottom directed water to another water feature below, a little *nymphaeum* set into a deep niche with an arched frame. The numerous complementary curving lines seen in this part of the garden were completed by the addition of a large demi-lune basin, which was itself enlivened by a centrally placed fountain, although not with the tall jet of water shown in one reconstruction drawing.[5]

FREE-STANDING WATER-STAIR FOUNTAINS

These are really an elaboration of the single water stairs often seen in association with *nymphaea*. These small decorative versions, however, are free-standing and basically four-sided; therefore they were not intended for a niche positioned against a wall. Today a simple example can be seen *in situ* in the lower garden of the House of Loreius Tiburtinus at Pompeii. This fountain had been one of the highlights in a series of interconnecting pools and was protected by a pergola covered by grapevines. It was placed on top of an island so that water could simultaneously tumble down its four little staircases and then drop into the water-filled basin below. Two water-stair fountains have similarly been found on an island in large type D-shaped basins at Cherchel in Algeria, and show that the setting for this very decorative feature applied to large as well as small properties.

This type of ornament was also thought suitable to adorn and enliven a small area such as a light-well, or *viridarium*, for one is recorded in the House of Apollo at Pompeii.[6] A larger pyramidal example survives at Chersonisos, Crete; this comprises water stairs on the four corners rather than in the middle, and the panels in between were covered by mosaic fishing scenes. It was found in a courtyard 'of a building of unknown function',[7] the size of which has not been given; presumably this courtyard may have been planned as a form of garden, either domestic or public.

To date fourteen of these fountains have been discovered and the range of locations show that they were to be found in the provinces as well as in Rome, where five have come to light. On average they are 0.50 m wide by 0.30 m high and have four water stairs alternating with panels of relief sculpture. Originally they were roughly pyramidal in shape but many, perhaps later versions, have more steeply sloping sides. In some cases the steps are nearly vertical and merely hint at their original purpose, to mimic a cascade. Characteristically we find that the exterior is divided into carved panels that are paired or alternating. Plain panels or, more typically, areas of high or low relief carvings alternate with decorative panels incorporating a sea shell above a flight of stairs. A number of these water stairs are themselves flanked by narrow panels containing either fluted pilasters, narrow rebated panels or a series of overlapping fish scales. The sculptural panels depict material or objects associated with nature and the deities and their attendants found in myths connected with the Roman garden (see chapter six). Thus we find shells, dolphins and putti which provide a link to Venus; animals associated with Diana; and members of the Bacchic throng or *thiasos* – Pan, satyrs and maenads. Of the three versions depicted here the uppermost shows alternately a winged boy and girl putto, the draped female holding a hare in her right hand while on her left shoulder she carries a basket of flowers or fruit. In the centre the panels depict three sirens, Odysseus and

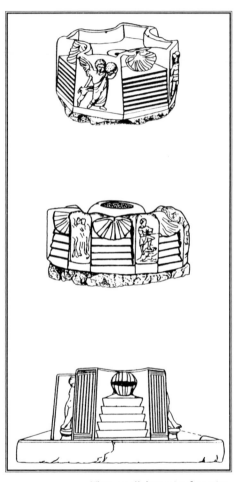

Three small decorative fountains incorporating water stairs. Above, Therme Museum, Rome; centre, Vatican Museum, Rome (h. 0.22 m, w. 0.48 m); below, Tarragona Museum, Spain (h. 0.38 m). Only the latter is complete with a lower water catchment basin. In the example from the Vatican the raised slightly domed area of the water outlet presumably allowed water to cascade all around the top before falling down the stairs.

Pan. In the bottom example there are high relief carvings of a pair of standing putti holding either a thyrsus wand or a rhyton drinking cup.

Presumably a small fountain figure or fitting was placed over the central aperture, to produce a small jet of water. Alternatively the slightly raised cupped central section found on three of these fountains might suggest that the water may have welled up to create a bubble-type feature, spilling over the cupped surface and into the upper catchment basin. A raised edge held water at the top and water from this pool trickled through a hole at the apex of each scallop shell, from where it poured down a steep flight of steps. The water then collected into another basin below, but most examples found have this part missing. There are two exceptions; one from Tarragona in Spain,[8] and the dog fountain in the British Museum (Inv. no. 2536) which both appear to sit in a much wider, shallow, square basin that was provided with an overflow outlet at one corner. A reconstruction of the latter, which is a truncated pyramidal version, is on public display in the Roman gallery and gives a rare opportunity to view one of these objects in full working order.

Many of these fountains retain some traces of a base or rough sections where the marble has been chipped away, presumably after antiquity, but this is not necessarily evidence that a lower basin was integral to the design. It is now clear that these fountains could be displayed in two ways: a water-stair fountain could be placed on an island in a larger pool, which became the catchment basin and the main point of interest; or the fountain could be put in a garden setting or court of its own without the need for a further water feature – in this case it would only need a small shallow base into which it could be slotted.

LARGE FOUNTAINS

Some water features were fitted with a number of *jet d'eau*. One of the most elaborate is found in the *nymphaeum* on the Palatine at Rome; this is one of a pair of island-like structures flanking the Imperial *triclinium* in the Domus Flavia. These combine a mixture of water features: a façade *nymphaeum*, a type D water basin and a monumental oval-shaped caisson. The tall boat-shaped island concealed a central oval plant trough that would have crowned the structure with greenery, today it is planted with irises. This is surrounded by an architectural façade of alternating curved and rectangular niches for fountain statuary. Each figure would have poured water into a shallow trough below. From there water somehow percolated into the decorative basin at its foot. Windows on both sides of the *triclinium* opened out on to this fine spectacle.

FOUNTAIN OUTLETS

Cicero mentions that his brother's fishpond had water jets[9] but unfortunately he does not specify which type. Many water outlet points would have been simple bronze nozzles with no additional adornment, as at the House of the Water Jets at Conimbriga. Sidonius Apollinaris, however, refers to a pool furnished with six water jets in the form of lion's heads.[10] In this case water would have poured out of the open mouth of the lion. These were perhaps the most popular type and examples have been discovered at Darenth (Kent)[11] and elsewhere. A lioness or panther's head type has also been found. Another form, that of a dolphin, was widely used and is recorded at Ephesus and Pompeii.[12] A bronze dolphin from Constantinople (Istanbul) is now on display in the British Museum (Inv. no. 1922). At Caerleon (S. Wales) a stone dolphin, although part of a statue group, was placed in a large *nymphaeum* so that water could pour from its mouth down a short flight of stairs and flow into an elongated pool running down the centre of the *palaestra*/garden of the fortress baths.[13] Other waterspouts, made mainly of bronze, include a raven found at Stabiae[14] and a peacock from Pompeii;[15] the water issued from the beaks of both birds. In some places we find a coiled serpent, usually shown about to strike. It has a wide gape and the water would spit out of its mouth as if it were venom.

Multiple jets were possible by combining two or three spouts on a shared stem, as in the triple dolphin fountain found in the House of Camillus at Pompeii.[16] Another popular method of obtaining multiple jets was by perforating a bronze or stone item with numerous holes. A pine cone is most often encountered and one originally from Pompeii can be seen on display in the British Museum (Inv. no. 2579). The pine cone was a motif that was charged with symbolism; its capacity to open its scales and shed its seed, even after a fire, was seen as a wonder and therefore it was associated with the concepts of fertility and rebirth. These ideas were acceptable to the Early Christian communities and we find that pine cone fountains continued to be used during the Christian era where they are seen in numerous Early Christian and Byzantine mosaics. An example depicted in a floor mosaic comes from Bordeaux in France and has been dated to the fifth–sixth century AD.[17] Here the pine cone has been placed on top of a tall stem situated in the centre of a tall urn fountain; ten streams of water are shown falling into the urn below. The pine cone outlet is also seen in church mosaics surrounding a baptismal area, as at Stobi in Macedonia, where there are four alternating scenes; two are set in a slender stemmed bowl and two in a tall urn. A large urn was found in association with this mosaic and one can speculate about whether this contained a device similar to that seen in the mosaic. Pine cones are also sometimes found in 'The Annunciation' scenes; one is found on the wall of the Byzantine church of the Dormition at Daphni.[18] Here four streams of water shoot upwards before falling into a small quadrilobe basin, then reappear at a lower level to pour into a second rectangular basin below.

FLUVIAL OUTLETS

A larger volume of water, or a broader flow, would be possible if a slot was used rather than a jet, and the fluvial mask was the ideal outlet for this. In these cases a slab of stone was carved to resemble a human face, usually a river god, who is often portrayed with wild eyes and curling hair, mouth slightly open to let the water issue forth and splay outwards with his curling beard. The large 'Bocca della Verita' in Rome is a fine specimen of its type; it was previously thought to be a drain cover, but the relief carving is too defined for that. Its large size may indicate, however, that it had been displayed in a public area rather than a domestic one. Some versions may have been street fountains but this form could equally have existed in a garden of some kind. Smaller ones are also found, such as at Carthage, where you are allowed to drink water from a spout concealed in an ancient fluvial mask placed against the side of the museum's WC!

The open mouth or gape of man or beast is an ideal medium to convey water to or from a pool. With statues of humans, as opposed to flat facial masks, it is rare to find a jet of water coming from the mouth, for this could appear as if the figure was spitting or vomiting. Therefore a face by itself was used for larger flows where it could be interpreted as a personification of a water source or spring, which was acceptable. For this reason we find that animals, birds and fish are more frequently encountered. Unfortunately statuary is rarely found in its original place, and this complicates interpretations. However, a large stone outlet that appears to resemble a carp has recently come to light at Tockenham (Wilts.); the scaly fish head with bulbous eyes and a wide open mouth would have been able to pour a large volume of water perhaps from a spring into a large pool.[19]

FOUNTAIN STATUES

A statue of bronze could be made with a hollow core that would accommodate a lead water pipe but it was more difficult to bore a vertical channel through a stone or marble figure. Perhaps for this reason numerous examples have a groove chiselled out of the rear so that a water pipe could be partially concealed behind. A horizontal or slightly angled hole was then bored right through to insert the rest of the pipe through the figure to emerge as a fountain. The outlet was often concealed, sometimes in an upturned urn or other vessel, so that the figure could appear to be pouring out the contents in a never-ending stream. One of the most frequent figures found is a small child or putto who appears almost weighed down by the large urn held aloft on his shoulder or in his arms. In a statue group the outlet was usually fitted through the head of an accompanying animal, bird or other object, and would then issue from the creature's mouth. In some cases the plumbing must have been visible and perhaps these statues may have been placed against a wall or in a niche which would help to conceal the pipes rather than let them be seen from all directions if they were out in the open. It possibly also suggests that some of these statues may have been used elsewhere before being converted for use as fountain figures.

Figures were placed in the open beside pools or else in a niche or recess, a setting that would in effect highlight the figure. Fountain figures could also be placed either in the middle of a pool, where they could appear to emerge from the depths, or on an island or pillar usually located in the centre of the water. Those that had been sited to one side of the water basin had an added advantage, for they would make the installation and maintenance of plumbing a great deal easier.

There is a great variety to be seen in fountain figures but they mainly comprise items that have a bearing on or some connection to water. Aquatic subjects are surprisingly numerous, from water nymphs, river gods and their attendants, to the fish and crustaceans living in the deep. A number of ancient mythological figures had adventures in the sea or in rivers and were also subjects for display as a fountain figure, but again these are often accompanied by an animal or object of some sort that represented the working part of the fountain. Fountain statues may be seen to play a dual role in the garden, being both ornamental and symbolic. But the same figure can also be found with or without a fitting for a fountain; to prevent repetition the iconography associated with deities and other figures found in gardens will be dealt with in the next chapter.

Fountains would add a sparkle to any pool and the pleasant sound of the trickling water would be relaxing. In hot climates the presence of cool water from a fountain would help to humidify the area and the change of atmosphere would have been both welcome and necessary.

A marble fountain figure of a putto carrying an urn from the Villa Cynthia at Tivoli, now in the Vatican Museum, Rome.

AUTOMATA

Automata are usually activated by a mixture of air and water and therefore it seems appropriate to include them in this chapter. Evidence for these contraptions is unfortunately confined to literary sources, such as Vitruvius, Athenaeus and Hero of Alexandria. Vitruvius confirms their existence,[20] but as he views them as frivolous he advises us to consult the works of Ctesibius which, sadly, have not survived. However, Hero of Alexandria, who is believed to have been a pupil of Ctesibius, wrote a very interesting and enlightening book on *Pneumatics*, which includes a section on automata. Athenaeus describes a statue of Nysa in Ptolemy's carnival-like procession that bears many similarities to features of automata described in this work. The statue of Nysa (who is connected to the myths of the god Dionysus/Bacchus) was said to rise automatically then, after a libation was given, it would sit down.[21] The addition of water would trigger the operation of a siphon which would

Drawing of an owl automata,
as described by Hero of
Alexandria.

force out compressed air to activate the figure. In other experiments
recorded by Hero a number of siphons caused birds to sing a song or
figures to blow trumpets.[22]

As several of the inventions contained in the book require running
water[23] many would surely have been placed in open areas, such as
gardens. Hero's experiment no. 47 specifically requires the 'action of the
sun's rays' for the function of such a device, and further evidence is
found in the description of experiment no. 14. Here Hero explains an
ideal situation for such a contrivance: 'The figures of several different
birds are arranged near a fountain, or in a cave, or in any place where
there is running water.' Because many of these figures were dependent
on movable parts – such as a turning owl – it is likely that they were
made of bronze rather than stone. Once removed from connecting
pipework, siphons and system of levers, their function would be less
clear, and they would subsequently resemble ordinary fountain outlets
rather than automata, which might be the reason why none have been
recorded. Apparently a working copy of Hero's owl fountain (a re-
creation of experiment no. 15) was installed in the Renaissance gardens
of the Villa d'Este at Tivoli, which would have been prior to AD 1580,
where it was observed functioning.[24] This at least proves that such
artifices were feasible.

The famous owl fountain is illustrated here. Instructions on how to
construct such devices were given by Hero, and a brief summary
outlines the stages of its operation. The water from the fountain flows

into a sealed rectangular chamber which contains a siphon. As the chamber fills with water the air it expels is piped to the birds, or at least the branches on which they sit, and produces an imitation of bird song. When the water in the chamber reaches the correct level the siphon empties it, causing the birds to fall silent, and the water falls into a lower chamber. The added weight pulls a cord that is looped around the column on which the owl stands, causing it to revolve towards the other birds until a second siphon empties the lower chamber. A weight at the other end of the cord then pulls it back and the owl returns to its former position. Hence the birds only sing when the owl is looking away from them.

CHAPTER SIX

Garden Sculpture

One of the characteristic features of Roman gardens is that many contained decorative items, frequently in the form of sculpture. Garden furnishings in stone – especially marble – bronze or terracotta introduced some life and variety into the garden. Many were used in imaginative ways and were placed to catch the eye, perhaps with the intention of providing a talking point, but in addition to being ornamental there were other reasons for their inclusion in the garden. This chapter will explore the various facets of Roman culture that inspired the character and symbolism of garden sculpture.

Evidence has been gathered from a number of sources, one of the most useful being the numerous surviving ancient frescos. They can supply clues to the way that certain items were used and displayed, and therefore their possible setting within a real garden can be judged. There are also a number of interesting small or miniature frescos depicting gardens that are compartmentalized by pergolas and trellis enclosures; in almost every case sculpture of some sort is found there. Items are placed inside and on the supports of the trellis itself, showing that the enclosures form ideal locations for sculpture.

In antiquity the large garden scenes painted in frescos could serve a secondary purpose as an alternative to actually owning any pieces. If a person could not afford to purchase sculpture, he could have them painted on to his garden wall instead. An artist would include the desired objects into a scene resembling a view of a garden, perhaps with a little barrier fence as well, and when seen from a distance they would serve as a good substitute. In this way he would at least be able to admire his painted works of art.

Sculpture and frescos are durable decorations but one of the simplest, though short-lived, ways to decorate a house and garden was with flowers and garlands. Cato mentions that the *matrona*, the mistress of the house, was responsible for growing and placing flowers on altars.[1] Quite often the flowers grown in the garden were woven with various pliant stems of foliage plants to form a garland, but in towns many gardens would have been too small to provide all the raw materials necessary and therefore the *matrona* would need to buy ready-made versions from street vendors.

On feast days the *domus* was also decorated and long garlands or swags were required to drape between the columns of a portico. Smaller ones were placed on altars or hung from a hook at the side. Pliny records that chaplets or *coronae* 'were used to honour the gods, the lares public and private, tombs and spirits of the dead'.[2] Therefore sacred statues may also have been decorated. Garlands by nature are ephemeral items and rarely survive but in Egypt the very dry conditions are conducive to good preservation, and some have been discovered in tombs dated to the Roman period. An example can be seen in the British Museum; this particular garland had been made with everlasting flowers, *Helichrysum Stoechas (L.)*. In this case the choice of flowers may reflect its funerary context but a number of Greco-Roman funerary portraits illustrate the deceased holding a garland in one hand. The dusky rose colour of the petals in these garlands indicates they were made entirely from roses. The rose was not just confined to funerary art. It has always been admired for its scent and beauty, and these garlands became extremely popular for use in the home as well, especially during the late Republic and throughout the days of the Empire of Rome. Literary sources describe different forms of garland, their use and components (see chapter seven), and a large number of frescos illustrate how garlands decorated architecture. Several frescos of garden scenes use them as a framing device or as a means of linking *oscilla* (small decorative marble reliefs) into the composition for otherwise they could have appeared to be isolated at the top of the panel.

Contemporary art as a source, although often an idealized one, is augmented by evidence supplied by ancient writers who mention sculpture in rustic contexts and public or private gardens. Virgil and Tibullus provide examples of rustic shrines that were usually in the countryside but could equally well exist on large estates. Martial, however, informs us that effigies of wild beasts adorned a grove of plane trees in a public park at Rome.[3] He describes one of these in detail, a large statue of a bear with mouth open as if growling in anger. One day his friend Hylas jokingly put his hand in its mouth and was unfortunately fatally bitten by a snake coiled up inside. A similar statue of a bear can be seen today in the Getty Museum.[4]

Archaeological evidence for sculpture, especially statuary, has indicated that a significant proportion has been found in association with dwellings as opposed to public monuments. Unfortunately the exact locations of the objects were until recently rarely recorded, beyond naming the site in general. Therefore sites covered by the eruption of Vesuvius are extremely valuable, for items were mostly found *in situ* and at least some were recorded adequately. This enables us to see the range available in garden ornamentation at that date and we can try to appreciate a sequence in their arrangement in the garden and also look for links between different items in each collection. The area serves as a model; it may be fairly representative of other periods. Many pieces of sculpture appear to have remained popular throughout the Roman period and are the result of centuries of iconographic development. This is a large subject in its own right and it is not intended to attempt an art historical study, but merely to show how certain items are relevant to gardens.

Today old photographs and the few plans that were made at that time need to be consulted for, with the exception of the House of the Vettii at Pompeii, all the sculpture is now in museums or storerooms. Sadly many items are stored out of sight as in general only a small proportion is on view in museums, and unfortunately even the museum of Pompeii itself is not open to the public. Garden objects taken out of context, unless well documented, lose some of their relevance; it is interesting, for example, to note the direction in which an item was facing as well as its location within the garden.

The House of the Golden Cupids at Pompeii may be used as an example. This archive photograph shows the sculpture *in situ* within the garden and the accompanying plan identifies each item. In this garden a number of *oscilla*, *pinakes*, herms, animal statuary and a sundial have been re-erected in their approximate original positions. As can be seen there is a large variety of items, most of which are small. In most cases they appear to have been placed so that they face into the garden, whereas in the collection at the House of Marcus Lucretius, also in Pompeii, they face towards the main rooms. This appears to suggest that the outward view from these rooms was of prime importance, and sculpture was used to enhance that view by often being placed in a direct line of sight. This is also noticeable in the location of garden structures such as *aediculae nymphaea* mentioned in chapter three.

The use of sculpture in large gardens can be revealing. Statuary was sometimes placed beside a water basin where reflections could add to the alluring quality of the scene; this is seen to good effect in the Canopus garden of Hadrian's Villa at Tivoli. The Romans might also have felt that the effect of multiple images from these reflections would double their value. Another means of display is seen in the Villa of Poppaea at Oplontis, in the large northern garden, where a row of herm statues lines a diagonal pathway. Presumably the large collections of herms found at other sites may indicate a similar pattern. At the Villa of Cassius, near Tivoli, the very large collection discovered in the eighteenth century may have formed what is termed a 'Hermgalerie',[5] where perhaps both sides of a path would be ornamented by herms. If we return to Oplontis and look at the large pool garden we can observe that the eastern side of the large *piscina* has a wide pathway lined by a row of statues on plinths, each one placed in front of a tree making a pleasant shaded walk. By this method the statues themselves would be shaded and protected by the tree trunk behind, and the dark trees would form a background against which the marble would be seen to advantage. De Caro, who excavated this site, points out that by setting the line of statues slightly at an angle in relation to the pool, they would all be visible from the principal rooms to the north.[6] Again this

Plan and view of garden sculpture at the House of the Golden Cupids, Pompeii.

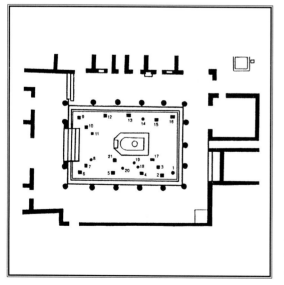

KEY TO LOCATION OF SCULPTURE

1. Monopodium
2. Herm of Dionysus
3. *Pinax*
4. Janiform herm
5. & 6. Herm of Dionysus
7. *Pinax*
8. Statuette of Omphale
9. Herm of boy
10. *Pinax*
11. Base
12. Janiform herm

13. *Pinax*
14. Sundial
15. Janiform herm
16. Herm of boy
17. Base
18. Boar
19. Rabbit
20. Dog
21. Herm of boy
There were also 5 mask *oscilla* and 2 circular *oscilla*

Plan and view of statuary at the House of Marcus Lucretius, Pompeii.

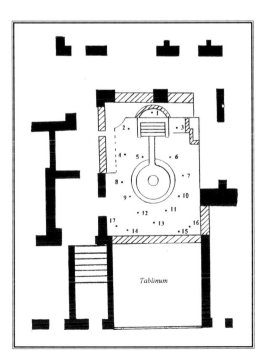

KEY TO LOCATION OF SCULPTURE

1. Silenus
2.& 3. Janiform herms
4. Satyr
5. Duck
6. Deer
7. Cow
8. Draped herm of satyr
   with goat and kid
9.& 10. Ibises

11.& 12. Hares
13. Group of satyr and Pan
   (reverse of that in the
   Vatican)
14.& 15. Dolphins with
   cupids
16.& 17. Janiform herms
There were also 5 *oscilla*

Drawing of a much eroded relief panel, now in the Louvre, showing statuary placed under a portico. From left to right these appear to represent: a figure now gone but its plinth is still preserved, above there is possibly an *oscilla*; an unidentified figure; a herm placed behind a ribbed vessel; Bacchus and his panther; another herm behind a fountain basin; Hercules with his club.

confirms that sculpture was placed in prominent places where, as objects of status, they could reveal the wealth of their owner.

On occasion sculpture was also placed at the edge of a colonnade. This means of display is shown in a relief carving now in the Louvre Museum. The worn nature of the stone makes it difficult to identify each object but the general effect that was intended is clear. Similarly an account by Athenaeus of the furnishings of King Ptolemy's pavilion set up for a festival at Alexandria shows that he also decided to place 'marble figures, a hundred in all', beside or near 'columns which supported the pavilion'.[7] In these cases statuary and other sculptures are individually shown to advantage by being isolated within a framework of columns and yet are linked to others by the very same colonnade. The carved representation indicates that the portico is further decorated by swags of garlands, these looped curves serve to break the strong vertical lines and introduce a softening touch while continuing to link the row of statuary. The statues would also be protected by the roof above from the worst of the winter rains. However because the statues in effect blocked access to the garden another part of the portico would need to be left open.

This means of display is on occasion seen in Pompeii, at the House of Ancora Nera, where one side of the sunken garden had been furnished by a row of statue bases protected by the arches of a cryptoporticus. At the House of the Vettii a number of small statues stood on bases placed immediately against a column, and several are paired so that two stood in the space of an intercolumniation. The statues would then have been standing facing each other and would almost appear to be leaning against a pillar. However, in this particular garden, which had four of these paired statuettes, the figures contained fountain outlets that had been placed there for convenience sake; it was then easier to connect them to water pipes laid along the gutter of the portico. Each pair of statues stood on either side of a rectangular water basin which could catch the arc of water playing from both fountain figures.

Apart from statues found in gardens at Pompeii and its vicinity, some of which are well recorded, it is difficult to determine whether an item found elsewhere ornamented a garden or a building, for their location is rarely given in excavation reports. There are, however, four main features which can be used to aid our identification; these are:

1. *Size.*
2. *Quality.*
3. *Association.*
4. *Rusticity.*

First, garden statuary is normally of a smaller size; however, their scale depends on the size of the garden. There is an obvious difference between the confines of a Pompeian-style peristyle garden and a large public park. Therefore it is understandable that in general the Capitoline triad (Jupiter, Juno and Minerva) is rarely represented, for these regal imposing figures, often of suitably Olympian size, were more fitting for public rather than private display.

Secondly, garden statuary is often seen to be of a mass-produced kind. Items contained in museums throughout the world show that a number of replicas were made of famous Greek statues. Several show minor variations of pose, and some are mirror images. Others show that they were inspired by an original, which in many cases became a standardized form, but there was obviously an allowance for artistic licence and perhaps for a patron's specific requests. With a large demand for statuary, workshops no doubt produced items of differing grades of workmanship and the resulting variations in price would suit a range of pockets. Some of the wealthier properties, however, would have contained masterpieces, such as the works of Praxiteles and Scopas displayed in the Gardens of Servilius, Rome, and described by Pliny.[8]

Thirdly, figures who are linked to a particular divinity associated with gardens, and some of the attributes of these deities, are represented in garden art. Their inclusion serves either to allude to the presence of that divinity or merely to accompany it. In larger gardens an area could be devoted to a form of theme garden, such as a collection of Egyptian-inspired statuary that could simulate the aura of Alexandria, Canopus and the Nile Delta in general. This is believed to have been the case in the Canopus area at Hadrian's Villa, Tivoli.[9] Alternatively statuary could be selected specifically to suit a particular location in the garden – for example, herms of philosophers in an Academy-style garden. Cicero provides an indication of this style of garden design; when ordering sculpture he directly specified that he desired subjects suitable for a gymnasium and *xystus*; also for an Academy, for which he stressed that Muses would be more suitable than Bacchantes.[10] However it should be added that gardens may have been ornamented by a mixture of pieces acquired over the years or generations, items that were available at the time as opposed to an exact choice. Sculpture was expensive so only the rich would have been able to afford to have a new collection to replace more old-fashioned pieces. All these factors could mask the original design or programme, if there was one.

The fourth element, rusticity, may be compared to our modern taste for garden gnomes. We do not usually place these little ornaments inside the home for to us they belong in the garden. In antiquity the Romans also did not place Silvanus, the woodland god, or the rustic but powerful figure of Priapus, for instance, inside a dwelling. Garden statuary was essentially connected to subjects that could be at home in an outdoor context, the countryside or sea, fields or woodland. At times one can feel there is a wish to re-create an Arcadian atmosphere, or a sacred grove within the garden.

Finally, there is a further feature which identifies a garden statue. If the figure is bored through to take a lead water pipe then it may be presumed to have been destined to serve as a fountain figure, and would have been situated close to a water feature of some kind. They may sometimes have been used to pour water into the *impluvium* in the *atrium*, but more often than not they were placed in a garden. The four criteria above would still apply to determine whether it graced a public fountain or a domestic one.

Several monographic works, such as catalogues compiled by Neudecker, Appelton, Jashemski, Hill, Bieber, Bellido, Kapossy, as well as collections held in museums, give a great deal of information on the range of items used and how frequently specific pieces that may be regarded as garden sculpture occur.

Grimal believes that the Roman love for 'naturalisme' pervaded all and he also thought that there was a religious aspect to sculpture. Jashemski sees the sculpture of Pompeii as having the combined functions of religion and ornamentation; by locating sites of altars in gardens, this has proved the worship of particular deities there. The approaches of both Grimal and Jashemski have much to commend them. The Romans were a very religious people and would see the presence of their gods in many things. Garden sculptures are ornamental items and their presence may reflect the fact that many Romans were sensitive to beauty and form, and could appreciate the decorative aspect of statuary while at the same time feeling that many of the items had sacred connotations.

Today we usually value a statue for its ornamental properties but in some countries sacred objects are still placed in niches or grottos, for example convent gardens in Italy, where a statue of the Virgin can sometimes be seen in an ivy-covered fountain grotto. This re-creates the cave at Lourdes, where the Virgin Mary appeared to St Bernadette, but the setting could be said to bear many resemblances to ancient Roman *nymphaea*. The figure is religious, yet by placing it in such a situation, it is also highly decorative. As can be seen, the setting around sculpture is important, revealing its connection – with Bernadette in this case; the setting adds to its religious significance as well as providing a suitable location in the garden for a small statue. Some saints, for instance St Francis, who was so in tune with nature, retain a holy yet rustic quality that would also make them a very suitable figure for display in a garden. He would become decorative but would still hold some sanctity for us. Numerous Ancient Roman statues of divinities were seen by the ancients in a similar light. However not all garden sculpture could be defined as having a religious context – the rustic figures of mortals and athletes, for example.

The appearance of secular as opposed to sacred items may be noted in surviving collections. These reflect a broader desire for ornamental objects, partly due to the Romans' approach to religion that changed over the centuries. Those of Epicurean or Neo-Platonic persuasion would perhaps be less concerned with statuary depicting deities. The syncretism that occurred throughout the Empire no doubt had an effect, too, with sculpture being tailored to suit individual tastes. Flora and Pomona appear to merge into the Venus figure, and are therefore under-represented in gardens. With the introduction of Eastern cults we see the inclusion of figures or the attributes of Isis, Osiris, and Bes; Attis and Orpheus are also sometimes encountered. There were many reasons for one's choice of statuary. The inference behind specific items will be examined later.

In table I (pp. 204–5), twenty different sites have been chosen from which there was sufficient documentation of large collections of sculpture. The first half (ten) are sites from the area covered by Vesuvius, so these form a fairly reliable control group. A mixture of small and large properties are included. The second half are from large properties in Italy for which documentation is unfortunately limited, owing to the fact that the ruins were excavated for the most part before AD 1900 and this was largely undertaken to acquire saleable commodities. Sculptural finds here, as on most sites elsewhere, need to be regarded as chance survivals after pillage in antiquity and later. Records rarely show if the sculpture originally belonged in a garden but the sites considered here contained certain features that could be found within the grounds of large Roman properties. Through lack of space the headings indicate only the most recurrent forms of sculpture.

The absence of altars on sites in the second group is perhaps partly due to a general preference to record statuary which are often of more interest to specialists studying aspects of Roman portraiture, monumental art and objects of fine quality. Over the years this had resulted in a lower priority being given to publishing the full details of all objects found, but modern recording methods are improving the situation. Likewise *pinakes* were probably omitted because they could appear to be a relief panel (and sundials a block of stone). These entries, therefore, can highlight the limitations of catalogues solely aimed at statuary. As can be seen there are few representations of Priapus but this may reflect the usual practice of installing a wooden statue rather than a marble one, and wood does not usually survive.

The table indicates the extent of the popularity of statuary depicting children/putti or animals. In a number of cases however there were statue groups composed of a child with an accompanying animal. Where these occurred they have been placed under one heading only, for children. Likewise any other combination with animals is placed under the respective heading, for example, Pan with a she-goat is included solely under Pan. This unfortunately does deplete the entry under animals but it is desirable to list items only once. The popularity of this combined group (animals with child) is, I feel, also partly due to the appeal of small creatures in reality, and for this reason it is not surprising that many are small in size. The heading of satyrs also includes groups of Bacchic content (for example, Pan and Satyr) and again these are counted as a single item. Satyrs often appear in the plural in mythology and this entry reveals another instance where Romans may have aimed to re-create myth in their gardens.

In table I, the ephebes and wrestlers are collected together under one heading for they appear to be related items which demonstrate an athletic image. Typically they show what was considered the ideal physique of comely, yet manly youth. The herms are a mixture of types, including Hermes himself. The full range will be examined later. After an inspection of the range and frequency of garden ornaments, and having established a mode of selection for such sculpture, the especial relevance of individual subjects is discussed in the following catalogue.

Catalogue of Sculpture Found in Roman Gardens

ALTARS

These are perhaps the earliest and simplest items of garden sculpture and are frequently seen in reliefs and frescos. A number of sacro-idyllic landscape scenes include an altar in the form of a small pedestal, often with a shrine, and our attention is drawn to its setting which frequently emphasizes a rural context. As such they belong to country villa estates as well as temple/shrine enclosures. Perhaps the earliest known inscription naming altars within a sacred enclosure is that of the Agnone tablet of about 250 BC (now in the British Museum) which reveals several divinities connected with agriculture, namely Ceres, Proserpina, Lympha-Rain, nymphs, Hercules, Genita, Flora and possibly Venus.[11] Of the literary sources, Varro identifies twelve deities that were considered appropriate to husbandmen, Jupiter and Tellus, Sol and Luna, Ceres and Liber, Robigus and Flora, Minerva and Venus, Lympha and Bonus Eventus.[12] These deities are of great interest for each provides an aspect of their cult that could be seen to have a connection to gardens, or horticulture in general. Varro has also provided each one with a counterpart, in many cases forming a male and female pair, but in all cases each couple is in some way linked.

A detail of a mosaic from Vienne depicting rural scenes; here two people give offerings and sacrifice at an altar shaded by a sacred tree.

The first pair, Jupiter and Tellus, were seen to fulfil the role of father and mother. Jupiter was the most omnipotent of all the gods and ruled the sky, whereas Tellus, the goddess of the earth, embraced 'all the fruits of agriculture'. Sol and Luna are a natural pairing; the first was the sun god and the second the goddess of the moon. Varro mentions that the course of their passage across the sky is 'watched in all matters of planting and harvesting'. Ceres, the mother of Proserpina, was the goddess of corn (and cereals in general when used for bread-making). Liber, a male divinity, was often equated with Bacchus, the god of wine, and Varro notes that this pair were to be seen as important 'because their fruits are most necessary for life; for it is by their favour that food and drink come from the farm'. Robigus was the god of rust and Flora the goddess of flowers, so 'when they are propitious the rust will not harm the grain and the trees, and they will not fail to bloom in their season'. The two goddesses Minerva and Venus were both highly honoured for 'one protected the oliveyard and the other the garden'. Lastly Varro beseeches us not to fail in our prayer to Lympha, the goddess of rain, and Bonus Eventus, the god who could ensure a good outcome, 'since without moisture all tilling of the ground is parched and barren, and without success and "good issue" it is not tillage but vexation'.

Gardens were essentially areas where plants were grown and therefore deities connected with agriculture still retained a hold, even on a small plot in town or country. But not all those mentioned above were transferred into the garden environment. Martial provides a list of the deities worshipped at altars on his Nomentean property, and these help to clarify which may be found: the Thunderer (Jupiter), Silvanus, Diana, Mars, Flora and Priapus.[13] On excavation it is not always possible to distinguish which deity was worshipped at an altar unless associated artefacts are found at the same time that could be attributed to a particular god or goddess but Jupiter is rarely identified in a garden context. It is possible however that a lightning bolt may have struck within Martial's estate and this altar would have commemorated the occasion. The other divinities mentioned by him are discovered occasionally but there were a number of others who may have a particular reason for their inclusion in the garden.

Statues of deities were sometimes placed beside an altar or in a shrine associated with it, and certainly several have been found in Pompeii.[14] The historians of the *Scriptores Historiae Augustae*, when recounting the lives of later emperors of the Roman Empire, mention how the mother of Marcus Antoninus was seen 'worshipping in her garden before a shrine of Apollo'.[15] Unfortunately they do not disclose if there was a statue of the divinity in this shrine but the immediate recognition of the deity as Apollo would imply that there must have been. Clearly religion pervaded all facets of Roman life. However, with the onset of a demand for the acquisition of status objects, statues that were placed in a garden take on a twofold meaning.

In a domestic setting altars were placed in the *atrium* or within the peristyle; sometimes they were painted on a wall or incorporated into an *aedicula* shrine (see chapter three). In the House of the Golden Cupids at Pompeii there were two altars/shrines, an *aedicula* or lararium on one side of the peristyle, and a painting in the corner of the opposite wall. The painted altar was shown in the middle, half on one wall and half on the other, between a pair of large snakes. Snakes were seen as benevolent and were commonly believed to ward off evil. These altars occasionally depict an egg or a pine cone for these were often used as offerings. Both the egg and the pine cone were powerful symbols of rebirth and the pine had an added bonus of having a high resin content, allowing it to burn well. The top of the altar usually had a circular depression to contain sacred objects, and for the sacrificial flame.

Altars were also located in the garden itself, against a garden wall or as a free-standing feature, often with a tree or shrub nearby which could give it some protection and shade. Pliny shows that large or beautiful trees were sometimes considered sacred,[16] a belief confirmed by finds of tree root cavities in close proximity to an altar at Pompeii.[17]

An altar flanked by two sacred serpents, detail of a fresco from Pompeii.

VENUS

This Ancient Roman goddess was the most important divinity in gardens. She was regarded as the protectress of the *hortus* and growing plants. An inscription on a vase from Pompeii refers to this connection.[18] Her role as the protector of gardens is mentioned by Varro and Pliny who also reveal that this valuable function continued even with the introduction of pleasure gardens.[19] Later she took on the attributes of the Greek Aphrodite and became associated with the fertility of man as well as plants. She also appears to have taken over many of the associations of Flora and Pomona. These chaste demi-goddesses retained an influence however, and Flora as goddess of flowers was worshipped in the festival of the Floralia that began on 28 April each year. Flora was usually shown crowned with flowers. Pomona presided over the orchard and could ensure the preservation of fruit. When depicted she is shown holding apples or a basket filled with fruit. Vertumnus, her male counterpart, eventually gained her affections. Silvanus, satyrs and even Pan tried to woo her but to no avail. Vertumnus decided to use various disguises but again was defeated, until he appeared in the innocuous form of an old woman. He gained her confidence and skilfully persuaded her as to the benefits of marriage, for with their union, the fertility of the garden orchard (under her care) would be assured.

A statue of Venus is found in numerous Roman gardens, which is testimony to her popularity. In a chapter on statues Pliny describes items of particular note and in his list he includes a celebrated statue of Venus at Athens that was known as 'Aphrodite of the gardens'.[20] But apart from naming the highly prized work of art he did not continue his description that could have informed us of the form in which she appeared.

The classic pose of Venus is a sinuous sensual form of a scantily clad or nude figure; she is often made to appear modest and tries to conceal her attributes. The version is the so-called Venus pudica and famous examples are named after the museums where they are now housed, such as the Capitoline Venus. This particular statue is of a monumental nature but suitably scaled-down forms would have been appropriate for a garden. Versions more commonly seen in gardens show Venus crouching down, perhaps to pick something (an example of this type is shown here), or alternatively she could be tying up her hair, putting on a sandal or as if emerging from the sea where she was born. Because of her associations with water, a half figure of the Venus discovered at Benghazi is believed to have been placed in a pool; in this position she would appear to be rising out of the water.[21] This type, plus the crouching Venus, would look very effective with their image reflected in water, and an accompanying dolphin could serve as the water spout for a fountain.

Marble statue of Venus, (Cordoba Museum).

Venus's associations with water are referred to by the inclusion in the garden of figures such as dolphins or other marine creatures, fish and crustaceans. A scallop shell is particularly emblematic, for Venus is often depicted emerging from such a shell. Larger sea creatures such as a hippocamp (a horse with a fish tail) are also shown in her entourage in many surviving mosaics. Her marine *thiasos* includes nereids, sea nymphs, and their counterparts, the mermen. Triton, the son of Neptune, is also seen at times. Marine sculptural groups include a hippocamp with a nereid rider. They are, however, usually seen in association with large water features, for example the pair of nereids that once stood at either side of a large pool in a villa at Formia, now in Naples National Museum.[22]

The presence of Venus could be symbolized by a dove, a rose flower or a sprig of myrtle, all of which were considered sacred to her. The animal used for ritual sacrifice in her honour was the hare (or the rabbit in Spain), whose fertility is well known, and was therefore highly suitable. In art hares are often shown eating grapes, the fruit of a highly prolific plant, and therefore would represent a fecund state. They also perhaps provide a second connection, this time with Bacchus, the god of wine. Bacchus was one of the deities named in a poem *The Vigil of Venus* where Venus bids her followers, including Ceres, Eros, Diana, Apollo, nymphs and the Graces, 'to go forth to the myrtle grove'.[23] All have links to Venus through myth, so their inclusion in a garden could form a theme. The Three Graces, Aglaia, Thalia and Euphrosyne, were the personification of charm, grace and beauty. These qualities were much admired in a woman, and their combination with Venus is understandable for her figure was and still is always seen as the ideal.

Another ancient myth recounts a competition, the Judgement of

Paris, to find which of the goddesses was the most beautiful: Paris had the unenviable task of deciding between Athene, Hera and Venus but of the three Venus was given the golden apple. These three are sometimes compared with the Graces but the addition of an apple to the narrative clarifies the rendition in fresco, mosaic or marble. Therefore Venus is sometimes depicted holding an apple, her prize in the contest, and this myth would supply a purpose behind the decision to include a figure of Paris in the garden of the House of the Vettii at Pompeii.

PRIAPUS

Priapus was believed to be the son of Aphrodite and Dionysus. This rustic divinity originated in Lampsacus, in Asia Minor, and replaced the old Roman phallic god Mutunus Tutunus whose potent member was widely used as a symbol to avert the evil eye. Such a talisman would ensure against the destructive forces of envy and malice. Priapus also appears to have taken over the role of the Roman god Vertumnus who was associated with the care of the orchard and fruit. The appearance of Priapus was sometimes made fun of by Latin authors for he was usually personified by a crudely made ithyphallic wooden statue, with a herm-like shaft. Sacro-idyllic landscape frescos often contain a roughly sketched outline of his form and nearly always place him close to a shrine or other building, but few actually depict him in an orchard or kitchen garden where he would be more at home. One notable exception is found in an old drawing of a miniature fresco, which places him in the middle of a small enclosed *hortus*. His statue, however, is shown larger than normal and what we are really seeing is his actual personification rather than a depiction of his statue. He guards the *hortus* but he also appears to fill the role of a work supervisor.

His well-endowed ithyphallic posture, as if by sympathetic magic, would ensure the fertility of the garden, orchard or vineyard where he was usually placed, and was believed to avert the evil eye. In one hand he carried a pruning hook, a reference to pruning and grafting techniques that increased the fertility of fruit trees and vines. This tool was also useful for his other major role, to ward off those intent on plundering the produce of the garden. Priapus's form also served as a kind of scarecrow for birds as well as humans.[24] There are many hilarious tales of his powers. Some are rather bawdy and others frankly and unashamedly pornographic and are the product of the times, which was largely a man's world. An extract from one of the milder versions in a poem called *The Priapea* illuminates Priapus's humble place in Roman society and some of people's expectations of him.

For these offerings Priapus must now make full return, and guard the owner's vineyard and little garden. Therefore, away! Boys, refrain from wicked plundering. Nearby is a wealthy neighbour, and his Priapus is careless. Take from him; this path of itself will lead you from the place.[25]

Drawing of a fresco depicting the rustic god Priapus keeping a watchful eye on workers in the *hortus.*

Not all of his statues were made of wood but as Martial jokes there were risks in owning a marble statue for such a valuable Priapus might be stolen.[26] A wooden version was less likely to disappear and therefore there was also less risk that the garden would be left without his protection. A large marble example, however, was discovered in the House of the Vettii, where his member served as a fountain outlet.[27] Several semi-clad stone statues of him exist; in this type he is often depicted lifting up his robe so that the fruitful produce of the garden might be displayed in the folds of his draperies, while at the same time revealing his symbolic potent ithyphallic character. Little children or cupids are sometimes shown lifting up his clothes.

The plant that was considered sacred to Priapus was rocket, thought to be the dyer's herb, or the sweet-smelling mignonette, which is also of the same family. The former, however, has tall spikes of flowers that could have been significant in his cult, and on occasions these were made into a crown to adorn his figure. The animal often associated with Priapus is the ass.

CUPID

Cupid, or Eros, was the love-child of Venus and Mars. Therefore he inherits certain characteristics of both parents; his use of bows and arrows from his war-like father and the ability to incite desire or love from his mother. This popular figure is found in many gardens and not unnaturally he is most often depicted as a chubby child with wings. Luxorius mentions a fountain statue of Cupid in a late Roman garden in North Africa[28] and in poem 46 he is shown to be at home in the garden with Diana, Nymphs, Venus and the Muses. This grouping of deities is similar to that in *The Vigil of Venus*, and their presence helps to confirm their suitability for a sculptural re-enactment of myth. Cupid is shown in a number of ways, sometimes stringing a bow, as in the example in the British Museum (Inv. no. 1673) or as a tired sleeping child, as found at Tarsus. The latter was also a fountain figure, the outlet being in an overturned urn. In a similar example from Nea Paphos, Cyprus, a shell appears to serve as a water outlet. Cupid is usually distinguished from statues of children by the presence of wings and a bow and arrows.

Cupid himself eventually fell in love with a nymph called Psyche who also sports a pair of wings. A delightful statue group of this youthful pair was found in Ostia, in a house now named after them; it captures a tender moment when the happy couple embrace. A similar group, although fragmentary, was discovered on the villa site at Woodchester (Glos.).[29]

CHILDREN

Statues or statuettes of children may have been a development from Cupid models and are often called erotes, putti or amorini; they are found both with and without wings. When portrayed in stone the children are mostly shown struggling or playing with animals, riding a dolphin or carrying an urn. Many functioned as fountain pieces, with the water outlet being in the mouth of an animal or vessel. These figures often show the various antics of young children with considerable realism. A mischievous child could be shown trying on an over-large theatre mask, or appears momentarily frightened by the sudden appearance of a frog – these are just a few examples of this pleasant genre. Another form frequently found is the sleeping child; this subject probably originated from decorative Greek funerary monuments, but the

Bronze fountain figure of a putto carrying a duck, one of a pair in the House of the Vettii, Pompeii. At the edge of the adjacent portico there is a three-legged marble table and a fountain catchment basin in the form of a two-legged table.

idea became quite popular and a number of copies exist. A rather sweet marble boy with a hooded cloak was curled up asleep at the edge of the *nymphaeum* in the garden of the House of the Small Fountain at Pompeii.

The children or putti mentioned above are usually plump little toddlers but slightly older infants, perhaps up to six or eight years old, are also found on occasion. An example would be the Maid of Anzio in the Therme Museum;[30] the Spinario, a slave boy extracting a thorn, seen in the Conservatori Museum, Rome, would really be classed as a rustic figure (for this category, see below). Older children that do not appear to have a particular function or distinguishing attributes may have been included in the garden as a reminder of a child's tender years that pass so quickly. These statues may then be notable in that they might bear some resemblance to a certain member of the household. An image of a plump well-fed child held an appeal then, as they often do today. The frequency and wide distribution of statues of young children is indicative of the popularity of this type.

MARS AND AMAZONS

Mars, although associated with war, was also connected to agriculture in the early days. An ancient prayer to the god Mars is preserved in Cato's agricultural manual and provides information on the rituals of land purification, where Mars was invoked to protect the household and associated land from sickness and disease, from barrenness and ruin, or invasion by insects, beasts and man.[31] He was in effect considered the father of the land (and farm) and the god of all growing things. The month dedicated to Mars offers further clues, for this important period coincides with the start of the agricultural year as well as heralding the season for campaigns of war. Martial mentions the worship of Mars on his estate at Nomentum but it appears that there was an alternative reason why the god may have been present on this occasion because he was also the patron of Martial's birth month.[32] This lends yet another dimension to the existence of certain forms of statuary in garden areas.

Mars's rustic background perhaps provides a reason why he is occasionally found in a garden context. One particularly fine example is actually from a fresco which depicts him as a statue. This is one of a set of three verdant frescos adorning the rear wall of the garden in the House of the Marine Venus at Pompeii. As the name of this house implies the central panel of the three was reserved for Venus; to her left is a garden scene and to her right her consort Mars, and as such he would still have a place in gardens. A second garden association is formed through Cupid, who was one of their children.

The Amazons, those fierce mythical warriors, seem to form a female martial counterpart and appear with Mars in a colonnade around the decorative water channel of the Canopus garden at Hadrian's Villa, Tivoli. A martial theme could also include Athene, the Greek goddess of wisdom and war (later linked to the Roman Minerva). She also has a war-like demeanour and is usually shown equipped for battle, wearing a helmet and holding a shield and lance. She is associated with the cultivation of olives, and therefore could be said to have a place of her own in the open green areas of gardens. A martial theme might on occasion also include Diana the huntress.

DIANA AND ANIMALS

Diana's image in the form of a garden statue is recorded in a poem by Luxorius and indicates her widespread appeal in the provinces.[33] She was the chaste maiden of the woods, the goddess of the hunt and mistress of the beasts. She often appears in frescos and mosaics depicting rural life, for hunting was a very popular sport. Diana usually wears a short tunic and carries a bow and quiver of arrows; often an animal connected with the hunt accompanies her. In his study of gardens Grimal believes that a garden could re-create her haunt in the country, the trees and shrubs would become the woods, teeming with animals.[34]

Diana the huntress (Paris, Louvre Museum).

A certain type of animal statuary, such as those most often sought in a hunt, for example, the boar or stag, could therefore be seen as another attribute of this goddess. Animals were a very popular art form in gardens, and we find all manner of hunting dogs or hounds, stags and hinds or boars, by themselves or as a group with hounds at bay. A famous example is the animated group of two hounds attacking a wild boar found at the edge of a pool in the House of the Citharist at Pompeii, now in Naples Museum.

Another interpretation includes the possibility that a garden could have been pictured as a miniature *paradeisos*, the aristocratic game park of Hellenistic rulers in the East, where a variety of exotic species were hunted.[35] A number of wall paintings depict *paradeisoi* hunt scenes, which include boar hunting as well as sorties after more exotic species such as lions. These are usually painted on the rear wall of the garden and were therefore thought to convey a scene where the game preserve was part of the general landscape beyond. Perhaps the owner of this house was wistfully thinking that he owned the territory where this would take place. Alternatively the garden could be made to represent those provinces where animals were hunted for the amphitheatre.[36]

All these theories could have some foundation, for a variety of animals are represented in gardens. The savagery portrayed in many sculpture groups, such as deer-hounds ferociously attacking stags, is reminiscent of the final stages of a hunt. But where exotic species are concerned, such as lions and tigers pulling down prey, these show an aspect of raw nature rather than a hunt. If a link is sought to Diana, and this could only be tenuous, then such scenes could relate to her role as mistress of the beasts, a concept more prevalent in the East. Another point that could be argued against this theory, and shows no connection to the cult of Diana at all, is that on occasion a number of wild and domesticated animals appear together in a garden. They could have merely served to decorate the area. But if a message was implied, and if the animals appeared to be calm, they could collectively be said to re-create a setting of a myth where Orpheus charmed the beasts with the melodious sound of his music, played on a lyre.

The garden could therefore be converted into a peaceful kingdom, where the lion could lie down with the lamb. This has Christian connotations but the idea of living in harmony with the natural world was a considered alternative approach that existed throughout the Greco-Roman period. It is found in certain philosophical ideals, and was part of the Orphic and Christian beliefs that became increasingly popular in the days of the later Empire. However a peaceful collection of domesticated animals could alternatively add a certain rusticity to the garden scene and they might recall a pastoral Arcadia. In this capacity they would then be linked to the rustic Arcadian god Pan rather than Diana.

Animals that could be considered pets were also displayed in statuary form and were more likely to be of a decorative nature. Dogs are numerous and seven fine examples were discovered near Lanuvio in Italy at a place dubbed Monte Cagnolo, the Hill of Dogs, after a large quantity of this type of statuary was found there. One of a pair of statue groups from this site, each portraying a pair of hounds, is illustrated here; this example is now in the Vatican and its partner is in London. Their original location in the ancient villa and garden is a matter of conjecture for they were discovered long ago, but one could well imagine how they could be shown to advantage, perhaps on either side of a path or feature in the garden.

A pair of greyhounds (Rome, Vatican Museum, height, *c.* 0.67 m).

APOLLO

Apollo was the twin brother of Diana and was considered the god of prophecy and healing. He also had artistic qualities and was the god of poetry and music. Pliny mentions the existence of a statue of Apollo in the Gardens of Servillius at Rome but this was probably an exceptionally fine statue.[37] These gardens contained a number of notable works of art but such high quality pieces were no doubt very expensive and perhaps of a more monumental nature than was normally found in domestic gardens. Apollo is usually shown as a naked or semi-draped youthful figure, representing the ideal handsome physique.

His connection with horticulture might be found in his links to Helios, the god of the sun, for Helios-Apollo would be seen every day coursing across the sky in a fiery chariot. The sun was one of the elements necessary for plant growth, and Sol (another name for Helios) is mentioned in Varro's list of twelve gods concerned with agriculture/horticulture.

Virgil implies that Apollo would be welcomed in gardens when he relates that 'my garden is Apollo's seat: I give him gifts – the bay tree and the hyacinth'.[38] The bay, *Laurus nobilis L.*, was considered sacred to Apollo and was widely planted in his honour. The hyacinth was named after a myth concerning his beloved friend, Hyacinthus, who was accidentally killed and his blood turned into the beautiful blue flower.

Apollo's presence in gardens, however, could relate to other myths that have horticultural relevance. In these a number of prominent figures would form a sculptural re-enactment, such as a scene taken from the musical contest with Marsyas. He dared to say he could play music better than the god Apollo, a rash statement that ended in a terrible punishment for the loser. A gruesome example from the Gardens of Maecenas portrays the actual punishment of Marsyas: he was tied to a tree then flayed alive. This is now in the Conservatori Museum, Rome. It has been particularly well executed; the sculptor has utilized marble with red veins that appears to portray raw flesh. The scene is recounted by Philostratus the Younger,[39] and is seen in relief sculpture. Companion pieces were a seated Apollo with his lyre and a slave whetting a knife. A number of seated Apollo statues survive and a slave from a similar grouping was found in the *Horti Luculliani*; this is now in Florence Museum. The tree reminds us of the outdoor setting and the fact that Marsyas was a satyr, a being associated with woodlands, helps to link this contest to a garden environment.

The slaying of Niobe's children was another myth of Apollo that exists as garden sculpture; items of such a group were discovered in the Gardens of Sallust at Rome.[40] Here individual statues portray wounded girls, some attempting to extract an arrow. Other mythical encounters could have inspired similar sculptural groupings.

HERCULES

The popular hero Hercules appears in one of the myths concerning Apollo where they struggle for possession of the Delphic tripod. This is but one of the Twelve Labours of Hercules, however, and his other labours are more relevant here. His eleventh labour set him the task of finding the Garden of the Hesperides and returning with the famed golden apples from this mythical place at the edge of the world. A fresco painting of this scene can be found in the villa at Oplontis. The narrative unfolds before one's eyes, a dark heavily built figure enters the garden, which is shown full of trees. To one side is a large rock on which we see the golden fruit freshly picked off the trees. The *hortus* could easily re-create such a mythical setting.

Hercules is often portrayed as a well-built bearded rustic character. He is usually nude or carrying his lionskin and club, which were trophies from his earlier exploits. Hercules appealed to the masses for a number of reasons – his strength and courage were legendary and the tasks set before him were arduous in the extreme – but he overcomes all and is rewarded. He fulfilled the classical role of a hero and was treated almost on a par with the

Hercules leaning on his club.

gods; he was considered the universal helper and was invoked at times of stress. However Hercules evidently had a number of human failings that added to his appeal. He was known to have a fondness for food and wine and when portrayed in garden statuary he was more often than not shown somewhat intoxicated. These aspects are reproduced well in the statue discovered in the House of the Stags at Herculaneum. At other times he can be found leaning heavily on his club.

The plant associated with the cult of Hercules is the white poplar, and the leaves of this tree are used as his emblem, as are his lionskin and large knobbly club.

BACCHUS AND HIS ENTOURAGE

Bacchus, being the god of wine and the vine, was understandably one of the most popular figures to be found in Roman gardens. He is the Romanized version of Dionysus, who had a great following in Greece and in the East where he is believed to have originated. In Rome Bacchus merged with Liber, an Italic god of fertility. Dionysus/Bacchus was also the god of drama, which was performed at his festivals; thus we find representations of theatrical masks and musical instruments in gardens, for these become symbolic of his presence. Another attribute, the vine, could be seen covering pergolas to give shade to summer dining areas in gardens. The consumption of wine at such feasts is reflected by the inclusion of drinking vessels in art such as a wine cup, rhyton, urn or a wineskin, symbols that also became connected with this divinity.

Another plant associated with his cult was ivy and its heart-shaped leaves were used as one of his symbols. These can appear similar to the poplar leaves of Hercules but ivy is usually given an extra curling tendril to indicate its climbing habit. Bacchus and his attendants are often shown wearing a crown of ivy leaves and flowers, although Bacchus himself sometimes has bunches of grapes dangling down his forehead. The leaves of ivy were also used to make the head of the thyrsus wand carried by the Bacchic throng. A thick stalk of fennel was used for the staff. Animals linked to Bacchus are dolphins, who represent the pirates who tried to abduct him at sea and were consequently turned into dolphins when thrown overboard, and a panther that was associated with the god's triumphs in India.

The *Triumph of Bacchus* is a scene often depicted in ancient frescos, mosaics and relief work and all of the figures associated with this myth appear to be at home in a Roman garden. They are represented either singly or in small groups. In statuary Bacchus is shown as a slightly effeminate young man; he usually carries a wine cup in his hand and is frequently depicted in the act of offering a drink or libation to his pet panther below. He is often accompanied by one or more of his attendants. Members of the Bacchic *thiasos* include Ariadne his consort, sileni, satyrs, fauns, Pan, centaurs, maenads, bacchantes, nymphs and at a later date Silvanus and Priapus, all of whom are creatures or beings associated with nature, woods or countryside. Alternatively Bacchus as an infant can be found in a garden context; he is differentiated from other children by his crown of vine or ivy leaves and he may be carrying a cup and his thyrsus; on occasion he is portrayed riding his panther. The young Bacchus would have the same appeal as other statues of children mentioned above.

In statuary many of the male figures of his entourage are shown in various stages of inebriation, presumably after wining and dining in their Bacchic revels. Satyrs and sileni are often shown staggering and leaning on or carrying a wineskin, which is sometimes used as a fountain outlet. In these cases the water pouring from the containers could appear to represent wine.[41] Some examples from the large variety of forms in this group are illustrated here. Many have been given a rocky base which gives them a rustic touch that matches their outdoor setting.

Ariadne is usually shown recumbent and is differentiated from reclining nymphs by holding her right arm over her head, so that she appears to be awakening. This statue re-enacts the myth of her abandonment by Theseus and subsequent encounter with Dionysus. Silenus was a foster father to the young Dionysus who always retained some affection for him. Statues portraying Silenus show a balding old man who is rather rotund and slightly the worse for drink. He is often being propped upright by fellow revellers, such as satyrs. Virgil mentions a scene where a rather drunken Silenus, still holding his wine cup, reclines half asleep in a grotto-like cave.[42] This image was partially recreated in garden frescos such as those at the House of Romulus and Remus.

Satyrs are the boisterous revellers of the woods; they have pointed ears and snub noses, and sport a goat-like tail. They are lustful creatures and

Pan extracting a thorn from the foot of a satyr, Rome, Vatican Museum.

are often found in pursuit of maenads. Pliny informs us that 'Only in gardens and the Forum do we see statues of Satyrs dedicated as a charm against the sorcery of the envious'.[43] This gives another indication of their popularity as subjects suitable for gardens. According to Propertius there was a famous statue of a satyr in Pompey's portico, the large public garden at Rome. This reclining fountain figure had been personalized and given the name Maro.[44]

Fauns were also creatures of the forest but were considered gentle and retiring. These are really a Romanization of the Greek satyrs, for Faunus himself was an ancient Roman god connected to agriculture and woodlands. Fauns have pointed ears and are often clothed with a *nebris* or fawnskin. A mirror image pair, with wineskins forming fountains, were found at the Villa Quintili, Rome, and are now in the Vatican Museum, Braccio Nuovo.

Maenads are often depicted in relief carvings, for example on the reverse of an *oscilla* in the Vatican Museum. In statuary form a seated Maenad exists in Brussels Museum; she was part of a group (with a satyr) known as 'the invitation to the dance', a scene known from carvings found elsewhere. Maenads and bacchantes are usually shown with wild flowing hair and swirling draperies, as if dancing. Bacchantes are, however, more often depicted in relief sculpture and on occasion are shown carrying parts of dismembered animals as a reminder of their frenzied role in the excesses of the cult of Dionysus.

Centaurs are creatures that are half-horse and half-man who are often shown pulling the triumphant chariot of Bacchus. They are seen both in frescos and sculptural form at Oplontis.[45]

Silvanus was the ancient Roman god of woodlands. Later he appears to join the Greek woodland throng of satyrs. His presence in gardens also indicates that he retained some influences in areas of garden covered by trees.

An assorted collection from this group, forming a Dionysiac theme garden, seemed to be quite popular. This kind of statuary appears pleasant and is often humorous, perhaps even slightly irreverent, but is in keeping with the carefree attitudes of Bacchus himself. Gardens were places for recreation or relaxation, where one could commune with nature growing all around; a Bacchic theme could be highly suitable.

PAN

This pastoral god originated in Arcadia and became symbolic of the Roman view of this place as a Utopia. He was essentially a rustic god, and appears in numerous representations of a country setting. He is usually shown half-man and half-goat. The upper part is more or less human but he has wild hair, a goatee beard and a pair of goat-like horns, while his legs are hairy and feet cloven. He was known for playing tricks and is often seen in the company of satyrs or nymphs. It is possible that his links with fertility brought him into contact with the cult of Dionysus/Bacchus. Pan was a popular god, strongly associated with nature; he would be symbolized by a set of pan-pipes and a pedum stick, the ancient shepherd's crook.

MUSES

The nine Muses are sometimes seen in gardens although not always together. They could promote aspects of contemplation and inspiration, and are linked to Apollo through his role as god of poetry and music. The Muses were the judges in the music competition between Apollo and Marsyas. Each Muse presided over a particular art and could be turned to when seeking help within their individual sphere. Calliope was known for epic poetry; Clio for history; Erato for erotic poetry; Euterpe for flute music; Melpomene for tragic plays; Polyhymnia for singing, harmony and lyric poetry (she was considered the inventor of the lyre); Terpsichore for choral dance and music; Thalia for comedy and bucolic poetry, and Urania for astronomy. In statuary each maiden is shown fully clothed and carries a symbol for her particular art. Several examples discovered in gardens depict someone deep in thought, perhaps composing her next play or poem. She is often shown standing, wrapped in her cloak and leaning against a rock, or sitting with one hand against her chin.

A Muse, Polyhymnia (Madrid).

Cicero and Varro both possessed a *museion*. This is a Greek term, and in Latin it is turned into a *museum*. This was literally a dwelling place for the Muses and their arts; it is fitting, therefore, that over the centuries our own museums are filled with objects of historical value, being under the sphere of the Muses, especially that of Clio. The ancient *museion* was in many ways also connected to *nymphaea*, traditionally the abode of nymphs.

NYMPHS AND RIVER GODS

Three nymphs, Philia, Coronis and Clyda, had been entrusted to nurse the infant Dionysus, and therefore they form a link to his cult. But unlike the fun-loving maenads, nymphs were modest young virgins. These beautiful young girls were considered immortal and were mostly associated with a particular cave and clear spring water. Therefore they were extremely suitable as a subject for a fountain figure. They are usually shown semi-clothed, and appear either standing or reclining. In the former they hold either an urn, a scallop shell or bowl, from which water pours; here the falling water would be symbolic of a sacred spring. A lovely example was found in Crete and is now in Istanbul Museum; it is approximately 1.10 m high. This statue type is also found in frescos; a pair is shown either side of the silenus in the House of Romulus and Remus. Statues of reclining nymphs are shown leaning on an upturned urn, which is used as a fountain outlet.

Reclining nymphs appear similar to the personifications of rivers which are also made to issue from an upturned urn. Statues of river gods are much larger and were more suited to public or Imperial display. The two river gods discovered at Hadrian's Villa, Tivoli, are a good example. Two bearded male gods, one personifying the River Tiber and the other the Nile, were positioned at either side of a broad pathway leading to the vast Canopus water channel. These were suitable in this setting and likewise the nymph who was associated with small natural sources of water, a mere trickle in some instances, is more suited for inclusion in a residential *hortus*, where a corner or wall could be utilized to form a cave-like niche or *nymphaeum*. Nevertheless some of these structures contained other Bacchic statuary, such as the silenus seen in the House of Marcus Lucretius, which is statue number one in the plan of this garden.

Masks of fluvial deities or attendants are another means of displaying the image of a river god but are discussed in chapter five. These could be large or small and were therefore appropriate in both private or public spheres.

RUSTIC GENRE (MORTALS)

This group includes a number of figures, usually peasants, that are portrayed with a realism that enhances their rusticity. Examples are statues of shepherds carrying young animals to market on their shoulders, and men fishing or in the act of selling their catch. A small bronze fisherman can be seen in one of the colour photographs here, from the House of the Small Fountain at Pompeii. This young fisherman had been placed on the edge of the fountain basin of the *aedicula nymphaeum* where he could appear to be casting his rod into the waters below. There were also small statue groups such as the fragmentary fishing scene found at Ostia, which once graced the courtyard of the Garden Houses. Sculptural relief panels were also placed in gardens (see under *pinax*) and these often depict rustic or sacro-idyllic subjects.

Rustic statuary could be seen as a desire to people an idealized landscape, as in the famous paintings of *topia* by Studius, described by Pliny.[46] Or they could symbolize the 'fruits of their husbandry', an aspect mentioned by Philostratus the Elder when contemplating the content of various famous paintings on display in a portico by Naples.[47] The 'fruits' perhaps refer to sources of family income, through the land or sea.

On first sight this genre appears to be ornamental but may have some connections to aspects within a rural Arcadia. However another aspect could perhaps be put forward. This type of statuary does not refer specifically to any of the pagan gods, and some Romans who may have needed to mask their religious beliefs (because of the threat of persecution) may have seen them with less aversion. In a world that loved decoration a total absence of works of art may have drawn suspicion in itself and rustic genre could seem more acceptable for display in some households under these circumstances. These figures are

Rustic genre, a shepherd going to market. He carries a hare bound to a stick in his right hand and a basket of produce on the other arm, while on his shoulders he transports a young goat. Found in the garden of the Villa del Pastore, Stabiae (Stabiae Museum).

not overtly pagan and could have therefore appealed to a number of fringe cults, such as the emerging Christian community for instance. A number of ancient iconographic details are known to have infiltrated Christian imagery and some of the pastoral statues, such as fish, sheep or a shepherd, could have represented Christ in the role of the Good Shepherd. Alternatively the shepherd could be seen to represent Orpheus to the Orphites, while fishermen could appear as 'fishers of men' (the Apostles). A small shepherd, 0.69 m high, from the Villa del Pastore at Stabiae, dates to pre-AD 79. This type remained popular and at a later date is found at Ostia in the Aula Bon Pastore.[48]

Ephebes, athletes, wrestlers

These figures are sometimes seen in association with bath buildings and palaestra, the associated exercise areas. When placed in the garden with philosopher herms or statues of philosophers they create a themed garden that could resemble the Athenian Academy or a gymnasium, where philosophers could commune with young men resting from their exercise training. An atmosphere such as this was noted by Cicero's friends, who exclaim how part of a garden at Tusculum was suggestive of the shady haunt of Socrates, an ancient Greek philosopher much admired by the Romans.[49] Large estates could contain several gardens and include areas with a selection of statues to enhance a particular concept. An example of this category is the pair of bronze wrestlers found in the large garden of the Villa of the Papyri, at Herculaneum, now in Naples National Museum.

Herms

Originally representing the Greek god Hermes, these were a very popular art form in Roman gardens, as can be seen by the number present in Table I. They consist of a bust of the god on a pillar-like shaft, which was set into the ground or slotted into a square base. A rather humorous touch was to add a pair of carved feet on the base, as in examples found at the Villa of Cassius, Tivoli.[50] Many herms had male organs, which were customary on the Greek prototype, or sometimes a triangular area of pecked marks. The shaft might incorporate a cross beam at the shoulder, originally to hold a cloak, but some Roman herms were carved already wearing a form of drapery. The type was adapted by the Romans into a means of displaying a portrait bust. Therefore we find famous and illustrious men portrayed; subjects ranged from Greek philosophers that were particularly admired by Cicero, historians, heroes, Hellenistic rulers or Roman emperors and their wives, to idealized portraits of men or women.

Numerous deities were also represented in the form of a herm, Athene or Mars for example. The most popular of this group are Bacchic subjects. Members of his *thiasos* were shown singly or paired. Therefore we find double or janiform herms, where two busts facing outwards share the one shaft. They often comprise a young and old Dionysus or a Bacchus and Ariadne. Others might show a satyr paired with a maenad, or a young satyr paired with a silenus. Like Janus, the two faces can present different aspects – here age or sex.

Herms are usually carved out of one piece of stone, often marble. However a number of small versions were carved from a more expensive coloured marble such as the yellow *gallio antico*, imported for the luxury market. Usually only the head and shoulder bust are on display in museums and therefore we cannot be certain that the post was always of the same material. Herms of bronze are known to have existed, one example being the bronze herm busts discovered in the large garden of the villa of the Papyri at Herculaneum. Cicero negotiated to purchase some herms, and one of his requests stipulated that they should be of bronze;[51] this is usually taken to mean the bust only and the lower part, the post, would be of marble. However a shipwreck discovered off the Tunisian coast near Mahdia was found to contain a great deal of statuary and sculpture, some perhaps destined for garden display. The cargo included a very fine herm made entirely of bronze; as bronze was expensive a large example would have been very costly and probably quite rare, even in Roman times.

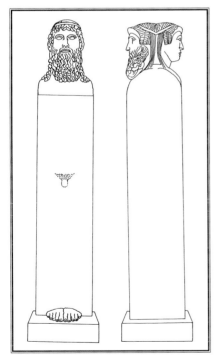

Drawings of herms. The first is a single herm set into a base with carved feet. The second is a janiform herm showing a young and an old Bacchus.

Herm taken out of a decorative wall, clearly showing slots on two sides of the shaft. The face of the herm has been weathered in antiquity; like all garden sculptures, they are exposed to the elements (Rome, Therme Museum).

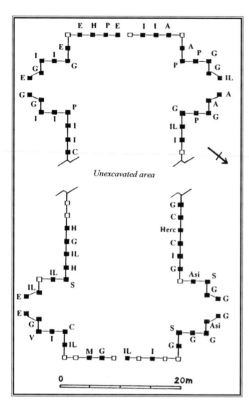

Plan of the ornamental pool at Welschbillig with a key to the number of herms incorporated in the surrounding wall.

KEY TO HERM TYPES

Asi	=	Asiatic
A	=	African
C	=	Cupid
E	=	Emperor or Hellenistic ruler
G	=	Germanic
H	=	Hermes
Herc	=	Hercules
I	=	Idealized portrait
IL	=	Illustrious personage
M	=	Mars
P	=	Philosopher
S	=	Satyr
V	=	Venus

Where herms were used as part of a decorative low wall, the shaft became the upright post, and the herm head the finial. We can see examples in both frescos and reliefs. Slim versions in bronze survive from the wreck of Claudius's luxurious boat recovered from the depths of Lake Nemi. These herms were janiform, draped, and the bust was of Silenus paired with a satyr or maenad. Several stone examples may be seen in museums and are distinguished from normal herms by beam slots for the wall on the shaft. Slots can appear on either side of the shaft or one side only, perhaps indicating that this particular herm was placed beside an entrance passage. Alternatively slots may have been cut into the side and front part of the shaft revealing that this herm occupied a corner position in a wall and that the wall changed direction, as seen in the example from the Therme Museum, Rome, shown here. A similar corner post in the Chiaramonti gallery of the Vatican portrays a satyr with a lionskin draped over his shoulder.

The large number of herms used in the decorative wall around the pool at Welschbillig provides a very good example of the range in existence in the fourth century AD. With 68 herms recovered out of the 100 thought to have existed the collection also provides an opportunity to try to establish if there was any detailed programme in the selection and positioning of the various examples of herms. They were preserved by either falling or being pushed into the pool and it has been possible to estimate their original location on the wall from the position in which they were found in the pool below. The herms appear to have been sited so that they would face on to the expanse of water. The busts comprised those already cited, plus ones with provincial features, such as Africans-Berbers, Asiatics with Phrygian caps or Germans with long hair and a torque. In a number of instances there are more than one of a particular herm type; in general these were not identical but a mirror image of the other, where the head is turned or tilted to the left instead of to the right.

As seen in the plan shown here it is difficult to pinpoint an intentional programme but the layout is not completely random either. In general two or more of each kind are not placed together and on a number of occasions you can see that there may have been an intention to group certain herm types together; for instance the lower half (on the plan) of the pool was lined by a number of mythological herms while the upper section appears to have only one, a cupid/child or a young Dionysus. There is also a greater concentration of Imperial or illustrious herms in the southern part; this could reflect the tastes of the owner or the architect/landscape gardener. But a detail such as this could also, perhaps, indicate the nature of any rooms in the vicinity, which are not otherwise known. The lower section however is believed to be flanked by the wings of the villa itself, for there are remains of porticos, whereas a large *nymphaeum* of basilican proportions is believed to have stood close to the opposite end of the basin. This bears some similarities to the 'Serapeum' at Hadrian's villa at Tivoli and may also have been a large summer *triclinium* with water features.

Herms remained popular throughout the Roman period, perhaps because of their versatility. They were a convenient way of displaying an illustrious image, partly because the bust was mounted on a simple shaft (decorated or plain) making it more cost-effective than sculpture in the round. Also, if a statue fell and was found to be unrepairable, all would not be lost, for the head could be mounted on to a shaft and could then continue service as a herm.

OSCILLA

As seen in several frescos, *oscilla* (singular *oscillum*) were usually suspended in some manner so that they could, as their name suggests, oscillate in a breeze. They were generally positioned in the space between the columns of a garden peristyle (in the drawing here). Occasionally they were sited in an atrium, as in the House of the Relief of Telephus at Herculaneum, although this particular *atrium* was furnished with planting troughs and would therefore resemble a small light-well garden. The circular *oscilla* in this house have been left *in situ*, and the gleaming white marble discs brighten the area considerably, even though they have been set higher than normal to secure them against theft.

The four versions of *oscilla* are illustrated below in a setting designed to resemble a garden portico. The size of *oscilla* varies greatly but a circular one would measure approximately 0.30 m wide. For the sake of

Different forms of *oscilla* suspended from a portico roof. From left to right: circular, rectangular, *pelta*, mask.

clarity they are depicted here disproportionally larger than the columns that frame them. From left to right there is the tondo or circular form, perhaps the most common variety found; a small rectangular version; a form shaped like a *pelta*, and finally those in the form of a mask. Most examples are of marble but some may have been made of wood or terracotta which do not survive so well. With the exception of mask *oscilla*, they usually had a plain border around their rim and are carved in low relief on both sides. Occasionally one face is carved in high relief and the reverse in low relief. *Oscilla* were meant to be seen from both sides of a portico, from inside the garden where carvings would be clearly visible in good light but also from inside the portico where the reverse side would be less well lit. The carving under these conditions would be more effective if it stood proud, but also as this side may have faced important rooms a higher quality carving was perhaps more desirable.

Oscilla are thought to have originated from the Greek practice of hanging trophies in a portico or on a tree beside a shrine. Virgil mentions that Bacchic objects were hung in trees,[52] and a number of relief carvings show these items dangling from boughs of trees. Usually a pine tree is depicted for this also features in the myth of Bacchus; interestingly we find that this tree is also used in the cult of Attis and the Great Mother Goddess for the display of their cult objects.

Because there is a Bacchic connection the subject matter depicted on *oscilla* is mostly confined to figures and motifs of the Bacchic *thiasos*, such as Silenus, Faunus, Pan, a satyr or maenad, an altar, theatre masks, a *tympanum*, *pedum* and so on. However, we also see attributes of Venus: for example, dolphins, sea monsters or hares/rabbits.

The simple geometric shapes of the first and second forms of *oscilla* more directly reflect the Roman use of trophies such as the shields or *clipeum* that were otherwise hung on house fronts to honour the achievements of family members or ancestors. The *peltae* form of *oscilla* is derived from a *pelta*, the mythical shield carried by Amazons. This was a motif that was often used for decorative purposes, and so continues the mystic or mythical associations seen in many collections of garden sculpture.

Peltae oscilla generally have griffin head terminals on either side of the shield and at the apex a palmette design from which the shield was suspended. Mask *oscilla* are lightweight in that they are concave in form, have an open mouth, and holes drilled for the eyes. The suspension point is usually found at the top of the head. Theatre masks are fairly common but there are masks of maenads or satyrs. *Oscilla* have been found in a number of provinces of the Empire, especially the circular, rectangular and *peltae* forms, which show that their use was widespread.[53]

Many *oscilla* were presumably broken on falling to the ground; reconstructed examples often show a break radiating from the point where the iron hook for suspension had been drilled into the upper rim. Traces of a hook are often recorded and in some cases were found *in situ* as in the mask on display in the British Museum. Cords or wire attachments do not normally survive but in frescos they appear as either a straight white line, which may represent a cord or a metal rod, but a plain link chain could be an alternative. A more decorative version is illustrated, however, and shows a bead and reel-like design.

Rectangular *oscilla* appear very similar to *pinakes* and evidence to differentiate the two depends on whether there were fixtures for suspension or provision for mounting on to a post, as is the case with a *pinax*. This is complicated by new evidence from a circular *oscillum* found at Bolsena, indicating that *oscilla* were at times reused. After this particular *oscillum* fell it appears to have been reused by inserting it into a horizontal surface, presumably the top of a post, in the manner of a *pinax*.[54] Alternatively *oscilla* could have been placed on a wall but most show no traces of mortar used to secure them into such a position. Rectangular *oscilla* and *pinakes* are both depicted in frescos and basically the size determines its function, for if a relief panel was too large it would be too heavy to suspend above one's head.

PINAKES

Like *oscilla* these were usually of marble and carved in low relief on both sides. They were frequently mounted on a marble post that was often plain but is sometimes decorated with carvings, mostly of foliage such as trailing vine. *Pinax* (plural *pinakes*) is a Greek word for a wooden board and stone examples do bear some resemblance, for they usually retain a rather thick outer frame. This is seen in frescos and stone reliefs where we may also note that *pinakes* were displayed in a number of ways. Normally the post of a *pinax* was embedded into the garden soil but at other times a *pinax* was placed at a higher level, such as on top of a decorative wall or fence. A relief panel of Bacchus visiting the house of a mortal, displayed in the British Museum, shows two *pinakes*; a large *pinax* appears in the foreground and was placed either on the top of the wall or on a tall post, while in the garden beyond a *pinax* on a short post is sited close to another building. *Pinakes* or decorative relief panels were also on occasion set into a wall. Cicero had this in mind in another request to his friend Atticus for more sculpture,[55] and examples of this type have been discovered embedded into the rear wall of the peristyle at the House of the Golden Cupids, at Pompeii.[56]

SUNDIALS

Sundials needed to be placed in an open area and the ideal place was in a garden or court. A simple dial could be made by scratching a series of lines on a sun-lit column of the peristyle[57] but in general they were carved on to a block of stone which, because it was free-standing, could be positioned to allow a correct reading of the time of day. In most cases this meant that they faced south but some versions were calculated to read the time from a sundial that faced north. A wide range of different forms have been discovered and of these the largest proportion of sundials were inscribed on a curved surface, as

A marble *pinax* displayed on a short decorative pillar, House of the Golden Cupids, Pompeii.

illustrated here. A similar example has been discovered in the garden of the House of the Golden Cupids (no. 14 on the garden plan). The lower portion of this type of sundial is usually plain and solid, forming a base, but sometimes this area is ornamented by a pair of lion's paws normally used in furniture; they do lend weight to the item and give the effect of supporting the dial above.

These dials, however, appear very different from those of the present day, for in the ancient world the hours of the day varied in length from month to month. Day and night were each divided into twelve hours, with the hours of day commencing at sunrise and ending with sunset. Therefore in winter the daylight hours were short and the night hours long, and in summer this was reversed.

On the sundials the hour lines were shown radiating outwards like a fan. In the example illustrated the wider spaces between lines near the outer curved rim matches the increased length of each hour during the days of summer. The lines crossing these – there are usually three –

mark the important points within the year. The central line marked the March and September equinoxes, while the shorter upper arc marked the winter solstice and the lower longer arc marked the summer solstice. For the period after the summer solstice the time should be read by retracing steps; just as we ourselves note that lighting-up time in the later part of October is similar to that of the beginning of February, the length of hours in those months would also be close.

The time was read by observing the position of the point of the shadow cast by a triangular metal gnomon or pointer which had been secured with lead into the stone dial. The point of the shadow could then tell the approximate time for the appropriate month. When a sundial was being made it was necessary to adjust measurements according to the latitude of its intended location. If this had not been done the shadow would fall too high or low on the face of the dial and the wrong hour would be shown. Therefore in a few examples, perhaps bought elsewhere, the time read would be very approximate. A sound knowledge of astronomy and mathematics was needed to construct a sundial and Vitruvius provides some of the equations needed. He lists several great men of learning who invented different forms. He also mentions a semicircular one that had been invented by Berosus the Chaldean;[58] his description of this sundial matches the version illustrated here.

A mathematical survey of the sundials in the Greco-Roman period has been made and numerous different forms identified.[59] For those interested in chronology details are given for the proportions of each type. Some were based on conical, cylindrical or spherical shapes but another form was inscribed on a flat horizontal surface. The plan of hours on these often resemble a pair of wings. In the planar sundial, seen in the second illustration, the line of the equinox is straight and runs right though the middle, whereas the two curved lines marking the solstices form the upper and lower end of the outstretched wings. The gnomon in this case is set vertically into the stone. A large horizontal sundial of this type was inscribed on to paving in the public park near the Mausoleum of Augustus at Rome. To provide a suitably large shadow a granite obelisk was brought from Egypt to make the gnomon.

A number of dials with Arabic inscriptions have been found at Cordoba in Spain; these appear similar to the basic design of the planar sundial shown here, and would suggest that the form was copied by later Arab invaders. This is perhaps a further testament to the usefulness of this ancient design.

Another method of telling the time is described in detail by Vitruvius, who introduces the water clock invented by Ctesibius.[60] Varro included such a clock in his elaborate aviary/dining room, within the garden.[61] In his example, however, the prevailing winds as well as the hours of day and night were shown. This, he informs us, is like the famous Tower of the Winds in Athens.

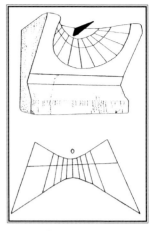

Two sundials, the dial is engraved on a concave surface in the first example and flat in the second.

CHAPTER SEVEN

Flora and Fauna in Gardens

T he defining feature of a garden is that it is a place where plants are grown and that these plants are selected by the gardener or the owner for the contribution they will make to the life and beauty of the garden, or for their usefulness in some other way. This applies whether the garden is large or small, urban or rural. Unlike static or hard garden elements such as paths, fountains or sculpture the plants are a constantly changing element of the garden, but they are also likely to need frequent attention. They will require trimming, beds occasionally need to be rearranged and at times certain plants may need to be replaced. But more than any other component the inclusion of plants can add life and colour to an area, and turn a plain court into an attractive garden.

The plants found in a Roman garden are mainly those originating in provinces within the Roman Empire, or in those areas that were in contact with it. For most purposes this means the regions bordering the Mediterranean, most of which had what we broadly term a Mediterranean climate, so a plant found in one area could frequently but not always be cultivated in other provinces. The range of plants used to stock Roman gardens was not so vast as today, for we have had the benefit of centuries of selection and hybridization. Plants in modern gardens come from places far and wide such as the New World, the Antipodes, South Africa and Japan; lands that were unknown in antiquity. Romans traded with tribes beyond their empire, and to some extent plants from places such as India were brought to Rome, but often this was for the spice trade and the plants themselves were not usually suited for cultivation in northern latitudes. The Romans, and to some extent the civilizations before them, experimented and cultivated a number of improved varieties. Their work was pioneering and in many cases appears fairly sophisticated for the times, but it must be remembered that these were early days in the science of horticulture, and many plants used to stock Roman gardens were perhaps only one or two stages away from their wild counterparts.

The identification of plant species used in gardens during the Roman period is at times made difficult because ancient authors did not have a standardized method of botanical nomenclature such as the Linnaean system in use today. Some Latin plant names are slightly ambiguous and others can appear to cover the family name, or genus, rather than a species within that group. Our most informative source is the *Natural History* of Pliny the Elder. His monumental work identifies and describes a wide range of plants and includes data compiled by several important figures, such as the Greek scholar Theophrastus. Pliny's descriptions have in some cases clarified which variety or species is referred to. This important source is complemented by a selection of drawings appearing in surviving copies of a herbal written by Dioscorides in the first century AD. Unfortunately the earliest of the copies date to the fifth century but some of these are thought to be a faithful rendition of earlier works. Dioscorides illustrates only plants with medicinal properties but as some of these were also used in a garden or *hortus* they are a useful additional source, and the named illustrations confirm which plant was concerned.

Drawing of a gillyflower from a herbal manuscript of Dioscorides.

Pliny's descriptions reveal that plants were mostly identified by the colour and shape of a flower rather than by the structure of the whole plant and its seeds. This can be noted in the varieties listed under rose, where Pliny includes a flower that 'springs from a stem like that of the mallow'.[1] This was not the mallow or hollyhock (*Althaea rosea (L.)*) for this is named elsewhere, so it may be a form of lavatera. The single flowered peony, or alternatively the rock-rose, may also have been considered a rose, for non-scented varieties are mentioned by Pliny. The island of Rhodes was said to have been named after the rose which abounded there but it is possible that this plant was the peony-rose or rock-rose that is considered endemic on the island. An image of this enigmatic flower was struck on to the island's coins, and it does appear to resemble a rock-rose rather than a true rose. Two little buds are shown to spring up either side of the main flower and this is a characteristic of the genus *cystus*. The rock-rose, however, was known as *ledon* by Pliny, so there is still an element of doubt on this matter.

We also find that a number of species are sometimes included under one given name when the species concerned all appear to have a similar shape of leaf. An example is the laurel which seems to include the bay (*Laurus nobilis L.*), the laurustinus (*Vibernum tinus L.*), butcher's broom (*Ruscus aculeatus L.*), a 'gelded laurel' which could tolerate considerable shade and may be the cherry laurel (*Prunus laurocerasus L.*), and a crinkly black-leaved variety from Cyprus, which so far remains unidentified.

The modern system of classification devised by Linnaeus in AD 1737 solved the obstacle of each country having a different word for almost every plant. He used a Latin nomenclature with the intention that it would become universal. Wherever possible he used an existing Ancient Roman Latin name, although some were Latinized Greek names. This in itself is a testament to the ongoing dissemination of species that Roman horticulturists had set in motion. If we use the *Viburnus tinus L.* as an example, we can clearly trace the changes Linnaeus made. Pliny acknowledges that although this bush was believed to be a form of laurel it was often called a '*tinus*' and was perhaps a 'separate kind of tree' because of its blue berries.[2] He was correct, for it is not actually a laurel at all. Linnaeus however retains the common name or epithet, *tinus*, by which it had been known. Plant species identified by Linnaeus carry a suffix L. and when used here this denotes a modern name as opposed to that used in ancient texts.

Some ancient plant names, however, are not as we imagine. For instance, when Pliny refers to the *rhododendron* this is not the plant of that name in our own gardens, for his version is commonly believed to have been the oleander, which in translation is sometimes called a 'rose-laurel'[3] (*rhodo* = rose, *dendron* = laurel). This is a case where an ancient Greek term has stayed in use or has been Latinized. Pliny does inform us that this was a Greek name and alternative names for it were *rhododaphne* or *nerium*.[4] As can be seen some plants can be confused by having several different names, and this might have come about from the different languages or dialects in the various regions where this species grew, with each locality having their own name for the same plant.

KITCHEN GARDEN PLANTS

Flowers are not generally mentioned in the context of early forms of Roman gardens for the plants represented would have been ones associated with an orchard and/or a vegetable plot. An exception is the poppy, the seeds of which were used in bread-making. A reference in Pliny shows that these flowers were grown in gardens at least as early as the sixth century BC when Tarquinius, who was armed with a cane, 'knocked off the heads of the tallest poppies in his garden'.[5] Cato, who wrote the earliest volume on agriculture, mentions the vegetable plants grown in the *hortus* in his day. These were, however, mostly varieties of cabbage which should be translated as greens, or brassicas, for several forms including kale are in this group; the only other vegetable Cato mentions is asparagus.[6] In his estimation the cabbage 'surpasses all other vegetables'[7] and he shows that over a dozen ailments could be cured by means of ingestion, infusion or application. This preference is also highlighted by Pliny the Elder who records eighty-seven medicinal remedies using cabbage.[8] Pliny describes various cabbages including one that formed sprouts. Vegetables were unfortunately only available in season; there were no freezing facilities and therefore several vegetables and herbs were pickled 'namely, sprouts and stalks of cabbage, capers, stalks of parsley, rue, the flower of alexanders with its stalk . . .'. The list continues and includes the flowers and stalks of fennel, parsnip, asparagus, mustard and samphire. All of these were preserved by using salt in the first instance and then brine and vinegar; they would be stored in jars for use later.[9]

Columella and Pliny give details of a large number of plants that could be grown in the *hortus rusticus* and also give advice on their culture. In numerous spheres our most comprehensive source is Pliny the Elder and data from his volumes is compiled into a table (table II) to establish the range of plants considered as garden plants. Different headings indicate the way in which each plant was used. Vegetables and fruit under cultivation in the kitchen garden were mainly for consumption and therefore appear under a heading to signify their culinary use. This list includes species used for their seeds, root or leaves. It is interesting to note that out of the wide range of vegetables mentioned in his numerous books Pliny informs us that in the early days garden produce was mainly of the salad variety because it required little cooking which, he says, also meant a saving of fuel.[10] If the greens were well watered they could be grown throughout the year and would remain fresh right up to the time when needed, which was an added bonus to growing these easy salad crops. Herbs were also grown in the *hortus* for seasoning as well as for other purposes. Interestingly some bushes such as myrtle were also included as a culinary plant. This is normally thought of as a decorative bush with aromatic leaves but its small white flowers were followed by a good crop of berries that were used as a form of pepper before eastern spices were generally available.[11]

Globe artichokes were also cultivated but were called *carduons* (cardoon). Those of Carthage and Cordoba were particularly noted. Mosaic detail, Bardo Museum.

PLANTS FOR MEDICINES AND CORDIALS

The Romans of the Republican and early Empire eras were essentially of a practical nature and therefore plants grown in a *hortus*, other than culinary varieties, were usually those which served a particular purpose. Some species were used in the preparation of medicines. Ailments and homeopathic cures are detailed by Pliny and these involve either internal or external application. He reveals that some plants could be used to cure several complaints. An example is mustard, which Pliny shows was used to cure snake bite, mushroom poisoning, toothache and stomach ailments. It could also ease asthmatics and epileptics, and soothed bruises and sprains.[12] Many remedies contain a number of ingredients, often including a sweetener of some sort, such as honey. Sometimes the various parts of the plant would be crushed to make a powder which could then be mixed into an oil for embrocation, or was added to wine to make a potion. At other times plant material was boiled down to make a liquid or paste.

Other plants were utilized to make cordials or wines. As grapevines would often have been allowed to grow over trellises in large gardens, many families would be involved in wine production. However, different wines were produced using fruits, such as apples or pears. Lesser known fruits were also selected; these include cornels, medlars, dried mulberries, service berries, pomegranates and carob.[13] A number of vegetables were used for wine-making too and yet others were distilled from aromatic herbs and certain shrubs. Pliny provides a few recipes, and one of the most straightforward is given here: 'they put two handfuls of herb into a jar of must [incompletely fermented wine], together with a pint of boiled-down grape juice and half a pint of sea-water.'[14] There was even a variety of wine made entirely with honey. Different methods of preparation are given and it is interesting to note that most, as with the honey wine, elect to use rainwater. Apparently this rainwater had either been stored for several years or if it was freshly caught it was repeatedly boiled before use.

PLANTS USED IN BEE-KEEPING

Pliny and others also include a section on species planted specially to provide nectar – food for bees. The production of honey was highly regarded by the Romans who used it as a sweetener (sugar was not yet available), and because of its value Varro advises placing hives near the villa for protection.[15] He adds that 'some people place the apiary actually in the portico of the villa'.[16] He also lists several different types of hive; there was one made 'of fennel stalks', which were made into a square shape, or there were 'round hives of withes . . . others of wood and bark, others of a hollow tree, others built of earthenware'. The last form was condemned by Columella for it would be too hot in summer and in winter it would not be frost-proof.[17]

An important consideration for the apiarist and horticulturist is pointed out by Palladius who mentions that the *hortus* should be placed in such a position that flying chaff and straw from a threshing ground would not blow on to plants.[18] This was a crucial measure because otherwise flowers, buds and tree blossom could be ruined. These were vital to provide nectar for bees to make honey and the bees in return would ensure a good rate of pollination for the production of fruit and seed, for consumption this year and to provide seeds for next year's vegetable and herb harvest.

Palladius advises his readers that the area reserved for bee-keeping should be screened; they should 'plant trees on the north side and bushes all about'.[19] The trees would protect the bees from strong winds, which they disliked, and bushes such as thyme (that all authors claim is the best for bees) would provide a ready food supply for them. Columella shows that to ensure the good health of bees it is wise to include species nearby that they could use as a form of medicine, such as the trefoil – he also included rosemary.[20] The latter herb is not mentioned as a garden plant by Pliny, which is unusual, but this suggests that the list in Table II may not be exhaustive, for this plant is also known to have an ornamental value. For instance it was used in hedges at Laurentum.[21] Rosemary appears in a medicinal capacity but is included with wild species,[22] perhaps indicating that it may not have been so widely cultivated at that time. Pliny shows that it was propagated by layering,[23] which implies that it must have been cultivated, so on reflection it seems best to include rosemary in Table II. Pliny mentions its scent was like frankincense and that it was alternatively known as *libanotis*[24] or *conyza*.[25] Under these two names it appears that it was used in chaplets, for bees, and as a medicinal kitchen herb.

PLANTS USED IN MAKING PERFUMES

Scented foliage and flowers, from trees and herbaceous plants, were highly esteemed. At first they were used as a means of freshening the air indoors, and later with the advent of a luxurious lifestyle for the making of perfumes and scented oils. Fragrant parts of plants, either the flowers themselves or aromatic leaves or roots, were boiled down and then mixed with oil obtained from a number of sources; for example, either olives, myrtle, laurel, cypress or terebinth-resin. Salt and gum were added to preserve the mixture and to stop evaporation. Scented oils were possibly made on a domestic basis but the majority of perfumes would have been manufactured from commercially grown plants. The most popular plant was the rose, which was grown extensively to make the justly famous attar of roses. Pliny mentions that Phaselis in Turkey was a centre for its production,[26] and it is interesting to note that it is still made in the hinterland today using flowers of the summer damask rose. Perfumes were also made from a surprising range of different ingredients, and the combined flavours could create a distinct scent. Many of these would include one or more of the following: balm, casia, fenugreek, iris, lily, marjoram, narcissus, nard, quince, saffron, spikenard or styrax.

FLOWERS AND FOLIAGE FOR GARLANDS

Many plants, however, owe their inclusion in a garden to the fact that they were necessary for making garlands, wreaths and also, at a later date, chaplets. Varieties used for this purpose are listed in Table II. In chapter six we saw that it was the duty of the *matrona* to grow flowers for garlands to hang by places of worship. In a number of frescos, mosaics and relief carvings, swags of garlands are seen decorating walls and spaces between the columns of a peristyle, and may have originally only been used on festive occasions (including birthdays). The large majority of the frescos illustrated in this book include a garland swag and on occasion the upper zone has also been decorated.

These long garlands would perhaps have been formed by utilizing the plentiful supply of ivy, which quickly produced long tendrils that would need to be cut back to control its growth. Strands of ivy, smilax or vine would have been interwoven with seasonal foliage and flowering plants. Some illustrations include fruit in garlands but these would not be suitable for use in a garden. They perhaps constitute a different meaning and the added items may represent offerings at an altar, or belong to a funerary context, in which case the fruit could allude to the afterlife. But fruit would not really be suitable for suspending above a walkway! They could do someone an injury.

Some of the long garlands appear to have one or two ribbons, or filets, draped over the swag and these dangle down, twisting as they fall and indicating just how light they are. These may be evidence showing that we have not one garland here but two. When garlands are made they are often tied to a branch with a cord or ribbon. A special fitting might have been built into one end but if the ribbons were retained people could have the choice of being able to tie them in place or hook them into position. Hooks were often fitted to the top of columns so that garlands or curtains could be attached. In this case each garland would have been attached to the top of a column and the two strands were just tied together in the middle, hence the double thickness at the centre of the swag and the two twisted ribbons, which would be the remaining end ties of each garland.

Shorter garland/wreaths and chaplets for wearing on feast days and at banquets were, on the other hand, more inclined to contain scented plants and otherwise more delicate species. At first *coronari* (crowns or chaplets) were honorific, and were composed of myrtle or the laurel we call bay; these shrubs have scented foliage and therefore must have been pleasant to wear. Pliny says in the earlier days, at least up to the Second Punic War (218 BC), one of the laws of the Twelve Tables controlled the wearing of coronari,[27] but later this rule was relaxed and decorative chaplets were more frequently worn. Sources indicate that chaplets and garlands could be formed by combining several stems of plants or young pliant branches of shrubs. A number of methods were used; some involved linking chains of flowers whereas other techniques included stitching or coiling, plaiting and weaving.[28] Theophrastus informs us that some people may have made a framework or 'hoop' of flexible wood first, he mentions mulberry or fig,[29] and this would have prevented an untimely disintegration of a garland or chaplet. Athenaeus mentions a number of named types of floral crown.[30] An example is one called *cosmosandala*, made with narcissus, roses, lilies and larkspur.[31] He also says that for a banquet one made of ivy would soothe a sore head, whereas one of gillyflowers, in Greek the λευκόϊον, would be too strongly scented and would oppress the senses. Decorative flowers and foliage were combined. When the seasons were unfavourable for the production of flowers garlands were made with dried flowers or dyed flakes of horn.[32]

Horace refers to the earlier practice of only having garlands made of myrtle or pliant parsley.[33] Yet in another of his *Odes* he adds ivy, showing that there were perhaps some further additions at times. He invites his friend to come out into the garden: 'in my garden, Phyllis, is parsley for weaving garlands; there is a goodly store of ivy, which, binding back thy hair, sets off thy beauty.'[34] Ancient illustrations often show people sporting a floral or foliate crown, and therefore one of the simple forms mentioned by Horace was re-created as an experiment; a chaplet of pliant

A chaplet of 'pliant parsley'.

parsley was chosen for the trial. Numerous flowering stalks were selected with the intention of plaiting the stems together. A garland could be made using the same method. When parsley is grown in a greenhouse or in a warm climate it will produce tall branching flower stems. Less than half of one plant was sufficient to make a chaplet, so there would be plenty left to provide seed. Ancient depictions of *coronari* indicate that flower heads were spaced out along its length. So with this feature in mind a number of florets were selected with stems about 30 cm long. To start with three were placed together, as if to make a bunch of flowers. Then leaving a gap of 6 cm three florets were added on to the others, making a staggered bunch of six stems. The combined stems below the second florets were now sorted into three pairs and plaited. Parsley, if picked while still green, is surprisingly pliant and bends without snapping. Three more florets were added after each interval of 6 cm, and additional flower stalks replaced earlier ones that became too short. Finally when the crown reached the desired size the stems were carefully plaited and woven behind the first floret. The beauty of this simple design is that no other materials were needed. The crown was light to wear and gave off a slightly aromatic odour that was quite pleasant and also cooling on the very hot summer's day of its trial. Parsley lasts well, it did not wilt at all, and after a month or so turned a colour resembling dried grass.

The most highly regarded and most widely grown chaplet flowers were reckoned to be the rose and the violet.[35] Apparently there was even a dance called 'The Flowers' and this really does highlight the esteem in which they were held. Revellers would recite these words 'Where are my roses, where are my violets, where my beautiful parsley . . . ?'[36] Again we hear of the parsley but many species were grown and picked for making garlands; these included the lily, narcissus, saffron and melilot which were also quite popular but as the range of plants used for this purpose is large – both flowers and foliage were utilized – a list appears in table II.

Sources inform us that of the different forms of rose the most favoured were those of Praeneste, which by all accounts was a late-flowering species, and the justly famous twice-blooming rose of Paestum, which was clearly a *Rosa bifera L.* Both of these were to be found in Italy, while the strongest scented came from Cyrene (in Libya).[37] Several mosaics depict garlands made of roses; the small mosaic tesserae used for these were chosen from an appropriate coloured marble in shades of dusky pink. One mosaic from Thuburbo-Maius in Tunisia was almost entirely devoted to the rose and the overall design is very effective. The pattern consists of a series of four vertical chains composed of sprays of rose linked together by horizontal swags of rose garlands. Rose garlands were even used to frame nine small figurative panels in the design, each of which contained a little bird, and every conceivable empty space was filled with rosebuds. The pattern of this floor mosaic would transfer well into a modern context and make a very fine carpet, and would retain the effect that it would have given in antiquity.

Of all the flowers of spring the rose was singled out to symbolize that season of the year. The seasons are often shown in mosaics and usually appear in four panels that are generally but not always sited at each corner. Each season is represented by a figure, usually female, wearing a chaplet made of plants considered important to her respective season. Spring, at the start of the Roman year, wears a chaplet of roses and often holds a single-stemmed rose in one hand; this must be seen as a mark of respect for this flower. Summer wears a crown made with ears of wheat, Autumn with vine leaves and bunches of grapes, and Winter olive leaves and berries. All four symbols are based on the plants or crops gathered in their respective seasons. Some mosaics also contain a small panel depicting some of the tasks of the year, and again spring is often referred to by a scene of people gathering roses or making garlands.

At the villa of Piazza Armerina in Sicily two large mosaics show young girls gathering roses and making the garlands and chaplets. The *coronariae*, or garland makers, tie one end of the garland to a branch of a tree, and

The Four Seasons based on Roman mosaics: Spring, Summer, Autumn and Winter.

Coronariae, garland and chaplet makers. Details from two mosaics found within the large villa at Piazza Armerina in Sicily. Top: Chaplet making. Bottom: Picking roses and making garlands.

while seated on a basket they fix on the flower heads. The garland was probably made by piercing through the centre of the flower. This concept of garland adornment, for the person or sacred object, is still in use today in some parts of the world, mainly in India and Nepal. In the mosaic large rose-coloured terminal flowers were placed at either end of the line of roses, with loose ribbon beyond to tie the garland round the neck. Pliny confirms the image seen in frescos and mosaic when he says that a *centifolia*, a 'cabbage' type of double rose, is placed at either end.[38]

A rose garland has actually been discovered in a tomb of the Roman period in Egypt[39] but in this case the method used in its construction appears to differ from that described above. It is interesting to note that the flowers had been picked while still in bud, and were attached to a core made with papyrus. Each flower was held in place by wrapping thongs around stem and core. This could be an actual example of a coiled wreath mentioned by Pliny. Further evidence of this technique could perhaps be found in a passage from Athenaeus who discusses an ancient common saying, 'rolling round and round in twists like a rolled out wreath'.[40]

Pliny mentions that there are roses with five, twelve or a hundred petals; some with a fiery colour, others less so, or white.[41] A variety of red and pink forms of rose appear in Roman paintings. The fresco from the House of the Wedding of Alexander, Pompeii, is thought by some to show a *versicolor* form,[42] and if so this may then be added to the other forms that may have existed. The majority of the species depicted in this fresco have now been identified but the term *versicolor* may have been given because the rose appears to be of two tones, the outer petals being red and the inner pink. However the artist may have painted in this fashion simply to clarify that there was a double row of petals. Species of rose cultivated in Roman times are believed to be: *Rosa gallica L.*, the apothecary rose; *Rosa phoenicea L.*, which originated in the Near East; *Rosa damascena L.*, of which the highly praised twice-flowering rose of Paestum was a cultivar; *Rosa moschata L.*, the autumn flowering musk; *Rosa canina L.*, the dog rose; *Rosa centifolia L.*, the cabbage rose, and possibly *Rosa alba L.* Modern botanists believe that the centifolia rose mentioned by Greek and Latin sources could be a form of *Rosa alba L.*

Violets were planted in gardens for the wonderful scent that they give, a scent that could fill the night air. References suggest that the Roman *viola* was not only of a purple colour but there were also some varieties with yellow or white flowers.[43] Descriptions of these three kinds have led us to the conclusion that again three or more species are involved. The purple form is thought to be the low growing *Viola odorata L.* but the yellow variety is believed to be the wallflower *Cheiranthus cheiri L.*, which is also scented; the white form may be the sweet-scented stocks *Matthiola incana L.*[44] Gillyflower is a common modern term used to denote several plants with fragrant flowers and this needs to be seen in comparison with the Latin *viola* and the Greek λευκόϊον. The latter is translated as the gillyflower and is variously thought to mean either stocks, carnation/pink, wallflower or even the dame's violet. There are suggestions that the illustration of the λευκόϊον in Dioscorides's manuscripts shows similarities to both the *Hesperis matronalis L.* and *Cheiranthus cuspidatus L.* According to Pliny the former 'has a stronger scent at night, from which fact it gets its name'.[45] Hesperis was the name of the night star. This species and the stocks both produce a number of mauve or white flowers with a good scent, and it now seems clear that the Latin term *viola* and the Greek λευκόϊον need to be seen in a slightly broader sense.

PLANTS FOR THE DECORATIVE GARDEN

Many of the garland flowers would also have provided scent and colour to the garden but a number of others were used in gardens purely for decorative purposes and as such were part of the *opus topiarium* – belonging to the realm of the *topiarius*, the landscape gardener. Pliny refers to this class of plants and they are listed in table II. Several do not have any special benefit to man, other than a pleasing appearance, but they were nevertheless considered worthwhile. An example is the date palm which was able to grow in Italy but was usually stunted and would not fruit.[46] Another is the acanthus which has a statuesque appearance and was highly valued. Pliny mentions that the Romans appear to have preferred to plant the 'smooth'- leaved form, rather than the spiny version found in Greece.[47] The Latin variant is thought to be *Acanthus mollis L.*, which is native to Italy. Apparently the acanthus and periwinkle were used as ground-covering plants on banks and in borders, or in the case of the latter where 'other flowers fail'.[48] Perhaps this means in dry shady conditions found under trees.

Many of the species grown in decorative Roman gardens were evergreen and the seasonal flowering forms would have relieved the scene. Contrasting foliage and grey-leaved varieties such as southernwood[49] were also used, however. Pliny mentions a silver-leaved shrub called 'Jupiter's Beard' that was clipped into a round bushy shape;[50] this may have been *Anthyllis barba-Jovis (L.)*, which also has attractive clusters of yellow pea- like flowers. The evergreen bay-laurel and myrtle were particularly favoured because of their scented foliage and the fact that they could be clipped to make chaplets when needed. It is recorded that on some estates large areas were converted into groves of these shrubs.[51] Box has a pungent smell and is hardy; this plant was also found to be tough enough to withstand the constant trimming required in topiary work.

Of the decorative trees, we hear that the pitch-pine was planted 'into our homes [gardens] because of the ease with which it can be clipped into various shapes'.[52] The cypress and box were also used for this purpose and the cypress was 'made into thick walls or evenly rounded off with trim slenderness, and it is even made to provide the representations of the landscape gardener's work, arraying hunting scenes or fleets of ships and imitations of real objects'.[53] The yew, however, was not utilized because of its highly poisonous nature. References indicate that people liked to sit beneath the shade of a tree but in the case of the yew it was thought this could be fatal.[54] Two species that were considered as harmful to man, the oleander and the strawberry tree (*arbutus*), were nevertheless found in many a Roman garden. The oleander provides a good show of flowers throughout the summer months and this is really the reason for its inclusion; however it did have a benefit for Pliny says this plant could provide an antidote to snake bites! The arbutus produces decorative fruits that are unfortunately 'difficult of digestion and injurious to the stomach'[55] but these did have some compensations for they were noted as being good food for birds. Their inclusion into the garden therefore indicates their decorative value was perhaps considered higher than their utilitarian properties.

Trees described as having 'an exuberance of spreading shady branches'[56] – 'often leaping across to the neighbouring mansions'[57] – were particularly useful. The plane was highly esteemed for this capacity, and also provided illusions of the plane groves in the Academy at Athens. It was brought to Rome by way of Sicily and Regium, and its widespread use was censured by some[58] as a worthless unproductive tree as opposed to useful species providing nuts or fruit. In contrast the prized lotus or nettle tree, *Celtis australis L.*, six of which grew in the garden of Crassus on the Palatine,[59] furnished small edible fruits (rather like cherries). These graceful deciduous trees belong to the elm family. When referring to these Pliny remarks that although 'no shady foliage is more short-lived. . . . No trees have bark that is more agreeable or attractive to look at.'[60]

Other species that were described as being a 'particularly good decoration for terraces'[61] were introductions to Rome (*c.* AD 23), such as the tuber-apple from Syria and the jujube from Africa, which produces small edible berry-like fruits. The cherry discovered in the region of Pontus (an area on the southern shores of the Black Sea) was brought to Rome by Lucullus in about 60 BC and was widely acclaimed, so much so that it was introduced to other provinces; varieties were grown in Germany and Belgium, and are recorded as being established in Britain by AD 46.[62]

Plants were sought from far and wide to extend the flowering or fruiting seasons, and to find new varieties with an improved flavour or larger fruit. Among the new species introduced during the period of the Roman Empire we have the peach, damson, citron and melon. New forms of rose were naturally looked for because this flower was in such demand, so much so that Horace became quite exasperated by these efforts; he cried out, 'A truce to searching out the haunts where lingers late the rose!'[63] In Egypt, however, conditions were different, and Athenaeus mentions that whereas in other regions the flowers would only be found during their regular season, in Egypt the soil and climate was such that plants could be grown all year round. He adds that 'it is not easy, as a rule, for the rose or wallflower or any other flowers to fail entirely'.[64] In those days the sight of such a wonderful mass of blooms would have been all the more remarkable, and the fact that many were normally out of season would have excited any visitors to those shores. Climate and geographical

Miniature fresco illustrating a *villa urbana* from the House of M. Fronto, Pompeii.

A garden with a complete peristyle, House of the Vettii, Pompeii.

Fresco depicting a grotto in a garden setting from the Villa of P. Fannius Sinistor at Boscoreale. (The Metropolitan Museum of Art, Rogers Fund, 1903 (03.14.13). Photograph © 1986, The Metropolitan Museum of Art.)

Statuary lining the large pool or *canopus* at Hadrian's Villa, Tivoli.

'Gutter' water feature running along three sides of a garden, House of the Ocean Gods at Vienne. Under the pergola there is an ornamental pool and earlier traces show that this was formerly the site of a summer dining couch.

Water garden with shaped islands filled with plants, House of the Water Jets at Conimbriga.

Mosaic-covered *aedicula nymphaeum*, House of the Small Fountain at Pompeii.

Fresco depicting a statue of Mars, House of the Marine
Venus at Pompeii.

Detail of a silenus head or mask water outlet, House of
the Small Fountain at Pompeii.

Garden scene, fresco from the Casa del Bracciale d'Oro, also known as
the House of the Wedding of Alexander, Pompeii.

Mosaic detail of a citron, the precursor of the lemon. It is a large fruit with a thick rough outer rind (El-Jem Museum).

Fresco with a rectangular *oscillum* and garlands above a fountain bowl supported by a Sphinx, provenance unknown (now in the Miho Museum, Japan).

Garden fresco from the House of the Marine Venus, Pompeii. From left to right the plants depicted are: ivy, myrtle, oleander, southernwood, rose, oriental plane, laurel, oleander, strawberry tree, myrtle and ivy.

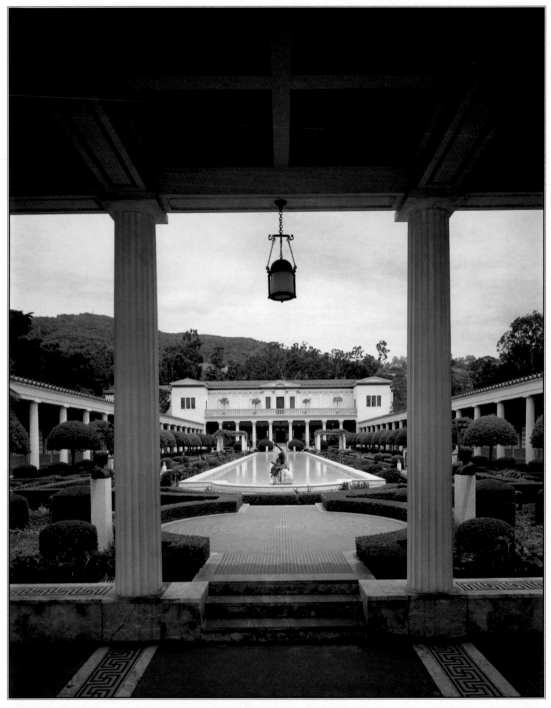

Reconstructed Roman garden at the John Paul Getty Museum, Malibu, California.

situation was really the most important deciding factor in what could be grown in a garden, and not all plants would grow satisfactorily in the different conditions found in other provinces.

The long winters and late frosts in Britain prevented a number of species being established here. Plants such as the stone pine and the beautiful pencil-like cypresses which are so familiar a landmark in Italy, then as now, were just too tender for the British climate and would have died after a prolonged frost. However plants such as the juniper, box, crocus and the humble leek, to name but a few, owe their existence here to the Romans. Recent research at Fishbourne[65] has identified the most important plants brought to Britain and the list is surprisingly long. Many belong to the fruit or vegetable class, and one can only guess at the changes made following this great improvement in the choice of food. It is hard to imagine a diet without many of these species that we take for granted nowadays. Apart from the sweet cherry mentioned above the Romans introduced the following species to Britain: almond, apricot, bullace, coriander, cucumber, dill, fennel, fig, garlic, grape, marjoram, medlar, mulberry, mustard, onion, orache, parsley, pear, plum, quince, radish, sweet chestnut, turnip and walnut. Also a number of native species previously not under cultivation were brought into Roman gardens; these are thought to include the wild strawberry, raspberry, blackberry, crab-apple and celery.

FRESCOS USED AS CONFIRMATION OF PLANT SPECIES

Literary evidence of species grown in gardens is complemented by their contemporary depiction in frescos. Some of these are painted in a rather naïve style, where the plant details are so simplified that they are barely recognizable, but these unsophisticated sketches still serve to give a general impression of a group of plants. There are however several notable frescos, some of which are illustrated here; these are of such meticulous draughtsmanship that a positive identification and analysis of species is possible. Unfortunately many frescos are now quite faded or have disappeared altogether, for some of the areas in Pompeii and elsewhere have been exposed to the elements for over a hundred years, and throughout this time the combined effects of rain and bleaching from the sun has taken its toll. Fortunately drawings of some of the frescos were made soon after their excavation and these provide a record of what once existed. However, caution is needed, for artwork is not always an accurate record. An example is the two paintings of an ancient fresco from the House of Orpheus at Pompeii which sadly no longer exists. The work of both Niccolini and Presuhn, dating to before 1879, is clear and informative but there are a number of features that have been interpreted in a different way. The paintings do however indicate the main features within the fresco in question and they are therefore still a valuable witness if used cautiously.

It is difficult to say if the verdant scenes in ancient frescos represent a

window whereby we can look into an actual Roman garden or if these
were an idealized vision of a sacro-idyllic scene. The fact that plant
species are shown flowering and fruiting at the same time makes one
suspect an idyllic garden like that of Alcinous may be implied.
However, statuary added to these scenes returns one to reality. Also with
the addition of a fence in the foreground, which often serves as a border,
one can visualize the garden continuing beyond, in the manner of *trompe
l'oeil* works of art. Because these scenes are mostly painted on walls
behind an actual garden or *viridarium*, I feel that they do imply some
elements of a true Roman garden. Jashemski is also of this opinion.[66]
She argues that Pompeian frescos could not be Greek or Alexandrian (a
suggestion put forward by some scholars) for some plants depicted in
the garden scenes were common to the area in Campania, for example
oleander, which does not grow in Alexandria. Painted garden scenes or
dados with plants have been discovered in other provinces of the Roman
Empire and are also referred to by Pliny the Younger, who describes a
room in his house at Tusculum decorated in a similar way. These would
confirm that this type of decoration is really a Roman fashion.

Some scholars have tried to find a meaning for each flower depicted in
the frescos, in a similar manner to the lore of plant names used during the
Middle Ages. This is probably out of place in a Roman context, although
some plants are known to be associated with various Greco-Roman gods
and their myths. However, the combinations found in many frescos are not
exclusively dedicated to a particular deity. A few plants were known to
have a separate meaning, albeit sexual rather than spiritual, and as these
frescos sometimes appear in dining rooms or *diaetae* such an interpretation
is possible although unlikely. For the most part the painted verdant scenes
simply represent a Latin view of a garden.

In the majority of garden scenes small plants are shown to the fore
and shrubs/trees fill the background, often with a blue sky beyond.
Some bushes are carefully painted and can easily be distinguished, with
individual leaves and flowers highlighting a selective number of plants;
others are less clearly defined and a green haze between generally
indicates a continuance of the shrubberies. The most common shrubs
depicted are laurel, myrtle, oleander and viburnum. Laurel and myrtle
look fairly similar but can be identified by their characteristic leaf
pattern; laurel being alternate and myrtle opposite. The former also has
red berries whereas the latter has black. Box would appear as a compact
version of myrtle, whereas oleander is shown with a closer leaf density,
slender willow-like leaves and pink flowers.

Of the trees, the most common appears to be pine or cypress. In many
fresco panels a large or particularly fine tree was sited in a central position,
as can be seen in the fresco from the Auditorium of Maecenas where the
pine tree is flanked by laurels. In the larger fresco from the House of Livia,
at Primaporta, Rome, the central tree is highlighted by a recess in the
decorative wall and fruit trees were the main accompaniment, in this case

Etching of a fresco
from the garden
room at the House
of Livia, Primaporta,
Rome.

quince and pomegranate. This fresco is one of six panels painted on to the
walls of a cool underground garden room used during long hot summer
days. It has proved to be of particular importance for the large number of
plant species and different birds that are depicted. These have been
studied in great detail and the wealth of species in the fresco illustrated
here (which is panel V) have been identified.[67] In front of the wall the
artist has sketched several clumps of iris, ivy, hart's-tongue fern and an
acanthus at the base of the pine tree; behind the wall and in the
foreground there are laurels, white daisies, red and pink rose bushes, box,
myrtle, chrysanthemums, periwinkle and poppies. In the middle ground
there are oleanders, laurels, two palm trees, arbutus and cypress. Fruit
trees were less common in frescos but a variety is shown in one house in
Pompeii and as a result it has been named the House of the Fruit Orchard.
Species depicted were apple, cherry, fig, lemon, pear, yellow and blue
plums, and a peach or pomegranate.[68] In the now quite faded fresco at the
House of Adonis, Pompeii, the relatively darker pigment used to paint
pomegranate fruits helps to locate the position of the tree.

Towards the centre of this composition a madonna lily can just be
discerned. The lily was considered next in favour after the rose,[69] and was
highly acclaimed for the purity of its white flower and for its perfume. A
succession of pristine white blooms is displayed to great effect in a
wonderful but fragmentary late mosaic found at Séviac in the Aquitaine
region of France.[70] Three tall lily plants weave their way upwards
between three fruit trees (a citron tree in the centre with pears on either
side). At their feet the artist has placed baskets alternately filled with
picked fruit or lily flowers. The lily plants may have only been included
in the design of the mosaic to fill the spaces between the trees, but might
also allude to a habit of growing these beautiful flowers in the shade of a
canopy of trees. This practice is noted elsewhere for vegetables and
certainly is frequently performed in warmer regions where the relentless

Lilium candidum, the Madonna
lily, mosaic detail, Séviac,
France.

Three zones of decoration in a fresco from the House of the Wedding of Alexander, Pompeii. In the middle zone the plants depicted are as follows: the tall bushes are sweet bay, laurustinus and oriental plane. In the foreground there are two date palms, roses, oleander, feverfew or camomile, marigold, periwinkle, two strawberry trees, variegated ivy and opium poppy. The lower zone, or dado, has hart's-tongue fern, iris and mounds of ivy.

sun can soon wither plants. Another variety, the red martagon or Turk's cap lily, is known from a number of references and also appears in some paintings, one of which may be seen on a low wall at Oplontis.

At the House of the Marine Venus the plants are not so accurately drawn but in the large garden painting on the right of the rear wall there are narrow elongated bushes of myrtle and oleander in flower, roses, and a grey-green bush with feathery foliage. This may be southernwood although this does not appear in Jashemski's table of plants represented in Pompeian frescos.

A detail from a large mosaic from Carthage. This roundel is thought to depict a person tending a lily plant.

Plants in the foreground of garden paintings were mostly low-growing varieties. They include plants with daisy-like flowers, ivy, lily, poppy and rose. Unfortunately the violet (the purple kind we understand by that name), which was much admired by the Romans, is not normally found, perhaps because their ground-hugging form would be difficult to reproduce successfully among larger herbaceous plants. In addition, sources suggest that there may have been a habit of having separate beds for these plants, and therefore they would belong elsewhere. *Violaria*, or violet beds, are specifically mentioned by Columella,[71] and in another volume he mentions that violets were planted in 'little trenches a foot deep'.[72]

Large garden scenes appear in the so-called third Pompeian style, which is thought to have been fashionable in about 15 BC to AD 62, but plant elements are found before and after this period. These frescos sometimes cover a whole wall or are confined to the larger middle portion of three horizontal zones. A painted fence would conveniently fit into the position of the lower zone, or dado, and several with this false barrier have been discovered, but at other times the dado is treated as a separate area of decoration. In many third style frescos this dado often displayed low-growing plants. Low garden walls (*plutei*) were treated in a similar manner and species were usually positioned in individual groups composed mostly of clumps of grasses or herbaceous plants. An example from the House of Adonis depicts an *Acanthus mollis (L.)* and hart's-tongue fern painted next to a white ibis or heron attacking a grass snake. Several plants cannot really be identified – they have large grass-like leaves but tall stems of daisy-like flowers and may well be the product of the artist's imagination rather than a lifelike study, or they may even record plants no longer in existence. Some however could represent a form of plantain, or perhaps the cynoglossum which is a member of the borage family. Both were regarded as a garden plant and Pliny goes as far as saying that the latter was 'a most attractive addition to ornamental gardens'.[73]

Ivy and smilax often appear in art and because of the ivy's link with the cult of Bacchus its inclusion could partly allude to a general Bacchanalian atmosphere. Smilax is in many ways similar to the ivy; both are twining and have a heart-shaped leaf, although the young leaves of the smilax are more pointed and arrow-like and the plant has many small thorns. The smilax is differentiated in art by its many corkscrew tendrils. It has glossy

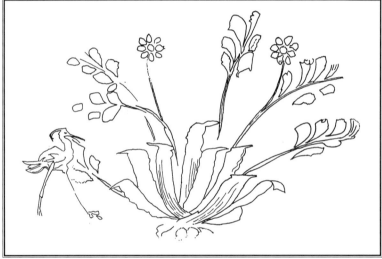

Roman flora and fauna depicted in the dado zone of a fresco in the House of Achilles, Pompeii. Accompanied by a drawing as the original is now very faded.

lime-green leaves and white flowers that were said to have the scent of a lily, and the plant later produces clusters of bright red berries. Because of its growth habit it was used as part of an effective green fence around the *hortus*.[74] Ivy is well recorded as a plant used for decorative purposes in gardens, to grow up trees and to link tree to tree in the manner of garlands. The ancients rather liked this spectacle and Achilles Tatius saw that the ivy could form 'ivy wreaths of honour for the tree' by itself.[75] A reference by Cicero informs us that ivy could also be carefully arranged to drape over statues.[76] Pliny shows that there were a number of different forms of ivy, the common green form and also a 'white' version,[77] which could be the variety in Virgil's *Georgics* which was referred to as 'pale ivy'.[78] Pliny also informs us that there was a form with a variegated leaf called Thracian ivy. He continues by saying that some 'differ in the arrangement of their markings'. A variegated form is depicted in the foreground of one of the frescos illustrated; this type is however less commonly painted. Interestingly the relatively more frequent renditions of ivy show it being trained to grow into a mound supported by a reed. Reeds were commonly used for this purpose as canes made out of bamboo were not yet in use. Bamboo had not yet been discovered by the Romans. Ivy mounds are perhaps more often depicted in the dado zone of frescos and can be seen at the House of Ceii or at the House of the Vettii where a portion of the supporting stick is still visible. Ivy has actually been planted and trained to grow in this way in a number of recreated gardens at Pompeii, although many are now quite overgrown.

ARCHAEOLOGICAL EVIDENCE OF PLANT SPECIES GROWN IN GARDENS

The largest proportion of our evidence comes from the area around Vesuvius where housing and the ground surface was covered by a thick layer of volcanic ash or debris which sealed and preserved the archaeological layers. Excavators noticed that after the ash and pumice had been taken away the original soil contours of AD 79 were revealed, showing in some areas rows or plots of garden cultivation. In some cases plant material was carbonized and fragments of tree branches, seeds and nuts of fruiting trees survived in places. These have provided a great deal of information about garden plants and of course the ubiquitous weeds of that day. Allowances have to be made, however, for the fact that some evidence for plant material may have actually been brought to the ancient site, and had been stored in the vicinity instead of growing there. This would include fruit, vegetables and other produce purchased elsewhere.

As the blanket of ash choked and killed all life below, the ancient Roman plants and trees of the area were either burnt into charcoal and preserved in that way or they slowly decayed through lack of light and air. The ash and lapilli then gradually infiltrated the spaces left behind. Many centuries later excavators came across some of these tell-tale signs and perfected a technique using plaster to fill the voids not completely choked by the lapilli. The ensuing casts have provided a record of objects usually too ephemeral to survive elsewhere. Wooden doors and window shutters have now been revealed as well as a series of gruesome relics in the form of humans and animals overcome by the catastrophe. The same technique was later used by Jashemski to go one step further, to reveal plant roots in Roman gardens. Here the lapilli below ground level were carefully removed, and the resulting voids were filled with a concrete mix. After setting the casts were cleared of soil and the shape of the roots were compared with present-day trees which led to their identification. Examples have been left *in situ* at the Villa of Poppaea,

A row of five root casts providing evidence for the existence of five large plane trees in the northern garden at Oplontis.

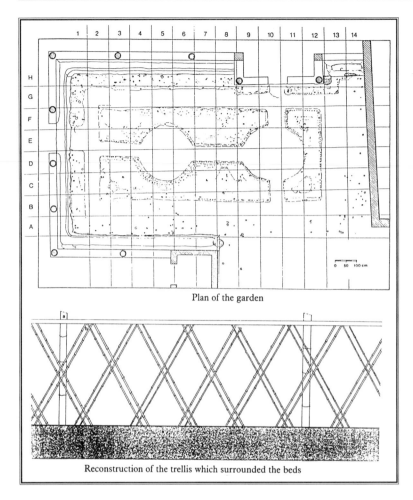

Plan of the garden

Reconstruction of the trellis which surrounded the beds

Plan of the garden and reconstruction of the reed fence found at the House of the Chaste Lovers, Pompeii, locating find spots of plant material.

Oplontis. The plan of this villa indicates the location of numerous find spots of tree roots in each garden area. In the large northern garden a row (running from north to south) of five very large root casts have been identified as plane trees.[79] These confirm the existence of mature trees with a large canopy that would have provided more than sufficient shade for the *ambulationes* beneath, and the adjacent garden portico.

An analysis of soil samples can reveal seeds and grains of ancient pollen, spores of fern or fungi, and remains of insects found in gardens. Some pollen from wind-blown varieties, however, may have come into the garden from elsewhere. This form of study can show a certain bias, for another factor that needs to be taken into account is that a number of plant species do not seed freely, and in some cases flower/seed heads are cut off prematurely or before flowering, as is the case with clipped box. This practice would tend to reduce the ratio of their presence in any pollen count. Jashemski has identified fifty-six genera from pollen found within the Vesuvian area and these appear in an appendix in her second book on the Gardens of Pompeii. Continuing work at Pompeii has revealed more and more data. At the recently excavated House of the Chaste Lovers, Ciarallo has drawn a grid plan of the garden showing the overall pattern of preserved root cavities. When compared with two tables, one detailing the microscopic analysis of carbonized wood, the other a pollen spectrum, they provide what must be the best indication of the appearance and distribution of plants in a modern excavation of a Roman garden. In the plan shown here macrofossils from rows C and F show that at either side of the central path there was a symmetrical arrangement of alternating juniper and rose bushes. A pollen analysis of the garden soil also indicates the presence of a number of ornamental species. The preserved pollen however was shown to relate to plants that were mainly in flower during August, which was the same month as the eruption of Vesuvius. These include southernwood, myrtle, members of the aster family, the pink family, mallow, *campanula*, *fabaceae*, *lychnis*, *cerastium* (the grey-leaved 'snow in summer'), ferns and plantains. There was also a low percentage of genera we would consider as weeds, and interestingly members of the brassica family were also present, perhaps showing that some food plants (or wallflowers that are of the same family) may also have been planted in this garden.

Many of the gardens at Pompeii were excavated without the scientific methods used today but in a few cases the presence of soil contours or a large carbonized tree root was briefly noted, although their significance was not at that time recognized. Jashemski has found that in gardens excavated more recently (within the last thirty years) a large tree, often fruit- or nut-bearing, was placed in the centre and/or one at each corner of the peristyle. Pliny mentions that at his Tuscan villa he had 'a small court shaded by four plane trees'.[80] Archaeological examples are found at Oplontis in one of the small internal gardens where three trees out of the four were planted, for the fourth would have blocked the entrance into that garden. However no two gardens are exactly the same. Houses elsewhere reveal that a number of trees were planted into their gardens to give shade and perhaps fruit. We must not forget that the blossom of fruit trees can be very attractive to look at, as is the rather gratifying sight of branches laden with ripening fruit. A good store of fruit to conserve for later use or to provide a little income was always an added bonus. The aromatic properties of trees and their fruit also need to be considered, for some fruits such as the quince were nicely scented and if placed on a dish in a room they would give off a pleasant subtle scent. The quince is often shown in frescos depicting still life and especially in a glass dish or bowl with other fruits.

Evidence found in the large internal courtyard garden at Oplontis indicates that a huge chestnut tree had been placed at its centre. The information here was retrieved from a root cavity and carbonized chestnuts were found at roof height.[81] The tree would have completely shaded the garden and portico, a feature repeated in many a home in the warmer areas of the Empire. Once mature, trees and drought-resistant shrubs would require little watering and were therefore not too much of a drain on precious supplies of water stored in cisterns. With the advent of a greater supply of water piped to houses from an aqueduct a more diverse planting scheme became possible, and lower growing shrubs and herbaceous plants were then more numerous. Some Roman gardens were laid out formally whereas others appear informal; there was evidently the mixture of tastes then that there is today. Many of the gardens at Pompeii have been replanted although a number of those kept locked are now quite overgrown. Often these reconstructions appear formal and symmetrical in design, following ideas prevalent at the time of excavation rather than as a result of evidence through archaeology. An example is that of the House of the Labyrinth, which had been named after a mosaic, and therefore the conservators incorporated a maze design in the garden for which there was no real evidence.[82]

Outside Campania the archaeological evidence for ancient plant material is considerably more limited. However at Thuburbo Maius in Tunisia Jashemski has discovered that where wind-blown soil has covered and sealed an abandoned site, ancient tree roots can be identified when soil of a different colour or texture has formed by the decaying process of woody material.[83] This is similarly observed in former post pits elsewhere. In these cases the wooden post may have rotted *in situ* and left a tell-tale dark patch, which again stands out against the surrounding soil. Another identifying feature of these pits is that large stones or rubble may have been rammed into the hole to steady the post. As these were usually left in place, even if the post had been extracted for reuse later, they could still reveal the location of a former post.

Apart from the use of posts in wooden buildings, a line of pits in what is believed to be a garden area could indicate the presence of a wooden fence. A double row might imply a pergola. Some pits are the sole reminder of a hole made when planting a tree, and the diameter of the planting pit would to some extent correspond to the dimensions of the ancient tree roots. These pits would reveal whether there was a random tree-planting scheme in that garden, or on occasions the direction of an alignment. But unless some dating material is included in the hole it would be difficult to assess when the trees had been planted, or even if this had actually occurred during the Roman period. Most excavation sites reveal many layers or periods of occupation and self-seeding weeds and trees would tend to confuse any remains of the original planting schemes.

In Britain, we have evidence from a modest sized villa at Frocester Court, where stake holes discovered in a number of planting pits are thought to have provided support for young trees.[84] The rough nature of the original ground surface in the front (south) garden has indicated that part could be interpreted as an orchard. At Fishbourne a row of posts alongside a portico on the east side of the large formal garden is believed to have supported a line of cordon fruit trees or vines.[85] At Piddington (Northants.) the alignments follow the line of the three porticos of the winged villa, and would in effect restrict access to the open space between the wings. These have been interpreted by the excavator as fences enclosing vegetable plots,[86] although they too could have provided a means of support for a decorative yet functional screen or trellis of fruit trees or vines. The same methods of detection have been used at Wollaston, in the Nene Valley,[87] where a vineyard has been detected. Several parallel rows of post holes (the supports) were discovered in association with long bedding trenches of a darker soil, marking the planting area for the vines.

As in the case above at some sites plant beds are identifiable by the long-term practice of enriching the natural top soil with compost or manure, or even the importation of better soil. These areas can therefore be traced by differential soil coloration, the darker soil normally being that of cultivation. A black earth theory is currently being used to reveal former Roman cultivation sites by comparison with field names incorporating the word 'black'.[88] This is more marked on otherwise poor land. At Frocester the land was fairly fertile but areas of enriched soil beside gravel paths (or cut into the gravel, as in the north rear garden) suggested the location of plant beds. The tell-tale mark of spade cuts into the subsoil in these regions further suggest deep digging in cultivated areas.[89]

At Fishbourne, where the top soil was thin and poor, the silhouette of plant beds was clearly visible by their darker coloration. Their highly decorative sinuous shape, in a typically classical rectilinear and curvilinear design, was suggestive of hedging. Cunliffe believes that the width and depth of the trenches would have been suitable for box[90] which, if trimmed, would retain the overall pattern. This assumption is supported by the number of clippings from box found at several other sites in Britain, for example, Frocester, Silchester, Winterton and Farmoor.[91] Ancient authors like Pliny attest to the practice of topiary using box. He reveals that it could be trimmed into tiers, obelisks, figures of 'innumerable shapes' or letters spelling out names.[92] At his house at Laurentum rosemary was an alternative, and was used to fill in gaps in the box hedge where the underlying soil was too dry.[93] In countries with shallow soil overlying rock, such as Malta, trenches were excavated into the bedrock and then filled with good loamy soil to allow sufficient depth for root growth.[94]

In Britain the identification of Roman garden plants by archaeological means is often reliant on seeds and pollen found in waterlogged conditions such as wells, ditches or pits, where preservation occurs because the soil becomes anaerobic. However, it appears that preservation can only take place if the soil also has a fairly low pH, in other words if it is acidic. Unfortunately fertile garden soil is more likely to be the opposite for lime and manure added to ensure a healthy fine tilth is not so conducive to preservation. Also a friable soil necessary for cultivation will let in air, and the constant turning of earth causes oxidization which destroys pollen and inhibits the survival of macrofossils.[95] The species that are more likely to be present in a soil analysis would therefore be those that prefer an acid soil, and cultivars that were wind blown as opposed to insect pollinated varieties

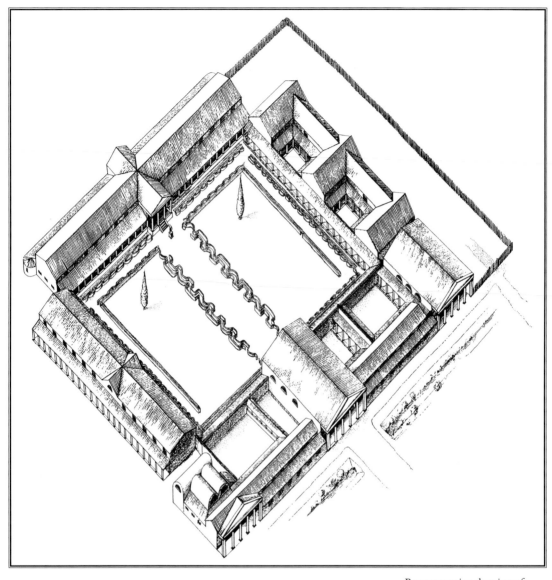

Reconstruction drawing of topiary hedges in the garden at Fishbourne in Britain.

which produce less pollen. Considering these limitations it is surprising that a range of garden plants can be identified.

Several garden species have come to light by examination of carbonized or charred material. Occasionally charred seeds have been found and may have survived a bonfire of garden or household refuse, such as is believed to be the case at Alcester (Warks.), where charred seeds of columbine, *Aquilegia vulgans L.*, were recovered.[96] Also wood burnt as fuel in the home does not always burn down completely and can leave carbonized remains and fragments of charred wood that would be thrown out with the ashes; these would have been used as a fertilizer mixed into the garden soil. However the presence of these remains does not necessarily imply their existence in the garden or even its vicinity, as evidenced from an analysis of the charred remains of wood from the Vigna Barberini, Rome (the presumed site of the *Horti Adonaea*). This survey has shown that the charcoal came from trees that did not grow there and had originated from non-resinous woodland trees found in mountainous regions. They were further believed to have been specifically brought to site from charcoal burners, rather than as green faggots and, after use as fuel, the residue with ash would have been added as fertilizer to plant beds.[97] This example highlights the importance of careful examination of evidence.

The number of plants known to the Romans in the first century BC is believed to amount to perhaps 475,[98] but this figure would of course include wild plants. A comparative list of plants known to the Romano-British, attested by archaeobotanical means, is at present being undertaken by staff at Fishbourne Museum.[99] A previous survey of 'garden and orchard crops identified from macrofossils at Roman sites in Britain'[100] listed thirty-two species; however they exclude ornamentals such as box, columbine and some 'exotics'. Some examples have come to light from an analysis of waterlogged material from wells at Chew Park and Low Ham.[101]

In my thesis[102] the archaeologically attested Romano-British flora were compared with two sites from the Gallo-Roman region, one in the north and one in the south. These were displayed beside flora found in the area covered by Vesuvius. What was immediately noticeable is that a number of the broad-leaved trees and fruit trees are found in all regions, the majority of vegetable species are also comparable, but flowering varieties are less well represented in Britain at present. As would have been expected the flora extracted from the site in northern Gaul shows that the area was climatically closer to that of Britain.

FAUNA IN GARDENS

A variety of creatures could be found in the garden and its adjacent porticos. The abundant bird population can be seen from frescos, and birds of many kinds are shown. This was not just a device to enliven the painting but it appears that birds were actually encouraged to enter gardens – the Romans enjoyed the pleasant sight and sound of these multi-hued creatures. In their frescos we see doves, pigeons, blackbirds, thrushes, yellow orioles, goldfinches, flycatchers, nightingales, buntings and warblers, to name but a few. The painted walls of Livia's Garden Room at Primaporta display a surprising quantity, a veritable flock of birds amounting to sixty-nine in all! They are shown flying in the air, alighting on bushes or fences or perched on stems. There are also numerous references recalling various singing or talking birds that were turned into pets – the most favoured of course being the parrot – but we also hear of magpies and starlings kept as talking birds. Doves were popular as pets and one was owned by Stella, Martial's friend, whereas a sparrow or finch such as that belonging to Catullus's girlfriend was more often given to children as a pet.[103] Of the larger birds the elegant peacock features in many frescos, partly for their ornamental value and partly because they were regarded as an exotic introduction to Rome. Varro informs us that Quintus Hortensius had created a precedent by serving peacock meat at a banquet, and thereafter they were considered a delicacy.[104] Small birds were also thought of as food to eat. Birds for the table may have been trapped or lured into gardens but the majority would have been purchased live and housed in the garden until they were needed. Therefore birdcages or aviaries (*ornithones*) could be found in some part of the garden or grounds of an estate. In some areas birds were bred for the table, but the birdcage or aviary could be both decorative and profitable.

Representations of birdcages show that most would have been made of wood or wicker, and are usually of a domed form. A small portable birdcage is depicted sitting on top of the low wall in one of the frescos at the House of Livia; they frequently appear as a motif occupying one of the many roundels of Late Roman mosaics. Unfortunately these light wicker frames do not usually survive the centuries but Statius informs us indirectly that some birdcages could have been made with metal when he refers to Melior's parrot that was housed in a cage of silver and ivory.[105] This bird was perhaps more fortunate than others.

A birdcage, detail in a mosaic from Carthage.

There is, however, more evidence for aviaries. Varro informs us that M.L. Strabo at Brundisium 'was the first to keep birds penned up in a recess in his peristyle, feeding them through a net covering'.[106] A similar arrangement is thought to have existed in the House of the Dioscuri at Pompeii.[107] In these cases metal or wooden brackets would have been fixed to walls or columns inside part of the portico; some would be attachments for the netting but others would serve as perches for birds. The position and arrangement of perches is mentioned by Varro when he describes his own aviary at Casinum.[108] The metal fittings or traces of them could survive but the net covering, which would have been of hemp, is too ephemeral, as were any wooden perches. However the base or foundations of a free-standing aviary could come to light, and the remains of a large circular structure found in one of the gardens at Pompeii is thought to provide an example, but it is not known whether it was for private or commercial use.[109]

From the earliest days pigeons and doves were encouraged to roost on the rustic steading and records show that originally pigeon lofts or dovecotes were located in the actual roof space of house or farm.[110] Later, special terracotta fittings were made to attach to the exterior of the roof, and these could provide nest sites for some of the birds in towns. Owners with larger gardens or country properties who had more refined sensibilities would be able to convert a *turris*, a turret or tower for their use, or could construct a specially designed *columbaria*. They were painted white and may be similar to that shown in the large Nilotic mosaic from Praeneste (Palestrina). This circular building with a conical roof can be identified by the six rows of nesting holes and birds flying around and alighting on its roof. Varro provides a description of such structures[111] that were designed to maximize the availability of fresh meat and eggs, but also to aid the gathering of their guano, which the agriculturalists reckoned to be the best form of fertilizer for gardens.[112] Ovid observes that these structures needed to be kept clean for the birds: 'You see how the doves come to a white dwelling how an unclean tower harbours no birds.'[113] Because of this, the guano would always have been cleared away for use elsewhere. Unfortunately this practice means that these buildings are difficult to identify archaeologically, for the accumulation of phosphates in the ground left by composted dung would ordinarily have left a trace.

The bones of numerous species of bird are also found on excavation in Britain and elsewhere,[114] although many may have been brought to site to provide food rather than having lived all their life in the garden. Birds, scavengers and insects would have helped to clean up scraps and debris thrown out on to the garden after meals.[115] Faunal remains found in gardens can be useful as 'indicators of features of the habitat'.[116] Wild fauna such as molluscs, insects, beetles, small mammals, amphibians and reptiles can on occasion throw light on species of plant grown in the garden: for example, some insects feed only on one plant and therefore would be indicative of the presence of that plant, whereas remains of fish, birds and mammals could reveal the way that the garden was stocked.

Cats, which could have reduced the rodent population, could equally kill the birds loved by Romans, but there is some evidence for their presence in gardens. One has been found at the villa of Montmaurin in Gaul[117] and although rare, cat bones have been discovered in Britain, at Silchester, for example.[118] Few mosaics depict a cat but these tend to show cats that are about to pounce on birds, or have just caught them. At the House of the Faun, Pompeii, the cat is shown devouring a bird, and another from Orange in France has caught a mouse.[119] Some cats, however, may have been considered pets, for one is depicted in the arms of a young girl in a stele from Bordeaux.

There is much more evidence for dogs as pets: for instance Martial mentions a lap-dog belonging to Publius.[120] There are also numerous representations in art of dogs either as companions, hunting dogs or guard dogs for flocks or the home. Bones of dogs have been found in gardens at Pompeii and a cast was made of one unfortunate victim of the eruption. The remains provide evidence that dogs of that period resemble those seen in Pompeian *cave canum* mosaics, which means literally 'Beware of the Dog'.[121] These were simple mosaics placed at the entrance of the house warning people that there was a fierce dog inside ready to protect the premises. The fictional rich freedman Trimalchio (in the *Satyricon*) had one of these painted on the wall by the porter's lodge, and it was effective in startling people on entry to the house.[122] Some of the dogs portrayed are shown baring their teeth, as at the House of the Tragic Poet; another appears alert and is chained to the door, but there is one where the dog is curled up and asleep, which would not be a great deterrent.

Many dogs were watchdogs guarding the premises and valuable garden produce from thieves. Larger gardens would have a dog resident in the garden itself, and evidence for the provision of a kennel was found in the Garden of Hercules at Pompeii.[123] Here half of a dolium, a large terracotta pot, had been cut lengthways and placed on bricks. Advice is given by Columella on the qualities thought desirable in a guard dog.[124] He adds that if the dog is tied up during the day when staff are about, it would be alert and on the prowl when let loose at night. Also if the dog is black would appear more fierce and would not be so easily detected by thieves – until it was too late.

A drawing of a mosaic depicting a fierce black guard dog protecting the entrance passageway of a house at Pompeii.

A large garden with significant areas under grass may have been stocked with one or more browsing animals, such as goats. They could keep down the height of grass but would need to be well supervised or tethered, for these animals would eat practically anything within their reach, and could wreak havoc if they strayed too close to a carefully tended flower bed. Pliny the Younger mentions how the centre of his hippodrome garden looked like a meadow and this could imply that the grass was not necessarily close cut. A goat or sheep would tend to leave the odd stalk and the 'cut' would be a bit uneven but could have saved many hours of work laboriously cutting the grass with a sickle or hand shears. The bones of a goat were found under the shade of a tree in the large garden at Oplontis, and if it was not there for this reason then it could only have been brought in to provide food at some future date.

Many gardens contained ornamental pools that would sometimes contain fish, and on more spacious country properties the larger fishponds and artificial lakes would be even more suitable for fish stocks (these are mentioned in chapter five). Likewise bee-keeping has been discussed but we must not forget that one or more beehives could have been positioned somewhere within large gardens, and at times could even be found under the protection of a portico.

Dormice (*Glis glis*, the edible variety) were considered a delicacy and were also perhaps kept in peristyles. Varro records that many were fattened in *dolia*, in villas.[125] He continues with a description of these specially designed receptacles that match the large pottery vessel seen at the Boscoreale Museum. This complete example with lid, in terracotta, is approximately 60/70 mm high. Breathing holes had been punched through the exterior while the clay was still wet. The interior was furnished with a spiralling ledge that gave additional living space for the dormice housed within. Nuts would have been placed in the central void. Because the diet of these creatures includes wood a wooden hutch would have been useless. At least three dormouse pots have been discovered in gardens at Pompeii.[126] A dormouse enclosure, or *glirarium*, was needed to breed these small animals and they were considered a profitable sideline on an estate. So too was a *locus Cochleariis*, a moated enclosure used for breeding edible snails. Descriptions of both are provided[127] but they would leave little trace archaeologically. Pliny

A large terracotta pot for dormice that could be kept under the garden portico. There was a spiral ramp inside so that it could house a number of these little animals (Boscoreale Museum).

records that before 49 BC F. Lippinus was the first to construct ponds for keeping snails.[128] An ideal location was at the foot of a rocky outcrop where the area was shady and damp. Water could be brought in if needed and a small nozzle at the end could direct the water to splash against a stone to create a fine mist or spray to keep the locality cool and moist. A moat would prevent them escaping and the odd leaf or two could be thrown in to provide extra food. To find such a site would be a real challenge for any archaeologist.

Hares were sometimes kept as pets and several are depicted in the arms of a child. Hutches would have been provided for them in gardens and certainly were used when fattening them ready for the pot, but more often they would be contained in a compound somewhere on an estate. Varro states that there were three divisions of villa husbandry which could 'afford him both profit and pleasure'. These were '*ornithones, leporaria, piscinae*', aviaries, warrens and fishponds.[129] The *leporaria* was originally an enclosed hare warren; rabbits were discovered by the Romans in Spain but elsewhere they were not as prevalent as they are now. Later the reserves were enlarged to accommodate a range of wild or semi-wild animals. The animals were fed and watered and by all accounts were tamed to come when summoned by the blowing of a horn.[130] Drinking holes or pools were also provided.[131] Some estates incorporated large reserves. Varro mentions one in Gaul that is thought to have enclosed about four square miles.[132] At Welschbillig, near Trier, the ancient walls commonly referred to as the '*Langmauer*' encircles an area of approximately 220 km². This area has been interpreted as an imperial game reserve.[133] They provided enjoyment for owners who liked to hunt on their own land and the animals kept there would also provide an extra source of food.[134] Varro reports some of the entertainments on offer when visiting the estates of some of his wealthy friends. In one passage he reveals that Quintus Hortensius would entertain dinner guests in his game reserve, while a servant provided music that charmed and attracted the beasts to re-create the myth of Orpheus.[135]

Frescos depicting gardens occasionally include Orpheus and the animals or scenes of hunting either from a leporarium or its more exotic form, an eastern style *paradeisos*. A more conventional tableau of landscape or plants is usually found beneath or beside these scenes, giving an impression that they are part of a large country garden. Thus the painting is linked to the actual garden below.

The Romans aspired to be in tune with nature, wild or domesticated, and pleasure gardens large or small were very much a living part of the *domus* or *villa*. They seem to have had a need to include in their life some of the rich flora and fauna native to their region and planted these beside the choice imported varieties from further afield.

CHAPTER EIGHT

Roman Gardeners, Their Tools and Horticultural Techniques

In the early days, before and during the Early Republican era, the traditional home was a farm or rustic villa, and society was largely based on a peasant economy where the population needed to be self-sufficient on a smallholding. Therefore the whole family would have been involved in the practice of *agri-* and *horti*-culture, with much of the produce coming from the *hortus*, the humble kitchen garden. However, during the Late Republic, Rome became increasingly affluent and property owners in many regions were able to possess or hire servants/slaves to perform various tasks on their estates, including staff specially trained to work in garden areas.

GARDEN WORKFORCE

Small properties may have had only one or two servants/slaves to help in the garden but villas with larger areas to maintain would have required a considerable workforce. There are many references concerning these people and they are complemented by epigraphic evidence from a series of funerary inscriptions. These indicate that on large properties such as the *Horti Antoniani* or the *Horti Sallustiani* in Rome, the grounds would be administered by a *villicus* and *subvillicus*.[1] Staff under their control were generally named after the role they performed; therefore one who tended vegetables was called an *olitor*,[2] a name derived from *holeris* which means vegetables. There are three funerary inscriptions from Rome that record the names of Ariarathes, Horatius and Sergius, each of whom had been described as being a *holitor*, which is an alternative spelling.[3] An *arborator*[4] looked after trees, mostly in orchards, and would be responsible for trimming and grafting. A *vinitor*[5] cared for vine plants and performed all the specialized tasks in a vineyard. Vines were also grown in garden areas and of course were the main climbing plant used to shade a pergola; this can be seen in the House of Loreius Tiburtinus and others. Some of the trellises were quite extensive, therefore the quantity of grapes produced would have been sufficient to merit the employment of a *vinitor*. An *aquarius* would be required to water plants; this may have been a humble occupation but when Ovid was in exile he wrote saying that if he was allowed to return home he would not mind undertaking such work.[6] A mosaic in the Vatican Museum shows a man watering a plant but the vessel in his hand appears to be a wine cup, whereas a watering pot would perhaps be larger. This mosaic could represent an occasion where the plant was given a tonic or simply a religious libation to the earth; these facets will be discussed later. There does not appear to have been an all-embracing term for a gardener, although there are some references to a *hortulanus*,[7] but these are thought to be late (second century AD) and may refer to workers in market gardens as opposed to ornamental gardens.

A *topiarius* was originally employed to clip hedges, *nemora tonsilia*, and his art gave rise to our modern use of the word topiary. He was engaged to maintain pleasure gardens, distinct from orchards and vegetable plots. The term also appears when referring to a landscape gardener, someone who created *opus topiarium*. Pliny provides a date for such work when he ascribes the introduction of the art of topiary to Gaius Matius during the reign of Augustus.[8] *Topiarii* seem to have been held in some regard and comments found in the letters of Cicero reveal aspects of their work that produced admiration. In one letter Cicero praises his brother's workman for creating a rustic atmosphere by draping ivy over statues and porticos, so much so 'that I declare the Greek statues seem to be advertising their ivy'.[9] Another passage, this time in a letter by Pliny, shows that it was permissible for gardeners to clip their own names alongside that of their master in box hedges. During the Roman period such a display of skill was evidently appreciated and clearly met with approval.

There is a surprising number of surviving tombstones recording *topiarii*, and this again demonstrates that these men had a certain status as craftsmen. Many had been commemorated by their former colleagues or family. A number may have been freedmen, for a couple of inscriptions appear to have originally been placed on a communal tomb, and list several men and women who were probably members of a burial club or alternatively were former staff on an estate.[10] Several headstones record *topiarii* in areas outside Rome, such as Lucrio from the area around Naples, or Fortunati from near Como.[11] As Pliny the Younger had several villas in the region of Como one could easily speculate and wonder if Fortunati had worked in one of them. His commemorative stone had been set up jointly by his wife and his pupil, providing an instance of someone in apprenticeship. Another records the existence of a principal gardener – unfortunately this fragment does not give his

Horticultural tasks, details
from a mosaic rustic calendar,
Vienne. From left to right:
sowing seed, gathering fruit,
grafting trees, taking out a
hurdle of manure to fertilize
the *hortus* or field.

name – but of the many fragments found elsewhere one perhaps stands
out, for he was appropriately named Florus.[12]

The various specialist gardeners mentioned above are at times
depicted in frescos and mosaics of genre or rural scenes. Some of the
scenes relate to the seasonal tasks to be performed on an estate and are
displayed in the form of a rustic calendar. Many could be considered as
agricultural in content but some of these tasks equally pertain to
horticulture. Examples are shown here such as sowing seed in a *hortus*,
hoeing, pruning or grafting trees, gathering fruit and transporting
manure to the garden/fields. Those that could be more specific to a
pleasure garden show staff picking flowers or tending potted plants. An
example from Carthage, which is just a small detail of a large mosaic,
portrays a man referred to as 'the lily grower'.[13]

GARDENING TOOLS AND EQUIPMENT

Cato lists a number of agricultural tools which are collectively called
ferramenta; again some of these would also have been used within the *hortus*.
Falces silvaticas were sharp tools like billhooks with a curved blade that
could cut down branches of trees. The *arborarias* was a smaller version used
when pruning bushes and trees. *Falculas viniaticas* were the knives used by
the vine dresser but similar ones would also have been used when making
cuttings, grafts or budding eyes of garden plants. *Ferreas* were metal forks.
The majority of these appear to have been furnished with three prongs, but
versions with only two are known and could be the '*bicorni*' mentioned by
Columella and Palladius.[14] The spade (*pala*) was sometimes of metal but
the vast majority were made of wood, *palas ligneas*. To strengthen the tip of
the spade that would get the most wear, and to get a good cutting blade, a
metal shoe was fitted on the lower half of the shovel. This iron fitting
would undoubtedly have prolonged its life, and was considerably less
expensive than a spade completely made of iron. This type of spade was
used in the Middle Ages and later and a number of manuscripts show
them in use; a good example is illustrated in a fifteenth-century copy of
Pliny the Elder's *Historia Naturalis*. Many of these, however, depict a spade

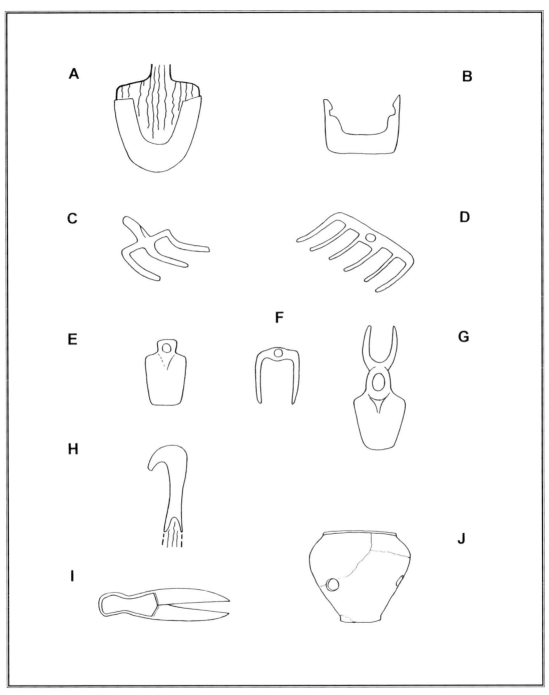

A selection of horticultural tools and equipment (not to scale).

A: *Palas ligneas*, a wooden spade, shown here with a curved iron shoe.

B: *Palas*, iron spade shoe.

C: *Ferrea*, iron 3-pronged fork.

D: *Rastrum*, 6-pronged rake.

E: *Sarculum*, hoe.

F: *Bidens*, 2-pronged hoe.

G: *Ascia-rastrum*, double-headed hoe.

H: *Falx arboraria*, pruning-hook.

I: *Forfex*, shears.

J: Earthenware flowerpot, from Fishbourne.

with a hand grip which was not usually fitted to those of Roman date. There are few illustrations of Roman iron-tipped spades or the more expensive type with a solid metal blade, but a weathered stone relief from Arlon, Belgium, reveals that they would appear similar to those in use in many parts of Europe today. Rakes were *rastros quadridentes* and as Cato implies were usually four-toothed; however rakes with more tines have been uncovered. *Crates stercorias* were hurdles on which manure was carried out to the *hortus* or field, *sirpiam stercorias* were manure baskets, and *quala sataria vel alveos* were the useful baskets or troughs used when planting out seedlings. A *situlum aquarium* was a bucket used to carry water for plants and a *nassiternam* was a watering pot. Unfortunately there is only one example of a watering pot known, from Arles, and there are some doubts as to its authenticity. Part of the pot would have been provided with holes and fragments were found but elsewhere these are usually attributed to being part of a cheese press. Once again, if we take a close look at a version depicted in a medieval miniature painting, we may find clues as to its form. This particular pot was held aloft by the neck and water rained down on to plants from numerous holes in the bulbous base. The *aquarius* would need to carry a bucket of water up to the plant bed and immerse the water pot into it; when full of water it could then be held directly over a plant. This would be especially useful for watering seedlings which require gentle treatment and could be irretrievably battered down if the contents of the bucket were poured all at once.

Various passages in Varro provide further evidence of the use of a larger selection of garden tools. To Cato's list we can add the *sarculum*, which had a long handle and either a pointed or straight-edged blade. This tool was the equivalent of a modern Dutch hoe or mattock. Different types of tools for weeding and loosening the soil are mentioned, including the *bidens*, which had two tines, and the *ascia-rastrum*, a dual-purpose tool that incorporated two heads (a *sarculum* and a *bidens*). Literary sources do not mention the tool used by *topiarii* to clip hedges but hand-held shears of the same type as those used to clip sheep's wool may have also served that purpose. What is immediately noticeable in the many illustrations of horticulturists at work, and from the range illustrated here, is that many of the implements believed to have been used in gardens appear similar to those of recent times – that is before mechanization – and this above all demonstrates quite clearly the effectiveness of their design; once introduced the basic form was passed on down through the generations of people working on the land.

Horticultural worker using a *bidens*, detail of a mosaic from Istanbul.

A number of these tools have been found on Roman sites in Britain and Gaul but few have specifically been noted in garden contexts; however at Frocester an iron shoe belonging to a wooden spade was found in one of the plant beds.[15] An *ascia-rastrum* and other tools were uncovered within the Roman towns of Venta Silurum (Caerwent) and Calleva Atrebatum (Silchester), evidence that could suggest they had been used in gardens in those towns but alternatively they may have just been stored there. In contrast in Campania a number of tools have been found in gardens, a *sarculum* in the Garden of Hercules, for example. Also, in the large internal garden at Oplontis, the excavators discovered 'a pointed hoe, a six-pronged rake and a pruning hook'.[16]

Planting troughs and baskets for gathering fruit or flowers were generally of wickerwork and making them was a task usually reserved for inclement days in the winter. The *arborator* would cut a plentiful supply of osiers and under the shade of a portico staff would be roped in to make panniers, troughs and baskets. Numerous mosaics and frescos depict these utilitarian objects. There were tall slim versions and varieties that are low and wide. Many are shown in scenes of people gathering fruit or flowers, while others are depicted separately and are filled with fruit freshly picked. Unfortunately wicker does not survive archaeologically.

Pottery on the other hand is very durable. It is easily broken but the fragments can be retrieved during archaeological excavations and if enough pieces are found the pot can be reconstructed. In some gardens, such as at the Roman Palace at Fishbourne, the excavators have found fragments of terracotta flowerpots. When pieced together the one complete pot appeared to be bulbous in shape and was provided with several round drainage holes in the belly and base. At Eccles ten pots with triangular holes have come to light.[17] Several have been excavated from within ancient gardens in Rome, Campania and at the Palace of King Herod in Israel: these show a range of sizes and a number of pierced holes for drainage. The pots vary in height from 12 to 18 cm, have three or four holes in the side and one below.[18] Roman and Greek flowerpots were primarily made for insertion in the ground and the inclusion of holes in the side of vessels may have, as Pliny implies, allowed the enclosed plant to breathe.[19] It is more probable that because of the quick root growth one sees in warm climates the holes would not constrict the roots to such an extent as would a pot with solid walls. Holes were usually round and appear to have been made while the clay was still wet.

At Oplontis, Hadrian's Villa at Tivoli, and the *Horti Adonaea* in Rome, the excavators also found broken amphorae that had been utilized as flowerpots.[20] The amphorae had been cut in half and turned upside down, with the open neck serving as a drain hole. Evidence shows that in the *Horti Adonaea* the 'normal' type of flowerpots found were used in the Julio-Claudian phase, whereas in the Flavian/Severan period reused amphorae were employed.[21] This practice would help in some way to diminish the growing pile of empty vessels if they could not be reused for food or liquid storage purposes. The use of both types of flowerpot dates at least from the Classical period in Greece. Adonis gardens planted in broken amphorae were pictured in the Karlsrühe Greek vase painting, and thick-walled flowerpots containing shrubs were placed in plant pits around the Hephaistion in Athens. However, these had no side holes.[22]

Large plant pots would have been used to grow shrubs and trees but are rarely identified. Nevertheless at Herculaneum a pair of large terracotta tubs were found by the entrance to the hanging garden at the House of the Stags but unfortunately we do not know what they contained. A literary reference provided by Palladius implies that planting pomegranate trees in pots would make them more fruitful.[23] Presumably the roots became pot-bound and this promoted flowering, leading to fruiting.

HORTICULTURAL TECHNIQUES

The greatest proportion of our evidence in this field has been gleaned from literary sources. These say that plants were increased in various ways. Seeds were saved to sow the following year and cuttings could be taken. Pliny mentions that various herbs were propagated by cuttings and that violets were usually increased successfully in this way.[24] Also slips with a heel were taken from the mother plant and planted in special nursery beds where extra care could be lavished on them. A good description of these beds and their culture is found in Cato.[25] The Romans noted that it was wise to plant cuttings in soil similar to that of its mother plant.[26] If the soil was similar there was a greater chance that the cuttings would be quicker to root. When the cutting had grown sufficiently the slips were marked with 'ochre or anything else you please'; alternatively notches were cut into the bark marking points of the compass.[27] Either of these measures would ensure that when the slips were planted they could be turned to face the same direction to which they had been accustomed; a practice designed to prevent the young plants being set back by winds coming from a different direction.

The Romans also made layered cuttings by burying the tip of a shoot or by air-layering. In some cases this involved feeding a selected branch into or through a flowerpot. Both Cato and Pliny describe all three processes.[28] The agronomists also say that a basket could be used to layer plants in the ground as an alternative to a pot. Soil was packed around the shoot and the pot or basket was then buried. When air-layering, however, the pot was left suspended on the tree until the cutting had taken root. After two years the layered cutting would have made sufficient root and was severed from its mother. The plant, still in its pot, was then planted into its new position. Nearly all the flowerpots discovered were broken but the Romans may have done this immediately before planting into the ground so as not to retard the plant's root growth, or the roots may have grown and broken the pot themselves. The latter is believed to have been the case in the pool garden at Oplontis, and was identified as a result of air-layering. The former method was used in the south garden where two rows of citron/lemon trees were planted, each in line with columns of the portico.[29]

Citrons are referred to by Pliny as a Median apple[30] and as such would have originated in the Middle East. These were valued for their medicinal properties, and may have been the prized golden apples of the Hesperides. They are thought to be the precursor of lemons. Citrons are larger than lemons, less acid, but have a thick uneven rind. They feature in several mosaics and their large knobbly appearance is quite distinctive. The citron was a new introduction that took time to acclimatize in Italy. If protected by being against a portico as at Oplontis, netting and reeds could be drawn across to protect the trees, enabling them to withstand the ravages of winter.[31] Some translations of Palladius have incorrectly interpreted the Latin word citron as an orange[32] but this fruit had not been discovered at that time and was only introduced to the West after the Arab conquests.

Horticultural workman carrying a hoe (*bidens*), detail from a calendar mosaic (February), Palestine.

Early crops could be protected in a similar way but the cover was laid horizontally, not vertically as was the case for tender trees. Columella describes his *modus operandi*: 'low trellises are constructed with reeds, and rods are thrown in and straw on top of the rods, and thus the plants are protected from frosts.'[33] Produce of all sorts could be forced into growth early, and for example to bring forward the fruiting or flowering of rose bushes or fruit trees they would pour hot water into a trench around the plant.[34] Another method was to use a *specularium*, a rather clever invention that was a miniature greenhouse on wheels. This machine was fitted with panels of transparent stone and could be wheeled around to follow the course of the sun. Columella records that they were used to provide early cucumbers for the Emperor Tiberius and Seneca mentions their use to force early blooms of lilies; we even hear from Martial that they protected tender fruiting trees from Cilicia.[35] The last example however refers to *specularia* 'facing the wintry south winds' and so to make sure that the trees 'may not grow wan and dread the winter' a shelter of some kind was constructed, which could imply that they were housed in some form of conservatory. If you wanted to retard a crop the same machine could still be employed by wheeling the crop around so that it would be in constant shade. It was noted that plants such as southernwood, which has soft feathery grey leaves, 'were chilly'[36] and that they needed to be placed in the sun, which is current practice today, for many grey-leafed plants are classed as being more tender than green varieties.

Trees and shrubs were improved by pruning out unwanted or less productive branches, and strains of good fruiting trees were grafted on to others. The Romans definitely believed that 'a tree which is engrafted is more fruitful than one which is not'.[37] Both Cato and Columella describe the techniques used in grafting and budding and the latter held the view that 'Any kind of scion can be grafted on any tree if it is not dissimilar in respect of bark'.[38] We learn from Pliny of experiments in producing different flavours when grafting plums on to apples or almonds on to plums.[39] On the other hand Calpurnius Siculus claims that crosses were made between pears and apples, and peaches and plums.[40] As these all belong to the *Rosaceae* family a successful graft might conceivably be possible. Sources also relate how peaches turn red if grafted on to a plane tree or similarly apples grafted on to planes produce fruit with pink flesh;[41] it was noted however that in the process the flavour had become impaired. Trees with several different fruiting branches were invented; some would have held a novelty value, as today, for if space is limited we can resort to a so-called 'Family tree' which often has two or three varieties grafted on to the one trunk. Pliny mentions a famous one at Tivoli that had 'nuts on one branch, berries on another, while in other places hung grapes, pears, figs, pomegranates and various sorts of apples'. With so many grafts it is quite understandable that 'the tree did not live long'.[42]

Romans searched far and wide to find new or better varieties and a programme of acclimatization was undertaken. Among the garden plants Pliny records the successful introduction of laurel to Corsica.[43] An indication of the extent of this programme is the number of fruits which have as their Latin name some record of their origin: the pomegranate commonly referred to as the Punic apple came from around Carthage; the apricot which was considered a variety of plum was called *armeniaca* and was introduced from Armenia; the damson or *damascena* from Damascus in Syria; and the peach or *persica* from Persia, although another variety was said to have come from Gaul. Various apples with different qualities were brought to Rome: there was one called 'the round apple' from Epirus in western Greece, a 'Syrian red', and the 'eunuch-apple of the Belgians is named from its having no pips'.[44]

New improved strains of fruit were also being produced locally. We hear of new varieties of apple or pear that were named by the owner of a particular estate where it was first produced, such as the Scaudian apple or Dolabellian pear, varieties that were later included in lists of the best fruit trees to plant in orchards.[45] Pliny reveals that such experiments were not confined to the aristocracy and he makes a point of mentioning that freedmen were also involved in the search for new strains. This service to Rome was highly regarded and a glance at the names of several prominent Romans indicates the extent of their families' involvement in horticulture/agriculture in the past. The Romans would change their own names at times to reflect a great deed such as a military victory, as in the case of Scipio Africanus, but also after a significant contribution to society. Therefore we have Stolon whose ancestor had invented a new process of pruning. *Stolon*, if the interpretation is correct, was the name for an unwanted shoot or sucker, the removal of which would promote better growth. There were also families with the name Piso, Fabius, Lentulus and Cicero, whose names derived from the cultivation of, respectively, the pea, bean, lentil and chick pea.[46]

Root pruning was performed and is recorded as an operation undertaken by *topiarii* to keep plane trees dwarfed.[47] Also the flowering of roses is reported as benefiting from regular pruning and 'burning'.[48] No method of burning is given but perhaps the growth of bushes that were close to wild varieties might have been sufficiently strong to survive such treatment. Sources suggest that roses were often grown in a separate bed and if the bushes were subject to a controlled burning, as we sometimes set light to areas of heather moor, the regrowth would perhaps reappear with new vigour. Some techniques appear somewhat brutal — for instance unproductive fruit trees were forced into fruiting by driving a stake into their roots.[49] A similar method was said to produce cherries without stones.[50] This sounds more like inflicting a punishment on the trees concerned but could have had the effect of root pruning which would in fact promote flowering.

At times the Romans espalier-trained fruit trees. Supporting evidence has been found at places such as Fishbourne, where trees would have been trained to grow against a row of posts at one side of the garden, and in the House of Julius Polybius at Pompeii a series of nails had been hammered into a garden wall so that branches could be tied up to it.[51] It would have been interesting to see whether the pattern of these nails revealed if the branches were trained in a fan or horizontally but the excavators have not disclosed these details. In most other cases the trees or bushes would be seen in plantations, orchards and vineyards and were planted in a *quincunx* pattern rather than the straight rows of the Greeks.[52] This formation was said to have a diagonal line of sight between trees which would imply that each row was staggered. This would ensure more root space per plant and make better use of the land.

Varro says that a 'sunny ground should be chosen for planting violets and laying out gardens as these flourish in the sun'.[53] However shady positions were thought suitable for asparagus beds. Roman plant beds are described by Pliny as having raised borders,[54] and the agriculturists' comments suggest that flower beds were treated in a similar manner to those containing vegetables. Columella advises to make these '10 feet wide and 50 feet long, to allow water to be supplied by way of the footpaths and to provide a means of access on both sides for the

Plants grown in beds with raised edges, as described by Pliny the Elder. A scene often encountered today in Mediterranean regions, in this case at Istanbul.

weeders'.[55] This would ensure that weeds could be reached without treading on plants. The depth of soil varied per plant bed: 4 ft was recommended for trees, 3 ft for roses and 1 ft for violets.[56] If the soil tended to be too damp Pliny recommends that you dig a planting hole to a depth of 4 ft so that brushwood, which would help to drain and lighten the soil, was placed at the bottom of the pit and the depth of soil would then be adjusted to about 3 ft 4 in.[57] Individual plants not in a bed were often encircled by a ring of raised soil, again to ensure that precious water would be directed straight to the plant and would not be wasted by running off elsewhere. This practice, which is still seen in areas with a dry climate around the Mediterranean, such as in modern Campania, Tunisia and Turkey, could also allow the plants to obtain moisture from dew collecting overnight in the trench encircling the plant.[58] Any source of moisture was sought and where possible all sorts of measures were employed to collect it.

Soil was improved in a number of ways, one being by the application of manure, and the merits of that obtained from different animals are discussed by Columella. Fertilizers such as ash and cinders were also added, and kitchen waste which could be made to incorporate bramble leaves and straw. Another method was to use a crop of lupins or vetch as a 'green manure'.[59] If the soil contained too much gravel it could be improved by applying clay, or vice versa.[60] Better drainage could also be achieved by planting a layer of potsherds or round stones at the bottom of planting holes,[61] a tell-tale feature that could be noticed on excavation. Archaeological evidence of plant beds and irrigation channels have been found at Pompeii. In the Garden of Hercules, which is believed to have been a commercial flower and/or vegetable garden, the cistern was not large enough to cater for all the family and the great number of plants in dry weather, so an elaborate system was devised to make the maximum use of additional water that had to be brought to site.[62] Channels were laid to reach each bed in turn. The natural gradient of the land was used to advantage, and large terracotta dolia sunk into the ground at each turn would slow the pace of the water and facilitate a change of direction for the life-giving supply. Remaining water passed through a hole in the wall to the next garden, lower down.

Recent excavations have also revealed that the plant beds in the Piazza d'Oro at Hadrian's Villa at Tivoli incorporated an ingenious system of irrigation built into the design of the ornamental garden.[63] This garden had a thin covering of soil so a network of planting holes and trenches had been excavated into the underlying rock. Water from the *nymphaea* nearby was directed into irrigation ducts and by the operation of sluice gates allowed to flow into the trenches; the plants could then be watered by capillary action. Remarkably the water then passed through a series of tubes under the long shallow *euripus* water feature in the centre of the garden and continued to irrigate the other side. This watering system is believed to have been labour-saving and as evenings are the traditional time to water a garden,[64] the reduction in

Grafted trees, a detail from the large mosaic at Mount Nebo in Jordan.

staff would save distracting the emperor and his guests when dining, in what was one of the prime banqueting areas of the villa.

Some gardening techniques can be seen in a number of frescos and mosaics. Many show trees that have few branches at a low level. This was partly because the leaves of many trees were cut to provide fodder for a variety of animals and were therefore pruned quite heavily but also because a browsing animal would reach up to help itself. This is actually shown in a few mosaics. A particularly interesting sixth-century example from Mount Nebo in Jordan shows a variety of fruit trees. This was a popular theme in Early Christian art and the most common and most easily recognizable fruits are apples, pears, pomegranates, citron and date palm. This particular mosaic includes what appears to be a row of grafted trees. The thick trunk of each tree bends slightly to the right and appears to have been cut off after a number of shoots or grafts had taken.

A couple of frescos illustrate how gardeners used stakes to protect, support or train a plant. One located in the dado zone of the peristyle wall at the House of the Vettii shows that a reed had been used to train an ivy plant to grow into the shape of a mound. The other, which is found in the beautiful series of frescos from the garden *diaeta* at the House of the Wedding of Alexander, displays a delicate pink rose deftly tied with string to a supporting reed. Palladius records that a split reed could keep a rose stem straight and the flower fresh.[65] The two halves would have to be held in position around the rose stem and unless the growth was very weak this would seem a little pointless, unless he is actually referring to flowers that have been cut and are to be transported.

Vines and gourds were allowed to grow over trellis-work to make arbours. Many frescos depict these and a mosaic at Aquileia shows the Early Christian scene of Jonah sitting or reclining under a trellis with gourds hanging down. Gourds come in all shapes and sizes and there seems to have been a great variety. Two are held aloft in a mosaic from Tegea depicting the month of August: both have broad stripes and one is long while the other is quite round. Some would have been dried and used as a container as an alternative to being eaten — in the case of the latter the long thin ones were considered more wholesome. There are also a number of mosaics that illustrate *xenia*, or guest gifts, and these are interesting for the collection of food items that are shown; there are many different types of fruit and vegetables. Some of these are placed in

August sees the ripening of gourds, detail of a calendar mosaic, Tegea.

Mosaic from the Vatican Museum, showing a plant being given a reviving drink of wine or water.

baskets, others are shown singly and among these are what appear to be long marrows stuffed to overflowing but two straps save their contents from spilling. Sources mention how gourds, melons and other forms of *cucumis* could be either grown on the ground or supported and allowed to climb. Even the cucumber was encouraged to climb and give shade.[66] The flowers of this plant are recorded as being placed into a shaped sheath or binding made of plaited wicker or knotted grass to produce fruit 'in the shape of man or beast'.[67] Apparently those shaped like a snake were the most popular.[68] Artifice and novelty are usually the most noteworthy but indirectly such references do demonstrate the advances in technological skills made by Roman horticulturists.

Due care and attention was given to the well-being of plants, and it is interesting to note that olive or wine lees were considered a tonic for ailing trees.[69] The minerals that these substances contain would in fact be beneficial to plants. The flamboyant lifestyle of some aristocrats like Quintus Hortensius, however, led to many criticisms. One example decried his conduct in leaving the senate early in order to give his plane trees their customary tipple. Such extravagances were naturally censured as an affectation that was turning 'even trees to be wine bibbers!'[70] This scene, or one similar, may be a more correct interpretation for the small mosaic from the Vatican; the man is still wearing his chaplet and has perhaps just returned from a feast, and steadily pours out the dregs of liquid from his upturned wine cup.

The control of garden pests and diseases was a problem and a number of 'organic' remedies are discussed. Several plants could be protected by sowing another in close proximity, so that bitter vetch would protect turnips, or chick peas could keep caterpillars away from cabbages.[71] Compounds or liquids containing the unsalted lees of olives or soot, and/or the juice of wormwood, horehound or houseleek were used.[72] The latter appears to have been the most effective plant for killing or deterring pests, and seeds could also be pre-soaked in this juice to thwart rodents from eating them once planted. In addition, heliotrope was recommended if plants were attacked by ants.[73] These potent plants were very useful additions to the garden. To eradicate insect pests such as aphids and greenfly a continual vigilance was needed, but because labour was cheap landowners could employ sufficient gardeners to make these daily inspections possible and they would be able to clear away all that appeared. However at certain times infestations of caterpillars or 'ground fleas' (perhaps thrips, leaf hoppers or aphids), and ground worms (possibly eelworm or carrot fly larvae) occurred. Therefore if all else failed it appears that ancient rustic rites were resorted to.[74] A skull of a female horse or the shell of a land crab was fixed on a post in the garden.[75] More improbable was the recourse involving a menstruating young girl who was requested to walk barefoot (and with hair loose) three times around plant beds and garden hedges.[76]

In the case of mildew and rust these were prevented by sacrifice to *Robigius* (god of rust).[77] During the festival of the *Robigalia*, held on 25 April, the rites demand the sacrifice of a rust or dun-coloured dog.[78] The presumed outcome was probably that like would cure like, the rust-coloured fur countering the appearance of that colour on the crop. A blight such as rust or mildew has the potential to damage or devastate the year's harvest, and taken in this light it would seem necessary to propitiate the god concerned. Rust is best avoided by strict crop rotation and this was also noted as a way to improve the fertility of the soil.[79] The other remedy would be to leave the land fallow for a time. This is more difficult to do in gardens where every part is used.

Columella and others provide a month-by-month calendar of work, detailing such things as the times to dig beds, sow seed, take cuttings, graft or replant. Most of the work was aimed to coincide with the change in weather at the spring or autumn equinoxes that are a feature of the Mediterranean climate. For instance, plant beds were made ready just before the autumn equinox – the hot dry weather was prone to change suddenly and heavy rain storms would make the conditions on the land just right for planting. The autumn, winter and spring were the times of plenty. With the summer fruit stored and the grape harvest gathered in, it was a time when most of the kitchen garden plants were grown. Another example is an entry saying that the kitchen garden and rose beds needed attention at the time of the spring equinox.[80]

The agriculturists also include some advice for colder climates in upland regions and they point out that various tasks needed to be delayed by a month, as would be the case in more northerly latitudes. The manuals were essentially practical and reflect the mixture of accumulated wisdom or science of horticulture that had developed under the Roman aegis, but at times they also reveal the underlying ancient lore of superstitious magic that was still prevalent at that time. However the following quotation by Columella remains valid and to me could also apply to Roman horticulturists.

Surely these examples remind us that Italy is most responsive to care bestowed by mankind, in that she has learned to produce the fruits of almost the entire world when her husbandmen have applied themselves to the task.[81]

The month of December, detail from a calendar mosaic, Palestine. A representation of work for that month. A woman goes out to hoe the vegetable garden or *hortus* with a *bidens* over her shoulder.

CHAPTER NINE

Non-Residential Gardens

Most people think of gardens in a domestic context but they also existed in the public sphere. Gardens played such a useful and important role that they were often incorporated into the design of buildings that served the community and its visitors. In many cases these areas of greenery would appear similar to their domestic counterparts but we often find that the building and garden would have been decorated to a higher standard by rich patrons who were keen to demonstrate their philanthropy and civic pride. In such places statuary (often with dedicatory inscriptions) may be of a more monumental nature, and might include figures of emperors.

This was also the case in corporate or fraternal buildings such as in the Schola of Trajan at Ostia, which belonged to the Shipbuilders' Corporation. Here the excavators found a large statue of the Emperor Trajan, hence the modern name for that building. At Ostia members of several private clubs and guilds, the *collegiae* or *scholae*, appear to have owned their own premises in common. Inside these we might find one or more communal dining halls where meals or banquets were served after meetings or were used for entertaining important guests. In many cases these imposing rooms opened on to a garden, such as at the Schola of Trajan, where the *triclinium* overlooked a long decorative water basin. At the House of the Triclinia, which is thought to be the guild house of a group of builders, the provision of communal dining rooms is quite clear. One room is larger than the rest and was given prominence at the head of the garden, while the ten other rooms on ground level are arranged along the sides; all open on to the peristyle garden in the centre. Five of these rooms still contain masonry dining couches.

Visitors to a town could be catered for in a *hospitium*, an inn, or a *mansio*. These are often found at the edge of a town and are usually situated on main routes so that travellers could rest and bathe before doing business in town. As always some were better than others; the more luxurious would have been provided with baths and rooms overlooking a pleasant garden. A number have been discovered in the provinces, such as at Caister-by-Yarmouth and at Godmanchester. *Mansios* were also specifically sited on trunk roads between towns to provide shelter for long-distance travellers, who could then rest overnight in comfortable surroundings, as found at Wall on Watling Street in Britain. The garden of this wayside inn was furnished by a demi-lune water basin (see chapter four).

GARDENS IN ASSOCIATION WITH DINING ESTABLISHMENTS

Cauponae, tabernae and inns that made provision for alfresco dining used these facilities as an added attraction, just as modern ones make use of an attached beer garden. Virgil reveals in the words of the Syrian Copa, a celebrated innkeeper, just how a garden in these establishments could be such an attraction. Staff of this inn would stand outside and invite potential clients through their door to sample their wares. 'There are garden nooks and arbours, mixing-cups, roses, flutes, lyres, and cool bowers with shady canes. . . . Come; rest here thy wearied frame beneath the shade of vines.'[1] Archaeological evidence has largely confirmed these inviting possibilities. You would be able to dine in the open air yet be shaded from the sun by a vine-covered pergola. Beneath this framework of greenery the owners of the establishment would have placed benches or couches for guests to dine from while being seated or reclining. In a *taberna* at Ostia permanent masonry benches were provided along one wall of the small garden in the middle of which a fountain played. The marble outer splash basin marking its location is still *in situ*. In a number of establishments in Campania we find both benches and masonry couches or *triclinia*; all of these would have been covered by cushions and drapery for added comfort.

MARKET GARDENS

A *hortus*, or more specifically *hortuli*, were terms that encompassed land used for market gardening. According to Cicero and Verro these establishments were to be found on the outskirts of cities where they would be close to a ready market. The short transportation distances would ensure that produce remained fresh and so would fetch a better price. Fruit, vegetables and flowers were grown in such districts; Cato specifies flowers used to make garlands, while Varro identifies two of these – violets and roses.[2]

In Pompeii several commercial gardens were discovered within the walls of the city. These, however, were mostly located to the south-east where housing was less dense. Such areas reserved for food or flower production in towns could also prove useful if there happened to be a siege, for any supplies that could be saved for emergencies would then prove very valuable.

A great deal of information derives from the large number of leases written on papyrus in Egypt where the dry atmosphere has aided their preservation. Several apply to land referred to as a garden but because they were used for commercial purposes the land was liable for taxation. The details of the conditions of lease are interesting. Some indicate a degree of specialization, such as a cucumber, narcissus or rose garden.[3] The level of tax for such areas varies of course but a lease of AD 141 indicates that an area devoted to commercially grown narcissi was valued at 60 drachmas. An apparently larger garden growing cucumbers, gourds and melons was valued at 300 drachmas per year. However this lease also contained a clause for a certain quantity of the produce to be delivered to the lessor on a daily basis.

A short letter written on papyrus from Oxyrhychus[4] indicates the scale of the internal market for flowers in Egypt. A lady named Dionysia wrote to a commercial grower asking for a supply of 2,000 narcissi and perhaps the same number of roses for her son's wedding. The reply to her request revealed that the grower could supply over 4,000 narcissi but only 1,000 roses could be found at that time. Presumably the season for roses had just begun, although some authors claim that roses could grow all year round in Egypt. In this instance it appears that demand may have outstripped supply. This letter does indicate, however, that large areas were under flower cultivation.

FUNERARY GARDENS

Tomb monuments were usually constructed at the side of the roads leading out of the city, where it was hoped that they would attract the gaze and thoughts of passers-by. Such gardens were almost always sited outside city walls for burials (both of cremation and inhumation) in general were not allowed within a town because of the risk of possible infections. Not all tombs were large enough to merit the provision of a garden area but in some cases where the owner had intended the tomb to resemble a house, one can appreciate a desire to include a garden area as well. Therefore we do find that a few tombs are sited within their own individual gardens. This was a particularly pleasant concept and a number of inscriptions associated with these tombs show that their owners went to great lengths to retain a link with their friends and heirs. *Cepotaphia*, as they were called, were the most developed form of funerary monument and often included a sizeable plot of land. This type was designed to provide enough produce from the land enclosed around the monument to sustain the shade of a departed person. Banqueting facilities were often included into its design for the benefit of family and friends when commemorating the deceased, and the insertion of a libation pipe or vessel into the grave would ensure that liquids such as wine could be poured down allowing the departed one to partake in the feast, ensuring that the past would still have a link to the present. A number of ancient inscriptions once attached to a funerary monument record that vineyards were sometimes planted specifically to provide wine for libations;[5] some people stipulated that profits from the sale of produce from their own funerary garden should be used for specific purposes or special occasions, for instance, 'from whose yield my survivors may offer roses to me on my birthday forever'.[6]

The fictitious parvenu freedman Trimalchio, while entertaining guests at a lavish banquet, discussed plans for his own funerary monument which included a garden. What he intended was a plot containing fruit trees and vines. He also reveals the plausible extent of such a *cepotaphia*, which may be typical of a number of others: 'a hundred feet facing the road and two hundred back into the field.'[7] This would be more than sufficient to provide offerings and any surplus produce could usefully provide an income for the heirs.

There are a number of leases preserved in Egypt that also relate to a funerary garden surrounding a tomb.[8] An inscription on marble concerning the funerary garden of Mousa[9] relates how this particular garden was leased and then illegally sold, later to be returned to the heirs. The laws governing such things were fairly complex and the lengthy procedures involved indicate that the land concerned was of considerable extent, sufficient to be profitable.

Cicero, after the untimely death of his daughter Tullia, recounts the difficulties involved in finding a suitable *hortus* near Rome where he could construct her funerary monument. He required a position outside the city limits, in a fashionable district to suit his station in life and her honour, but at an affordable price. Cicero[10] mentions that he had found an ideal garden belonging to Cotta, a prominent Roman, but following difficulties with this sale others were considered – such as the *Horti Scapulae*[11] – but these later proved unwise to buy when he realized that he would be bidding against Caesar. He then resolved to find a suitable site on his own land where on reflection he would be able to visit the grave monument more frequently.

Archaeological evidence of a small funerary garden was found at Scafati.[12] Here the partially excavated enclosure measured 8 m by more than 20.5 m. As six large tree roots were discovered, Jashemski believes that the area under the shade of those trees would have been 'planted with fragrant flowers'. An indication of the most favoured plants that may be found in funerary gardens is found in the *Culex*, a satirical poem to a dead gnat:

Here are to grow acanthus and the blushing rose with crimson bloom, and violets of every kind. Here are spartan myrtle and hyacinth, and here saffron . . . soaring laurel . . . oleander and lilies . . . rosemary and the Sabine plant . . . marigold, and glistening ivy . . . amaranth . . . and ever-flowering laurestine . . .[13]

Mausoleum of Augustus and its associated walks (as reconstructed in the Model of Imperial Rome in the Museo della Civiltà Romana).

How these plants were grown or displayed in the garden is difficult to ascertain but two valuable maps of funerary gardens survive, for they were engraved on marble. One in Perugia Museum[14] outlines a range of buildings on the plot that may be a complex for ritual funerary banquets, and also perhaps accommodation for the slaves and equipment to maintain the funerary garden. The second, found at the necropolis on Via Labicana near Rome,[15] provides a plan locating the monument to one side and a series of lines and rows of dots that would appear to indicate pathways, plant beds and rows of trees or vines.

The most famous funerary garden was the *silvae et ambulationes*, the woods and walks, associated with the mausoleum of Augustus at Rome. This large circular monument, like ancient Etruscan tumuli, was surmounted by a mound of earth. Ancient sources[16] say that a grove of evergreen trees was planted above the tomb and a bronze statue of the Emperor crowned the summit. Suetonius[17] mentions that the surrounding area was left open to the public as a park. The reconstruction drawing shown here, as interpreted in the model of Rome, indicates the possible appearance of this monument built in the area of the *Campus Martius*.

PUBLIC PARKS

From time immemorial the public had access to areas considered as sacred woodland, a *nemus* or *lucus*, inhabited by spirits such as a *numen*.

As time went by many of these areas were eaten into with buildings as land was valuable. As the density of housing increased green areas within cities were correspondingly more important, therefore the creation of parks expressly for the use of the public was seen as a humane act of beneficence to the populace, as well as being good propaganda for the donor. Archaeological evidence for parks is extremely rare but in some instances boundary *cippi*, or stone pillars, record an edge of the area in question. Fortunately, some details survive in ancient literature relating to Rome. The first public park was that of Pompey the Great (this example will be discussed later). Not to be outdone, Caesar made provision in his will to open his gardens at Trastevere to the public.[18] Later Augustus planted the *Nemus Caesarum* by the Naumachia,[19] as well as the *silvae et ambulationes* around his own mausoleum.[20] Agrippa also willed his *thermes*, a large bathing complex with attached gardens, to the public;[21] this was later called the *Campus Agrippae*. Martial reveals that these were much frequented; and Ovid when in exile recalled their beauty with nostalgia; he tried in his mind's eye to visualize the spectacle once more – the greensward of the *Campus* with its beautiful gardens ('*pulchros spectantis in hortos*'), with the *stagnum* and *euripi* watered by the Virgo.[22]

The *stagnum* or artificial lake within this park was a location for Nero's infamous night revels, mentioned by Tacitus;[23] both this and a long water basin, the *euripus*, were fed by the *Aqua Virgo* (mentioned in chapter four). Strabo[24] places a fine statue of a lion, plundered from Lampsacus, between these two water features. There was also a *nemus*, a wood, which may have been the grove of plane trees adorned with animal statuary recorded by Martial.[25]

To establish further the possible appearance of these parks, we would need to include paths and perhaps shrubberies and flower beds, also areas covered by grass. A number of sources mention sitting upon flower-strewn grass,[26] and the climate would allow for the possibility of a greensward, although in high summer it would have appeared yellow. Martial[27] indicates that seats were included in such areas. Although parks contained statuary and features of an appropriate monumental nature, they could in many cases be said to resemble large domestic gardens, and some had originally been private gardens before being opened to the public.

PUBLIC PORTICO GARDENS

These soon became the favoured haunt of many Romans and were in reality an enclosed public park. They could in some ways be compared with the garden areas found within older residential squares of London. There were a large number of portico gardens in Rome. Fortunately we are able to reconstruct five of these: the *Porticus Pompeii*, the *Templum Pacis*, the *Divus Claudius*, the *Adonaea* and the *Porticus Livia*. These examples help to give an understanding of the concept and to see how they may have been planted.

The first public portico in Rome was the *Porticus Pompeii* constructed in 55 BC by Pompey the Great, who is thought to have based his design on the Hellenistic theatre complex at Mitylene, in Turkey.[28] As in that example the portico garden was an adjunct to the theatre built by Pompey. It was an area enclosed by covered walkways, *portici*, designed to give shade from the sun and shelter from rain when the audience retired between performances in the adjoining theatre, an architectural device described by Vitruvius.[29] The adoption of Hellenistic porticos to enclose the garden within a *peristylium* was perhaps partly motivated by the need to separate the garden from the surrounding streets and buildings, and maps locating the ancient portico gardens of Rome indeed reveal their close proximity to other structures. The porticos of Pompey's much esteemed garden were united into one entity and thereafter the term *portico* was used to indicate an enclosed garden of this type.

The area of Pompey's Portico is today hidden from view under housing but Propertius describes some of the characteristics of the famous garden. There were shady columns and an 'avenue thick-planted with plane-trees rising in trim rows'[30] as well as water features with statues. Fortunately a plan of this important garden can be drawn from relevant surviving fragments of the Severan *Forma Urbis*, a map of Rome engraved on marble that was once placed on public view by the *Templum Pacis* in Rome (*c.* AD 200). Opinions differ on the interpretation of lines and dots within the ancient plan. One version interprets the four centrally aligned rows of squares as representing pollarded plane trees around two large rectangular water basins.[31] Another interpretation,[32] however, visualizes these two features as the site of a *nemus duplex*, the double grove of trees mentioned by Martial.[33] The squares could then indicate that each group of trees was flanked by a row of statues set on plinths. A series of *exedrae*, semicircular and rectangular recesses, probably provided seating or *scholae* on the outer margins of the garden. Fountains are mentioned by Propertius and may have been situated in proximity to larger water features or they may have been placed to the rear of the theatre façade, as at Perge in Turkey, but any interpretation will have to await confirmation by archaeological means. The *Porticus Pompeii* may be a more elaborate version of a Greek-style *palaestra*, an area in which youths and men would exercise, and in Roman times these were usually found next to a public bath suite. Vitruvius describes their ideal qualities:

> Three of the sides are to be single colonnades; the fourth which has a south aspect is to be double, so that when rain is accompanied by gales, the drops may not reach the inside. . . . On the other three sides, spacious *exedrae* are to be planned with seats . . . double

colonnade walks in the open are to be planned [*xysta*] . . . . The *xysta* ought to be so laid out that there are plantations or groves of plane trees between the two colonnades. Here walks are to be made among the trees with spaces paved with cement . . .[34]

The *hectatostylum*, a colonnade of 100 columns, is marked on the Severan Marble Map as adjoining Pompey's Portico immediately to the north and provides a double colonnade. Plantations could refer to box, which was a feature of 'sun warmed Europa', a portico garden mentioned by Martial,[35] or the laurel bushes that adorned the *Porticus Vipsania*, which Martial was just able to see from his garret window.[36] Alternatively there could be vines grown on trellises, such as protected walkways in the *Porticus Liviae*.[37] Other sources mention two myrtles in the shrine of Quirinus[38] and a lotus tree in the precincts of Vulcan.[39] Pliny also reports that 'different kinds of trees are kept perpetually dedicated to their own divinities, for instance, the winter-oak to Jove, the bay to Apollo, the olive to Minerva, the myrtle to Venus, the poplar to Hercules . . .'[40] This could perhaps indicate that each species was planted in different areas within a sacred garden or that plantations of a specific species associated with a particular divinity could be found in, or as a grove outside, their respective temple precinct. Other porticos may have contained a combination of bushes such as laurel, myrtle and box trees, which are mentioned in a 500 ft long portico garden proposed by Gordian III (*c.* AD 238–44). The project did not materialize but the brief description is useful in comparison with those built earlier. Gordian also intended to have a statue-lined central path leading up to a basilica and bath complex 'so that the pleasure-parks and porticos might not be without some practical use'.[41]

The components of the *Porticus Pompeii* may be compared with later portico gardens for which it provided a model. This type of garden increasingly became associated with a number of important public buildings, such as theatres, bath complexes, libraries, temples, or they could stand on their own. They became fashionable places in which to stroll or sit, where one could be seen; they also served as a venue for assignations, as revealed by Ovid in his *Ars Amatoria*.

In the provinces there are large theatre portico gardens at Italica and at Mérida, in Spain. The former is at present under restoration but the latter which has been partially restored and replanted gives us a marvellous insight into the scale and usefulness of these green areas. At Mérida the visitor can visualize how effectively the garden can beautify an already superb monumental theatre façade. The garden and porticos were separated by a deep gutter basin as seen at Vienne in France (chapter four). Examples of gardens in association or close to public baths are those at Conimbriga in Portugal,[42] Aphrodisias in Turkey, and Thuburbo Maius in Tunisia. In the former a small garden area was found inside the bath complex, in the *palaestra*. At Aphrodisias the so-called

Portico of Tiberius is conveniently near the Baths of Hadrian. Here the long garden was provided with stone benches (similar to those at Phaselis) facing on to the large central water feature which almost fills the open garden space. The pool is in many ways reminiscent of the Canopus at Hadrian's Villa at Tivoli. Excess water was directed from the baths to the basin/fish pond, keeping the level high. This in turn added to the supply of water for a *nymphaeum* at the opposite end of the portico. In Tunisia the Portico of the Petronii at Thuburbo Maius is likewise close to a bath suite, the summer baths. Inside this portico is a relief of a nymph standing and pouring water from a conch shell, a decorative motif often found in garden contexts, and a large room perhaps for dining opened on to this enclosed area that appears to have been a garden in the form of a *palaestra*.

Excavations at Athens have revealed that the Library of Hadrian was provided with a portico garden.[43] This had a single colonnade on all four sides but was provided with a series of *exedrae* where people could bring out a library scroll to sit and read in good light and fresh air. There was a plantation in the open interior and by positioning the elongated water basin (type C) on the central axis a *nemus duplex* was created.

A number of temples were sited within a sacred enclosure or portico and evidence increasingly shows that this reserved area may have been used as a sacred grove or garden. Sites include the temple at Didyma in Turkey where a plantation of bay trees is thought to have existed in the sacred area, and the sanctuary of Munigua in Spain where excavations have revealed a series of tree-planting holes on the lofty temple platform. In Britain the Temple of Divus Claudius at Colchester may have been designed along similar lines to those at Rome, and perhaps specifically to the temple of *Divus Claudius* in the capital. Details of this are fortunately engraved on the Marble Map. Here the temple has been placed near the centre of the garden but the close spacing of a number of incised lines, rather than holes, has indicated a planting scheme

The public portico garden attached to the theatre at Mérida; looking towards the exterior façade of the theatre. A 'gutter' water basin ran along three sides of the portico garden but was interrupted by this wide central path.

composed of hedging not trees. This information has been used when making a reconstruction of this temple for the model of Rome housed in the Museo Romano, Rome. Ancient literary sources mention that this portico garden was furnished with fountains and *nymphaea* under Nero after he extended the Aqua Claudia to supply the gardens, which he altered to incorporate into the domain of his Domus Aurea. Archaeological evidence suggests that along the eastern (rear) colonnade water from the aqueduct fed a series of niches,[44] in what may have been a façade type *nymphaeum*.

Fragments of the Marble Map also reveal the garden in front of the *Templum Pacis*, also known as the *Forum Pacis*. This type of garden forms a *temenos* or *atrium* outside the Temple of Peace (as one finds in later Christian churches). Two rectangular *exedrae* were built into the lateral walls. In the centre two areas of irregularly shaped rows of boxes would suggest a *nemus duplex*, or alternatively flower beds.[45] Pliny reveals that apart from the spoils of the Jewish War, statuary and paintings from the demolished Domus Aurea appear to have been put on public display here.[46] He also mentions a statue of Venus in the precincts of the Temple of Peace and a Nile 'with 16 of the river-god's children playing around him'.[47] The 'Nile' is probably the recumbent river god in the Vatican Museum, Braccio Nuovo. Such large works of art were suitable for display in gardens of the public sector. Procopius mentions the existence of a fountain and statuary here. He notes that the fountain, in the form of a bronze bull, was sited in front of the temple.[48] Pliny indicates that the whole complex was aesthetically pleasing and he counted it as one of the three most beautiful buildings in Rome.[49]

The *Adonaea* is another sacred enclosure or portico garden mentioned by Ovid[50] as a place much frequented. This area was the main site in

The *Divus Claudius*, a temple dedicated to the deified Emperor Claudius set within a public portico garden (as reconstructed in the Model of Imperial Rome in the Museo della Civiltà Romana).

Rome for the cult of Adonis. A quotation from Philostratus does help to locate it on the Palatine hill; he records that the *aula*, or hall, was in the vicinity of Domitian's palace. It was 'bright with baskets of flowers, such as the Syrians at the time of the festival of Adonis make up in his honour'.[51] We are fortunate that a plan survives on the Marble Map. It appears to have had a wide colonnaded entrance and the first encircling row of dots could indicate porticos. After an interval, three further rows of dots are thought to represent trees or vine-covered arbours in the open courtyard.[52] An elongated rectangular feature across the centre of the garden could be a *euripus*, and the series of irregularly shaped boxes that surround it may be flower beds. However, four blocks, each of four lines (with serifs) have remained a puzzle; these perhaps detail benches or beds upon which the pots containing 'Adonis Gardens' could have been placed. After the plants had died they could then have been thrown into water, in this case the *euripus*, to complete the full ritual.[53]

Recent archaeological research in the *Adonaea*[54] has confirmed evidence that porticos existed from the time of Emperor Septimus Severus and several rows of half amphorae used as flowerpots have been discovered on what appears to be alignments similar to the lines engraved on the map. The pots had been set in the ground into a bed of marble chippings and because they were placed so close together, the pots may have served as receptacles for plants associated with the cult of Adonis. A wider spacing would indicate permanently planted pots of flowers or shrubs instead and in such instances the pots are usually found to be cracked open by root growth, although some pots would be pre-broken so that growth would not be checked.[55] Incidentally the *Adonaea* is thought to be the garden on the Palatine where St Sebastian was tied to a tree and martyred, hence the Christian church dedicated to him within its walls. This story, however, does suggest that at that time (during the Great Persecution of Diocletian *c.* AD 304–11) there were still a number of trees in the garden.

A number of porticoed gardens were named after their donor. In France, at Vaison la Romaine, there are remains of a portico garden constructed by the Pompeius family who had been prominent Gauls. Trogus Pompeius, presumably of the same family, was listed as a historian during the reign of Augustus. The use of Pompey's name indicates that they must have gained citizenship while under his command in the army. The north-east wall of the portico has been restored and stands to a height of 4 m. It was furnished with three recesses that today contain casts of appropriate monumental sized statuary, although these may have originated elsewhere in the town. The impressive colonnades looked out on to a garden containing a large fishpond with a central island, although unfortunately only half of the garden has been excavated.

The most famous donor portico was at Rome, the *Porticus Liviae*, Livia being the wife of the Emperor Augustus: unfortunately its exact location in the city is not known. This was one of the most popular resorts mentioned by Ovid, Martial, Pliny and Strabo.[56] This version of the same theme demonstrates that such gardens are not always connected to public buildings or monuments but were in fact classed as public monuments in their own right. This garden was planted with vines or rather one large old vine, 'that protects the open walks with its shady trellises, while at the same time it produces twelve amphorae of juice yearly'.[57] Such a garden may have been intended in the now badly faded fresco found in the Gnostic catacomb in Rome, which appears to depict paths covered by arched pergolas. Funerary representations often have a spiritual context and in this case the enclosed area may have been intended as a representation of heaven, a garden paradise. If this interpretation is correct then the portico garden was seen as an ideal resort or amenity area, a greatly loved space that the people could claim as their own. It had become the ideal form of Roman garden.

Evidence shows that planting schemes within portico gardens are arbitrary and ephemeral – details can easily change over the centuries. But it appears that gardens played an important part, as a complementary adjunct to architecture and to beautifying their surroundings. The contrasting colour and texture of the green foliage would act as a perfect foil against which the white marble or stonework would be shown to advantage. Another aspect revealed by Vitruvius[58] is that such areas in a fortified town could prove valuable as sources of wood during times of siege, when these localities could be converted for food production.

CHAPTER TEN

Conclusions

The Latin word *hortus*, like the English word garden, is an all-embracing term and can have a range of different meanings. In the first instance the word can be used to imply either a domestic or public space where plants were grown. However these two areas cover a variety of forms; a *hortus* could be either a place that we would consider a kitchen garden, market garden, green funerary enclosure or an urban park. Gardens also appeared in certain inns and corporate buildings, and were often included in temple complexes or other public structures. Likewise the domestic garden is found in all shapes and sizes, for example, plants graced a *viridarium*, or small internal court, or a large area could be made available for the benefit of the family and their guests. There are also obvious differences between many of the gardens found in the towns, which could be quite cramped, and those of the villa in the country where there was more space and scope for the landscape gardener. Therefore, if one was asked to specify the appearance of a Roman garden it would be a difficult task, for they were many and varied. One would be justified in saying 'Which type of garden?' However, research indicates that many of these green areas share elements in common, and these can be used to visualize their appearance.

To define the characteristics of a Roman garden several factors need to be taken into account. One aspect is that the Roman period extends over many centuries and therefore garden details vary with time. Gardens of the Late Republican Era, for instance, differ from the humble *horti* preceding it, and from those of the late Empire. Also great differences are apparent between gardens that are fed by water drawn from a cistern and those having piped water from an aqueduct. This crucial element, water, could affect the range of plants that could be grown and the way in which they were planted. In general where there are limited water resources the gardens tend to be more informal with a larger part occupied by mature bushes and trees that are less prone to drought, whereas formal plantations and bedding patterns often require low-growing plant species which tend to need more watering. Insufficient water would also restrict the installation of fountains and water basins.

Each has great implications for the overall form of the *hortus*. The most influential element, and the most unpredictable, is that gardens reflect the owner's taste and aspirations: some people carefully tend and furnish their gardens while others are less keen and merely mow the lawn, and we are all familiar with neighbours who neglect their own. Such is human nature and to some extent, then as now, a garden is an expression of the owner. In Pompeii the shape and appearance of gardens is varied.

When attempting to date the defining features of these gardens it was hoped that a perusal of the many archaeological site plans and reports could reveal a pattern of trends within the long timescale of the Roman period, such as appears in comparisons between different types of water features. To a certain extent it appears that *oscilla* and *pinakes* date to the earlier centuries, that is during the Late Republic and Early Empire, but apart from these few items the picture is too incomplete; so few gardens have been adequately excavated and recorded. With the more stringent archaeological recording procedures today, however, this may in time be resolved.

For many years a number of scholars have believed that the houses and gardens in the area of Pompeii and Herculaneum were based on Greek principles because this region had been settled by Greek colonists centuries before. Because of this care has been taken to see if the gardens in this region are in fact representative of those found elsewhere throughout the Empire or if they were the result of a local or Greek style. All the evidence does seem to show that these gardens are in no way similar to those of the Classical period of Greece, although there may have been some influences drawn from the later Hellenistic period. Gardens in the provinces have been found to be basically very similar to those in Italy and Pompeii. However in the East this may be less so for it appears that in many town houses Greek tendencies for paved courts may have persisted. Many gardens in various countries have been studied and numerous examples inspected, and with this exception evidence shows that in general Roman housing, like other forms of buildings in the provinces, tends to follow the fairly standardized patterns set by Rome. Therefore, it is not surprising to find that gardens from other provinces bear many similarities to those of Pompeii, and other regions in Italy.

The Empire covers a large number of climatic zones and so one point to consider is how far the character of an individual Roman garden was influenced by the climate of the province in which it was located. In regions with a drier atmosphere, such as in parts of North Africa, certain measures were taken, such as the provision of large cisterns. Also notable is that in general smaller water basins were installed in these areas for they used less water. Some gardens were at a lower level than their surrounding peristyle to conserve moisture, and in places the soil around plant beds or even individual plants could be contoured and the edges raised to prevent water running off elsewhere. In areas with very dry conditions the centre could also be made to slope downwards and would act as a funnel to make sure that precious water would collect at the base of the plant and would be absorbed straight away by its roots, making the maximum use of the water available – in those conditions every drop counted. The agriculturalists, although referring to conditions applying in Italy and Spain, noted that gardens planted in cooler regions, such as in inland areas or on higher ground where no benefit could be had from the warmer air coming from the sea, needed to be treated slightly differently and planting and flowering was at least one month behind. In such locations some of the more tender species such as the citron could not survive the winter. In dwellings located in a more northerly latitude there would have been further differences; the winters were longer and severe frosts would have limited the introduction of 'exotic' species of plants, and could damage exposed pipework and fine statuary. One modification to provide protection from cold north winds is that houses and villas are more likely to have partially enclosed colonnades bordering gardens as opposed to those in the south.

Most Roman gardens contained some structures, even though the item most likely to survive in the archaeological record is one or two pathways. Where there was an adequate supply of water a number of gardens excavated were shown to have at least one water feature that held a special place as a focal point and was a means to decorate the garden. Shrines and altars are found and there could be evidence of post pits to indicate the existence of a shady pergola or a wooden or trelliswork fence. At times seats and tables would have been placed in the garden and sculpture was spread out among the greenery in such a way that it ornamented the garden and could enhance particular views. Owners made use of architecture and landscape to improve the vista of the house and garden, of both the exterior view of house and garden and the view from the house looking outwards.

Why did the Romans need gardens? There are many answers to this question. First the nurturing of living green plants fulfils a basic instinct for a closeness to nature, often associated with the idea of a wholesome country life. Many people were required to live in cities so the garden could play an important role in providing a little *rus in urbe* – a sense of country in the city. The Roman love of nature and growing things is shown in the many areas that were given over to greenery in Pompeii and elsewhere. It is also interesting to note that evidence shows gardens were not just the preserve of the wealthy, for even those living in smaller properties were able to include a corner of greenery, or even a few plants in containers or a window box, which could give joy and would relieve the tedium of their cramped conditions. The possession of a garden, no matter how small, would give some release from the pressures of an urban existence. Also a sense of space could be created if a verdant painted backdrop was provided. A *trompe l'oeil* work could extend a garden or, if employed behind just a strip of plants, the illusion of a garden could be created.

Another benefit in owning a garden was that many of the plants grown were scented varieties so that the area would be fragrant and could freshen any stale odours that came from the house. Gardens in internal courtyards would also allow more light and air into rooms facing on to it, and the surrounding porticos of a garden made an ideal extra living space or workplace that was used to advantage. Evidence of loomweights at Pompeii suggests that the women spun and wove in gardens or in the spacious porticos where there was good light but shelter from rain or the fierce sun of summer. Garlands could be made there and vegetables prepared for meals. Fish for later consumption could be kept fresh in a fishpond in the garden and likewise birds for the table could be housed in an aviary. Pets could also be housed in the garden and its associated porticos. Plants were grown for effect and yet provided food and medicines. Bees were welcomed into gardens to pollinate food plants and to convert nectar into honey, while flowers and foliage provided materials for making garlands to decorate the building, shrines or the person. So the garden was an additional living area for man and the birds and bees. As it was an area that required frequent attention it was a place of work for some, and therefore it was necessary to provide accommodation for those occupied in its maintenance; this fact was a valid consideration when Pliny the Younger was considering buying a villa.[1]

Archaeological discoveries confirm textual evidence that a garden was an ideal location for parties and feasting, especially in summertime when most use would be made of alfresco dining areas. A place within the garden, perhaps a *diaeta*, *pergula*, or other shady location, would also have been allocated for study or relaxation, contemplation and inspiration. Numerous references are made to time spent relaxing on the grass or a seat under the shade of a tree. Cicero mentions how peaceful one particular area in his country villa was, where he was wont to go and sit in a little glade on an island in a river flowing through his property; and there were several other occasions when he and his friends went for a walk to have a discussion in the garden.[2] Ovid and the younger Pliny both reveal that they gained inspiration when working in their garden,[3] so gardens could revive the spirits and also be seen to have health-giving properties. Maecenas, the friend and patron of Horace, was recorded to have been fond of 'honouring the Muses and Apollo in luxurious gardens, he reclined babbling verse among the tuneful birds'.[4]

A villa and garden in the country could have other attractions; many Roman writers hark back to earlier generations or centuries when the traditional *mores* of ancient Rome were adhered to and society as a whole lived closer to nature. A peaceful existence in the country therefore beckoned to some, especially in dangerous times under tyrannical emperors, and could be a refuge for those who could afford to retire from city life. Pliny recommended retirement and even the Emperor Diocletian expressed his desire to retire to his palace at Split so that he could grow cabbages, which perhaps suggests that retirement was considered respectable, if time would be spent in one's *hortus*.

With an increasingly wealthy society the nouveau riche of the middle classes and freedmen aspired to own larger properties or *villae urbanae* which had previously been the preserve of the landed gentry, who in turn vied to own larger estates than their rivals. Sources indicate that many former properties in Italy were turned into vast pleasure gardens and this indirectly threatened the economy of Rome. One of the most outspoken critics was Horace who speaks out, 'the lonely plane-tree will drive out the elm; then will beds of violets and copses of myrtle and the whole company of sweet perfumes scatter their fragrance amid olive groves that once bore increase to their former owner'.[5] The Elder Pliny also laments that 'large estates have been the ruin of Italy',[6] so much so that a significant proportion of provisions then needed to be imported. The decline of agriculture in many areas may have contributed to the eventual fall of Rome.

During the late Empire, which was a period of general unrest and the danger of barbarian tribes was a distinct threat, there was a tendency to construct town walls and fortify country villas. Unprotected gardens were now very vulnerable and may have shrunk in size but to some extent this fact seems to have been compensated for by a concentration on or elaboration of architectural designs in courtyard gardens. In this period many late gardens were provided with façade *nymphaea* or ornate fountains and pools. Large pleasure gardens became less practicable and many would have shared a comparable fate to those at the villa on Via Gabina, where the once decorative terraced gardens overlooking Rome returned to agriculture. Also it appears that from the fourth century many people from the countryside flocked into towns where they could feel there was a certain amount of safety behind the high walls.[7] The shortage of accommodation soon became acute and these people often had little recourse but to set up some sort of squatter hovel in spaces within public buildings and in large houses of the former middle classes. It appears that if gardens were kept they would have been shared with more than one family or even this area was likely to be taken over by squatter buildings. Therefore any remaining gardens would probably have belonged to the large *domus* of local magnates, who now basically ruled from their homes and needed audience chambers and the space to entertain petitioners and dignitaries. So, as the quality of urban life decayed, many gardens in town and country houses, other than those of the ruling class, may have been converted to the provision of food or were abandoned altogether.

SURVIVALS OF THE ROMAN GARDEN

A simple form of garden in a peristyle appears to have survived in the atrium or outer court of early Christian churches. These gardens were very similar to those seen in public porticos attached to temples and theatres. It is not surprising that the Christians followed earlier principles, for everyone of that date would be familiar with the way in which these gardens formed a forecourt to the public monument, and these were ideal places where people could gather before and after services under the shade of trees or the colonnades. These porticoed courts would seem unfurnished without a plantation or a variety of plants. In the Byzantine and Medieval periods these cloister gardens were often called a 'paradise' or a Garden of Eden. In the fifth-century AD account of the *Life and Miracles of St Thecla* the miracles are mainly set in garden areas or an atrium attached to the church at Meriamlik, in southern Turkey. In Miracle 24 the atrium was described as containing an assortment of birds; they mention that several species were reared there such as doves, pheasants, swans, geese, cranes and perhaps ibis from Egypt. In Miracle 26 we find that there were numerous trees and flowers, a flower-bedecked lawn and water playing in the background. The scene has been likened to a *paradise*.[8]

Some elements of a Roman garden were even taken over and integrated into Christian iconography, such as a well or fountain which became the fount of life. Birds in the garden, especially doves and peacocks, were turned into symbols of peace or eternity, which indicates that these creatures were at least considered wholesome, unlike idolatrous statuary such as Pan who became the very image of the devil. Monastic establishments continued the tradition of a cloister garden and the medieval *Hortus Conclusus* may owe some of its design to the gardens within fortified Roman villas.

Another surviving remnant can be found in the enclosed water gardens of the Arab invaders of the late Roman and Byzantine Empire. These people kept the tradition of elaborate water features and continued to value a knowledge of horticulture which was re-introduced into Spain following their conquest there. The formal geometric nature of many Arab gardens tends to recall those of earlier days and the long water features would seem to echo back to the *euripi* of Rome. These interconnecting pools were enlivened by multiple water jets which also had many precursors in Roman gardens, at Conimbriga for example.

In most of Europe horticulture was thought to be almost non-existent during the Dark Ages until surviving ancient texts were examined anew in the late Medieval period. Cato, Varro and Palladius were especially read at this time and we hear of the effect this had on Petrarch and the Age of Humanism.[9] During the Renaissance ancient sculpture was increasingly collected and studied. The ancient myths gave the figures a new meaning and consequently they were no longer profane images to be broken up. Instead, gardens were created in which these *objets de vertu* could be seen and admired. Works of art such as the Bacchus by Michelangelo were commissioned by Jacopo Galli (*c.* AD 1497) to act as a focal point in a linked Bacchic theme. Gardens were constructed on terraces and in the sixteenth century elaborate *nymphaea*, grottos and water features were added. In gardens such as the Villa d'Este their architect P. Ligorio (*c.* AD 1568), who was also an antiquarian and excavator, modelled his work on archaeological remnants found at Hadrian's Villa and at Rome. His knowledge of Classical texts was combined with an adaptation of the spectacular examples that had survived from antiquity. From the list of plants chosen to decorate this garden it appears that he actively sought to further the atmosphere of a Roman pleasure garden by including species mentioned by ancient authors. Plantings in Italianate villas tend to favour clipped evergreen bushes or trees, so much so that these gardens and their furnishings could well resemble the splendid grounds of an ancient Roman *villa urbana*.

In Britain Castell published a volume in 1728 on Ancient Roman villas based on the literary references of Varro and Pliny the Younger. He attempted to reconstruct the plans of whole estates, including garden structures, and set them into a rather fanciful landscaped design. His interpretations are believed to have contributed to a new style of horticulture, where large country parks were landscaped and dotted with Classical ruins and pavilions. The movement towards Classicism continued with the construction of a great many neo-Classical buildings but their gardens tended to have wide open views and there was a tendency to plant a more 'natural' looking landscape. However, at Port Lympne in Kent, the owner (in about 1919) specifically decided to re-create a garden in the Roman style, where tiers of topiary recalled descriptions by Pliny the Younger. Here the Italianate gardens with terraces of topiary overlook Romney Marsh and the sea beyond, in the spirit of a *villa maritima* or *littorale*.

INTERPRETATIVE ARCHAEOLOGY AND ROMAN GARDENS

Today there is a general interest in ancient societies and one aspect of this is to re-create the past in the form of reconstructions of a variety of Roman buildings. To further the atmosphere of the past these buildings are decorated as far as possible in the style of the originals. Such areas would appear more complete if the associated open areas or gardens were also reinstated following the same principles. If we wish to re-create a Roman garden today we must first determine the elements that were characteristic of the period. This task has been achieved in Pompeii although to a great extent only the latest reconstructions are archaeologically accurate, and in these cases sculpture is usually omitted for security reasons. However this is not such a problem inside the controlled environment of a museum. The J. Paul Getty Museum in California was modelled on the Villa of the Papyri discovered by tunnelling at Herculaneum in the eighteenth century and with such a comparably warm climate garden furnishings were included to provide an atmosphere of authenticity. The new villa and its associated gardens are very effective and the pristine state of the building and its collection enables you to visualize the whole as it would have appeared in antiquity. However the gardens here contain a number of items that belonged to other Pompeian gardens. One example is the *nymphaeum* constructed in the east garden, which does not appear on maps of the Villa of the Papyri, but is a replica of that in the House of the Large Fountain at Pompeii. The gardens display a range of Roman garden furniture rather than those items found in one villa but this is a museum after all, and as a whole it is very representative of elements found in a wealthy fashionable Roman garden.

In Britain the cooler climate would mean some adaptations are necessary. The Corinium Museum at Cirencester, which has a small irregular shaped courtyard, has opted for a style similar to that found in Campania, and the result is somewhat crowded but successful. On the other hand the Roman garden at the Birmingham Botanical Gardens is misleading on several points, for example the use of yew and York paving. One needs to take into account the practices of the relevant period. One example is the treatment of pathways. At Vienne they have been restored in sand as Vitruvius recommends, whereas at the Archéodrome in France a pebble surface is used. Pebbles, gravel or finely broken stone are common on many Roman archaeological sites and the choice of any of these materials could help to re-create a more authentic image. Medieval gardens, such as the one re-created at Winchester,[10] are perhaps more successful partly because they draw on the many details shown in illuminated manuscripts. A similar use of contemporary illustrative material (from frescos) has not been attempted for the Roman period and, apart from Fishbourne, the garden areas on archaeological sites open to the public are usually simply covered by grass for ease of maintenance. One also needs to bear in mind that machine-cut grass is much shorter than it would have been in the past.

Roman gardens, then, are an important source of information on the Roman way of life and numerous facets of their civilization can be found within the confines of the *hortus* itself. In order to gain an understanding of how the garden was used one is brought into contact with many areas of study, such as botany, the Roman diet, geology and geography, agriculture and horticulture, but also one needs to explore the role of architecture, art, literature and religion, and trace their effect on the garden.

Evidence shows that religion pervaded the area and we find altars, shrines and statues of deities. Ritual was observed and superstitious precautions taken to avert the evil eye away from growing plants, or the family in general. Architecture is ever-present in gardens and the growing importance of the garden could be said to have had a profound effect on the architecture of the Roman *domus* and villa, and to some extent even of certain public buildings, influencing the way their design changed over the centuries to adapt to new tastes. The garden could be classed as one of the most important spaces in the house for it is very noticeable that prestigious rooms such as *triclinia* and *exedrae* were usually designed so that they would open on to the garden. At times the garden was also used as a room and in summer dining was carried out under a shady vine-covered canopy. Some gardens contained pavilions or *nymphaea* bringing architecture into the garden and features that had been originally designed for inclusion in a *hortus*, such as *nymphaea*, in turn infiltrate decorative schemes inside rooms.

Art in gardens is displayed in the form of decorative frescos that adorned architectural elements within the garden, *plutei* and the walls of peristyles, while mosaic was used to ornament *nymphaea* and some water basins. In many cases the subjects chosen were taken from themes associated with gardens, such as the verdant scenes of flora and fauna, attributes of deities of the *hortus* or elements in some way connected to water, which was such an important feature in gardens. In the case of sculpture it appears that the garden was an ideal place to display items; this is confirmed by comments made by Pliny the Younger. He mentions that an acquaintance 'on the very day he bought a large garden he was able to beautify it with quantities of antique statues'.[11] This perhaps indicates that a garden would obviously appear incomplete without statuary. Evidence for the mass production of specific forms depicting rustic qualities shows that a large proportion of sculpture had been made specifically for a garden and, together with other garden furniture, they would have complemented the scene as a whole. All of these items would form components of a typical Roman garden.

A study of the ancient sources reveals that gardens and gardening appear as a subject worthy of mention. Just one example is Pliny the Younger who takes pains to reveal in his letters that to him his garden was as important as his house, and the beauty of his garden was evidently a feature that he wished to bring to the attention of his friends.

Literary references can put the flesh on the bones found through archaeological means and both are important sources of information leading to an understanding of an artefact or feature, its mode of employment and the context in which it appears. Each field needs to be studied thoroughly, and new inroads are being made by the use of modern scientific methods of archaeology. Techniques used in the study of the environment have now been applied to the previously neglected area of the Roman garden, and the relatively new field of garden archaeology holds great scope for the further understanding and interpretation of this area and aspect of the past.

FEATURES THAT COULD BE INCORPORATED INTO A MODERN
GARDEN TO EVOKE THE SPIRIT OF A ROMAN GARDEN

Many gardens today are quite small in size and because space was often
restricted in urban Roman gardens a number of Roman features, if well
arranged, would not look out of place in a modern context. For instance
a loggia or colonnade could be constructed alongside the house or
against a boundary wall/fence and would recall a Roman portico. The
siting of such features in Britain and other northern countries will of
course depend on the aspect of the garden, whether it faces north or
south for example, and will be more effective if placed in the sunshine.
Unfortunately the majority of plants suitable for growing in a Roman
garden are sun lovers and this may create problems in more northerly
climates.

If the garden faces south a portico built along the rear of the house
would catch the sun, and would make a pleasant alternative to a
conservatory. Opening doors (such as patio doors) could be made to
resemble the access point to a peristyle from an *oecus* or *triclinium* dining
room, and features in the garden should be placed with this line of sight
in mind. The spaces between the columns or posts of the 'portico' could
be fitted with a low wall that would provide extra seating when needed,
and would be more comfortable if cushions were brought out for the
occasion. The spaces above would provide an ideal location to hang
oscilla, from a centrally placed hook fixed firmly into position on the
underside of the beam. If there is a wall on the short sides of the
portico/loggia this could be ornamented in a number of ways. First a
relief panel could be set into the fabric of the wall; secondly a niche or
plinth could be provided for a statue; thirdly an *aedicula*, a shrine-like
structure, could be built against one wall.

A terrace could provide the necessary hard standing for seating or an
alfresco dining area. The large summer *triclinia* found in Roman gardens
would not be very comfortable for us today, for we are used to dining
seated rather than reclining, but a pair of bench seats with a small table
nearby could be most useful. A light open pergola could be fitted over
the seating area and would set the scene for feasting in the Roman style.

A trellis or pergola could be built along one side of the garden, or to
the rear, and again could provide a means of displaying *oscilla*, as seen in
some of the fresco vignettes. A trellis of some kind could support a
rambling rose or a vine; the latter would also provide the household
with a supply of grapes, and could add that extra touch of authenticity.
Frescos show a variety of designs in trellis-work and larger versions
reveal that the upper part of the framework could be either curved or
flat. This allows a certain flexibility in a modern reconstruction. Some
wooden archways and panels can be purchased ready-made from garden
centres or specialist manufacturers.

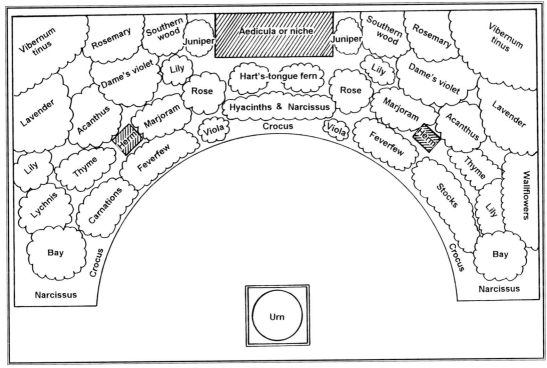

Botanical names for the plants
mentioned above

Acanthus	(*Acanthus mollis*)
Bay	(*Laurus nobilis*)
Carnation	(*Dianthus caryophllus*)
Crocus	(*Crocus sativus*)
Feverfew	(*Chrysanthemum parthenium*)
Hart's-tongue fern	(*Phyllitis scolopendrium*)
Hyacinth	(*Hyacinthus orientalis*)
Juniper	(*Juniperus communis*)
Lavender	(*Lavandula spica*)
Lychnis	(*Lychnis flos-jovis*)
Madonna lily	(*Lilium candidum*)
Marjoram	(*Origanum vulgare*)
Narcissus	(*Narcissus tazetta* or *poeticus*)
Rose	(*Rosa damascena bifera* 'Quatre saisons')
Rosemary	(*Rosmarinus officinalis*)
Southernwood	(*Artemisia arborescens*)
Stocks	(*Matthiola incana*)
Sweet rocket or Dame's violet	(*Hesperis matronalis*)
Thyme	(*Thymus vulgaris*)
Turk's cap lily	(*Lilium martagon*)
Laurustinus/ Viburnum	(*Viburnum tinus*)
Violet	(*Viola odorata*)
Wallflower	(*Cheiranthus cheri*)

A simple bedding plan for a
Roman style garden (suitable
for a small garden). Pot-grown
lilies, Madonna and Turk's cap,
could fill gaps after spring
bulbs have finished flowering.

When constructing a covered walkway try to incorporate a decorative feature, a niche or item of sculpture at the end, for this will add interest and draw the eye. A niche, arbour or shrine-like structure (an *aedicula*) can also be in the open, as often seen in small Roman gardens, and could be placed against a wall where it would provide one of the necessary focal points in the garden. It would make a fitting frame for a statue, perhaps of Venus so that she could preside over her garden domain. If space permits a fountain and centrally placed pool of geometric design should be sited so that they would be seen to good effect from the house. Many Roman gardens contained sculpture of some form and any modern garden could also be enlivened by the addition of one or two items. Italianate sculpture is available in Britain today from reputable garden centres and through mail order, but care is needed to choose items that could be applicable to Roman times – many statues on offer are in fact Baroque versions of more ancient forms. Statues could be set at the edge of a pool or against a background of shrubs/topiary where they would stand out against a green backdrop. Herms are ideally seen in company and they could be set along one side of a gravel path or placed either side of a particular feature in the garden.

Those fortunate enough to own a walled garden could reserve one section for a fresco painting of a landscape or garden scene in the Roman style. These images are extremely useful when trying to find means to extend a small garden. Unfortunately frescos might need some protection from the rain and sun, for they tend to fade quickly if exposed to too much direct sunshine. Owners of large gardens could reserve an area of their garden that could be screened to provide a 'room' devoted to the Roman period. The room could be surrounded by tiered topiary hedges or if a pergola or trellis fence was used it could be made to resemble a decorative enclosure garden illustrated in several miniature Roman frescos.

The garden could include topiary figures or obelisks as mentioned by Pliny and a box hedge could outline a path or plant bed. Box could be planted and clipped into a sinuous geometric pattern and recesses could be made in a design (as at Fishbourne). A list of plants that were grown in Roman gardens can be found in Table II and any of these would be appropriate for inclusion in a modern planting scheme. Unfortunately no bedding plan survives from antiquity and therefore any modern reconstruction must be used as a guide only. Individual plant beds for roses and violets are mentioned in ancient sources and others may have been planted between or in front of trees or bushes which, then as now, were the main framework of the living garden. There appears to have been a preference for foliage plants and scented forms were highly favoured. With these features in mind a simple plant bed of species used in the Roman period can be suggested but in this case it is composed of varieties suitable for a more northerly climate. A hardy alternative to bay would be clipped box. In garden centres today there are numerous varieties of plants and it is always necessary to search for the earliest forms. Many are herbs and these at least are readily available today. Some, such as the rose, may need to be obtained from a specialist establishment. Species such as *Rosa bifera* 'Quatre Saisons' is an ancient form that could be included, and *Rosa gallica officinalis*, the Apothecary Rose, can be ordered from Peter Beale's Roses.

A Selection of Roman Gardens Open to the Public

Britain

FISHBOURNE ROMAN PALACE

A large topiary garden re-created from archaeological evidence found on site. To one side there is a museum dedicated to Roman gardening; associated with this are a number of display beds containing plants of the Roman period.

CAERLEON

The courtyard or *palaestra* of the Fortress Baths was enlivened by a long rectangular pool and *nymphaeum*.

CHEDWORTH

A large villa or shrine complex, apparently built on terraces, it includes a garden court (under grass). A spring still flows to the *nymphaeum* by the bath building.

CORINIUM MUSEUM, CIRENCESTER

A small irregular shaped courtyard garden, decorated and ornamented in the manner of Pompeian gardens.

BIRMINGHAM BOTANICAL GARDENS

A small garden court with plants that could be found in a Roman garden (excluding yew).

WALL

The peristyle court of the *mansio*, within the Roman site, contains the remains of a demi-lune water basin. The remainder of the garden is covered by turf.

France

ARCHEODROME

An archaeological reconstruction park, sited on the rest area off the route national to Provence (north of Lyons). The museum on this site has been partly constructed to represent a Roman villa with a semi-enclosed peristyle court. For security reasons plate glass has been added on to the *plutei* or low walls of the peristyle. The open court contains a pebble path (following evidence from a Roman site nearby) and plant species of the Roman period.

SAINT-ROMAIN-EN-GAL (VIENNE)

Once a large Roman town. There is a district of houses and gardens located on the western bank of the River Rhone. The majority of gardens here display the distinctive 'gutter' type water features. Two houses were furnished with a summer *triclinium*; one can be seen *in situ*.

VAISON-LA-ROMAINE

A large excavation site divided by a modern road. Several Roman houses and gardens can be viewed and a public portico garden.

Greece

OLYMPIA

The Leonidaion or Roman period guest house contains a type F pool.

Italy

OSTIA

This Roman town has a variety of Roman dwellings, some with gardens, and there is an interesting selection. There are façade *nymphaea* in the House of Cupid and Psyche and the House of Fortuna Annonaria. The garden in the House of the Thunderbolt has a shrine and altar, plus a summer dining area furnished with a *biclinium* near a raised rectangular pool. There are remains of *aediculae nymphaea* in some properties and in the House of the Round Temple there was a fountain set on a small decorative indented island in a marble-lined pool.

OPLONTIS

Between Pompeii and Herculaneum there is a large Roman villa with numerous gardens, many restored faithfully following archaeological evidence.

POMPEII AND HERCULANEUM

Both Roman towns have many houses with gardens. A range of garden forms is found there, but they are too numerous to list individually.

ROME

The Imperial Palace and its gardens on the Palatine contain numerous features of note: a hippodrome garden, a Cyzican triclinium, a type F water basin and several type D pools. The Auditorium of Maecenas is a splendid example of a large basilica form of *nymphaeum*. Also large domed *nymphaea* can be seen in the so-called Temple of Minerva and in the ruins of the Gardens of Sallust.

SPERLONGA

Part of a large villa can be seen together with an interesting cave beside the sea this has been enhanced into a grotto with dining facilities. Fish were kept in sea-water pools by the *triclinium*. Access to the cave is by a narrow path leading from the garden.

TIVOLI

At Hadrian's Villa there are several notable garden features that are on an exceptionally large scale. The grounds are extensive and with few restrictions on space we can appreciate how water and landscape had been used in imaginative ways. There are numerous pools and fountains here, such as *aedicule*, façade *nymphaea* and water stairs. In the Canopus valley a large sheet of water is ornamented by an elaborate colonnade with statuary. The gardens contain pavilions, temples, belvederes and a grotto. In the 'stadium' the remains of the pavilions are only a few feet high but the semicircular end was fitted with a combination of tiered plant beds and water cascades. Today this theatre-like setting is covered by grass. The whole site has a special quality that is enhanced by the fine prospect over surrounding countryside.

Portugal

CONIMBRIGA

A Roman town with several large houses containing pools, one of type B, one of D but the majority are type F.

Spain

ITALICA

This Roman town, the birthplace of the emperors Hadrian and Trajan, had a number of large luxurious houses that contain gardens. Many were furnished with pools and two were provided with a summer dining area, a curved *stibadium* placed beside the pool.

MERIDA

In the heart of the town lies the spectacular Roman theatre and public portico garden that has 'gutter' type water features. These water basins can also be seen at the edge of the forum and in two large Roman houses nearby: the House of the Amphitheatre and the House of Mithras. A type B basin can be seen in excavations by the former and in ruins found below the museum (these have been left *in situ* and can be seen in the crypt).

Turkey

SIDE

Two small houses have paved courts in the Greek style but one was furnished with a small Roman façade *nymphaeum*; only the catchment basin survives.

North African Provinces: Morocco

VOLUBILIS

This Roman town has a number of houses with peristyle gardens, many of which contain water features.

Tunisia

CARTHAGE

There are a couple of large Roman houses with gardens in a residential area near the Roman theatre. At the House of the Aviary a narrow internal court was provided with a large water feature, giving the impression of a façade *nymphaeum*, while in the peristyle court there is an interesting raised hexagonal garden.

DOUGGA

This large site contains a number of Roman houses, some of which contained gardens. Several were furnished with a demi-lune water basin. In the House of '*Omnia tibi felicia*' the small court was lined with plant troughs.

THUBURBO MAIUS

Again this is a very large archaeological site containing many Roman houses and garden areas, some containing type E basins. There are also public gardens such as in the Portico Petronni and recent excavations have located traces of plant pits in the courtyard surrounding the east temple but none of the gardens have been replanted.

UTICA

Many of the Roman houses contain gardens furnished with pools, some of which were type E basins. In the House of the Cascade there are several water features, a mosaic-covered fountain basin, a type E and type F. A sundial can be seen in the peristyle garden on an island in the large central pool.

Table 1

A SAMPLE OF ANCIENT ROMAN SITES AS AN INDICATION OF THE RANGE AND FREQ

Site	Altar	Venus	Priapus	Cupid	Children	Animals	Diana	Apollo	Marsyas	Muses	Hercules
Villa of the Papyrii Herculaneum (Neudecker)	–	–	–	–	6	4	–	–	–	–	–
Villa of Poppaea, Oplontis (De Caro)	–	1	–	–	2	1	1	–	–	–	–
House of Camillus, Pompeii (Dwyer)	–	1	–	–	2	5	–	–	–	–	–
House of the Citharist, Pompeii (Dwyer)	1	–	1	–	–	6	–	1	–	–	–
House of Fortuna, Pompeii (Dwyer)	–	–	–	–	2	–	–	–	–	–	–
House of the Golden Cupids Pompeii (Dwyer)	1	–	–	–	–	3	–	–	–	–	–
House of Marcus Lucretius, Pompeii (Jashemski)	–	–	–	2	–	7	–	–	–	2	–
House of Loreius Tiburtinus, Pompeii (Jashemski)	–	–	–	–	3	3	–	–	–	–	–
House of the Vettii, Pompeii (Appleton +)	–	–	1	–	6	–	–	–	–	–	–
Villa Sora, Torre del Greco (Neudecker)	–	–	–	–	2	1	–	–	–	–	1
Imperial Villa, Anzio (Neudecker)	–	1	–	–	1	1	1	1	–	–	1
Imperial Villa, Castel Gandolfo (Neudecker)	–	–	–	2	–	2	–	–	1	–	1
Monte Cagnolo, Lanuvio (Neudecker)	–	–	–	1	3	9	–	–	–	–	–
Horace's Villa, Licenza (Neudecker)	–	–	–	1	1	6	–	–	–	–	–
Voconius Villa, Marino (Neudecker)	–	–	–	1	1	2	2	2	1	–	1
Villa Maxentius, Rome (Neudecker)	–	3	–	–	–	–	–	–	–	–	–
Villa Quintili, Rome (Neudecker)	–	1	–	1	6	–	2	1	1	5	–
Tiberius's Villa, Sperlonga (Neudecker)	–	–	–	–	6	3	–	–	–	–	–
Villa of Cassius, Tivoli (Neudecker)	–	–	–	–	–	3	–	–1	–	9	–
Villa Cynthia, Tivoli (Neudecker)	–	–	–	–	1	–	–	–	–	1	–
TOTALS	2	7	2	8	42	56	6	6	2	17	4

Bacchus	Pan	Silenus	Satyr	Maenads	Nymphs and River Gods	Ephebe	Herms Double	Herms Single	Oscilla	Pinax	Sundial	Urns
–	1	–	2	–	–	3	–	32	–	–	–	
–	–	–	1	–	–	1	–	7	–	–	1	1
–	–	–	–	–	–	1	–	1	–	–	–	–
–	–	–	–	–	–	–	2	2	12	–	–	1
–	–	1	–	–	–	–	–	2	16	–	–	–
–	–	–	–	–	–	–	3	6	7	4	1	–
–	–	1	2	–	–	–	4	1	6	–	–	–
–	–	–	1	–	1	–	–	–	3	–	–	–
1	–	–	2	–	–	–	2	–	–	–	–	5
–	–	1	4	–	–	–	7	1	–	–	–	–
–	–	–	1	–	–	2	–	4	–	–	–	–
1	–	–	5	–	2	6	–	1	–	–	–	–
1	2	–	–	–	–	–	1	4	–	–	–	2
–	–	–	–	–	–	–	–	2	1	–	–	–
–	–	1	–	–	–	5	1	7	–	–	–	1
–	–	–	–	–	–	–	–	11	–	–	–	–
–	1	3	2	4	1	–	3	19	–	–	–	–
–	–	–	–	–	–	–	–	11	2	–	–	–
1	–	–	3	–	–	–	1	34	–	–	–	–
–	–	–	3	–	–	4	–	8	–	–	–	–
4	4	7	26	4	4	22	24	153	48	4	2	10

Table II
GARDEN PLANTS MENTIONED BY PLINY IN HIS *NATURAL HISTORY*

Names of Plants	Ornamental	Chaplet	Wine	Bees	Medicinal	Culinary
Acanthus	x	—	—	—	x	—
Adonis	—	x	—	—	—	—
Almond	—	—	—	—	x	x
Amaranth (*Immortales*)	—	x	—	—	—	—
Anemone	—	x	—	—	x	—
Anise	—	—	—	—	x	x
Anthyllis (*barba-Jovis*)	x	—	—	—	—	—
Apiastrum	—	x	—	x	x	—
Apple	—	—	x	—	x	x
Asparagus	—	—	x	—	x	x
Basil	—	—	—	—	x	x
Beans	—	—	—	x	x	x
Beet	—	—	—	—	x	x
Blite	—	—	—	—	x	x
Box	x	—	—	—	—	—
Brussels sprout	—	—	—	—	x	x
Cabbage	—	—	—	—	x	x
Caper	—	—	—	—	x	x
Cardoon	—	—	—	—	x	x
Carob	—	—	x	—	x	—
Caraway	—	—	—	—	—	x
Carrot	—	—	x	—	—	—
Casia	—	x	—	x	—	—
Catmint	—	—	x	—	x	x
Cedar	—	—	x	—	—	—
Cerintha	—	—	—	x	—	—
Cherry	—	—	—	—	x	x
Chervil	—	—	—	—	x	x
Chestnut	—	—	—	—	x	x
Chicory	—	—	—	—	x	—
Chives	—	—	—	—	—	x
Chrysanthemum (*parthenium*)	—	x	—	—	—	—
Citron	x	—	—	—	x	—
Convolvulus	—	x	—	—	—	—
Coriander	—	—	—	—	x	x
Cornel tree	—	—	x	—	—	x
Cornflower (*Cyanus*)	—	—	x	—	—	—
Cress	—	—	—	—	x	x
Crocus	—	—	—	—	x	x
Cucumber	x	—	—	—	x	x
Cumin	—	—	—	—	x	—
Cunila	—	—	—	x	x	—
Cyclamen	—	x	—	—	—	—
Cynoglosum	x	—	—	—	—	—
Cypress	x	—	x	—	x	—
Dill	—	—	—	—	x	x
Dittany	—	—	x	—	—	—
Elecampane	—	—	—	—	x	x
Endive	—	—	—	—	x	x

Names of Plants	Ornamental	Chaplet	Wine	Bees	Medicinal	Culinary
Fennel	–	x	–	–	x	x
Fig	–	–	–	–	x	x
Gallic nard/Valerian	–	–	x	–	x	–
Garlic	–	–	–	–	x	x
Gentian	–	–	x	–	–	–
Germander	–	–	x	–	–	–
Gourd	x	–	–	–	x	x
Ground pine/pine	x	–	x	–	x	x
Hazelnut	–	–	–	–	x	x
Heliotrope	–	–	–	–	x	x
Hemp	–	–	–	–	–	x
Hesperis (Dame's violet)	–	x	–	–	–	–
Holly	x	–	–	–	x	–
Horehound	–	–	x	–	x	–
Hyacinth	–	x	–	–	x	–
Hyssop	–	–	x	–	x	–
Jujube tree	x	x	–	–	–	–
Juniper	–	–	x	–	–	–
Iris	–	x	–	–	x	–
Ivy	x	x	–	–	–	–
Laurel (bay)	x	–	x	–	x	–
Lavender	–	–	x	–	–	–
Leek	–	–	–	–	x	x
Lettuce	–	–	–	–	x	x
Lily	x	x	–	x	x	–
Linseed	–	–	–	–	x	–
Lovage	–	–	–	–	x	x
Lychnis	x	–	–	–	x	–
Maidenhair (*Adiatum*)	x	–	–	–	x	–
Mallow	–	–	–	–	x	x
Mandragora	–	–	x	–	–	–
Marjoram	–	x	x	–	x	x
Mastic tree	–	–	x	–	–	–
Medlar	–	–	x	–	x	x
Melilot	–	x	–	x	x	–
Melissophyllum (balm)	–	–	–	x	x	–
Mint	x	x	x	–	x	x
Moss	x	–	–	–	–	–
Mulberry	–	–	x	–	x	x
Mustard	–	–	–	x	x	x
Myrtle	x	x	–	–	x	x
Narcissus	–	x	–	–	x	–
Nettle tree	x	–	x	–	x	–
Oleander	x	x	–	–	x	–
Olive	–	–	–	–	x	x
Onion	–	–	–	–	x	x
Orache	–	–	–	–	x	–
Orage	–	–	–	–	–	x
Palm (date)	x	–	–	–	x	–

Names of Plants	Ornamental	Chaplet	Wine	Bees	Medicinal	Culinary
Parsnip	–	–	–	–	x	–
Parsley	–	–	x	–	x	x
Partridge plant	–	–	–	–	–	x
Peach	–	–	–	–	x	x
Pear	–	–	x	–	x	x
Pennyroyal	–	–	–	–	x	x
Pepperwort	–	–	–	–	x	x
Periwinkle	x	x	–	–	x	–
Plane tree	x	–	–	–	x	–
Plum	–	–	–	–	x	x
Pomegranate	–	–	x	–	x	x
Poppy	–	–	–	x	x	x
Purslain	–	–	–	–	x	x
Quince	–	x	–	–	x	x
Radish	–	–	–	–	x	x
Rape	–	–	–	–	–	x
Rocket	–	–	–	–	x	x
Rose	x	x	x	x	x	–
Rosemary (*libanotis/conyza*)	–	x	–	x	x	–
Rue	–	–	x	–	x	x
Saffron	–	x	–	–	x	x
Sage	–	–	x	–	–	–
Service tree (*Sorbus*)	–	–	x	–	x	x
Smilax	x	x	–	–	–	–
Sorrel	–	–	–	–	x	x
Southernwood	–	x	x	–	x	x
Spalax	–	–	–	–	x	–
Squill	–	–	–	–	x	x
Strawberry tree	x	–	–	–	–	–
Summer beet	–	–	–	–	x	–
Sweet rush	–	–	x	–	x	–
Terebinth	–	–	x	–	–	–
Thapsia	–	–	–	–	x	–
Thyme	–	x	x	x	x	x
Tree medick	–	–	–	x	–	–
Tuber apple	x	–	–	–	–	–
Turnip	–	–	x	–	x	x
Vetch	–	–	–	x	–	–
Vine	x	x	x	–	x	–
Violet	x	x	–	x	x	–
Walnut	–	–	–	–	x	x

References (from Loeb editions)
Plants that ornamented gardens: Volumes IV, V, VI.
Garden plants used to make chaplets: Book XXI.
Garden plants used in making wines/cordials: Book XIV.
Garden plants for bees, to make honey: Book XXI, 41, 70.
Garden plants with medicinal properties: Book XX–XXIII.
Culinary garden plants: Book XIX.

Notes

Introduction

1. Jashemski, 1979, 25.

Chapter One

1. Hugonot,1992, 38.
2. Kramer, 1958, 112–14.
3. Hyams, 1971, 11.
4. Iraq, XIV (1952) 33, ll. 38–48 cited by Wiseman, 1983, 142.
5. Strabo, XVI, 1, 5.
6. Diodorus Siculus, II, 10.
7. Homer, *Odyssey*, XXIV, 225ff.
8. Ibid., VII, 112ff.
9. Carroll-Spillecke, 1992, 86ff; Wycherley, 1976, 177–80.
10. SEG XIII, 521.11.158–61 cited by Carroll-Spillecke, 1992, 100, n. 12.
11. Athenian Constitution, 50.
12. Gleason, 1989, 285.
13. Thompson, 1963, fig. 11.
14. Theophrastus, *Enquiry into Plants*, VI, 1.
15. Pliny, *NH*, XIX, 19, 51.
16. Xenophon, *Oeconomics*, IV, 21.
17. Plutarch, *Lives, Alcibiades*, XXIV, 5.

Chapter Two

1. Pliny, *NH*, XIX, 19, 50.
2. Ibid., XIX, 19, 57.
3. Gracie & Price, 1979, 13.
4. From the Villa of Dar Buc Ammèra (Aurigema, 1960, pl. 123).

5. Cato, *RR*, I, 7.
6. Pliny, *NH*, XIX, 19, 49.
7. Virgil, *Georgics*, IV, 130ff.
8. Jashemski, 1987, 64 –71 and fig. 32.
9. Columella, *RR*, 10, 25.
10. McKay (1975, 21) mentions three prototype *atria*, which can be dated to the fifth century BC at the Etruscan city of Marzabotto.
11. Jashemski, 1979, 16, and Carroll-Spillecke, 1992, 94 respectively.
12. Ibid.
13. Diodorus Siculus, V, 40, 1.
14. Vitruvius, *De Arch*, IV, 9, 5.
15. Ibid., VI, 5, 1.
16. Martial, *Ep*, XI, 18.
17. Juvenal, *Sat*, III, 270–1.
18. Pliny, *NH*, XIX, 19, 59.
19. Seneca, *Ep*, 122, 8, and *Controv*, 5, 5.
20. Varro, *RR*, I, 13, 6.
21. Cicero, *De Leg*, II, 2, 5.
22. Varro, *RR*, III, 2, 3–10.
23. Platner & Ashby, Vol. I, 1929, 264 –73.
24. Vitruvius, *De Arch*, VI, 5, 2.
25. Pliny, *Ep*, II, 17, 17.
26. Vitruvius, *De Arch*, VI, 7, 5.
27. Varro, *RR*, II, Intr., 2.
28. Pliny, *NH*, XVIII, 1, 7.
29. Horace, *Odes*, II, 15.
30. Plutarch, *Lucullus*, XXXIX, 4.
31. Varro, *RR*, I, 13, 7.
32. Pliny, *Ep*, IX, 40.
33. Ibid., IX, 7.
34. Ibid., V, 6, 1.
35. Gorges, 1979, 121, fig. 19.

36. Lengyel and Radan, 1980, fig. 33.
37. Zeepvat, 1988, fig. 1.
38. Varro, *RR*, 1, 23, 4.
39. Columella, *RR*, I, 6, 1.

Chapter Three

1. Pliny, *NH*, XIX, 6, 24.
2. Clarke, 1991, 160. Cf. Wallace-Hadrill, 1988, 82.
3. Cicero, *Ad Att*, I, 10.
4. Willems & Kooistra, 1987, 139, Afb. 2.
5. Brulet, 1996, 1, 74, fig. 3.
6. Pliny, *NH*, XIX, 20, 60.
7. Ciarallo, 1993, 110.
8. Morel, 1993, 431.
9. Vitruvius, *De Arch*, V, 9, 7.
10. Gracie & Price, 1979, 13.
11. Pliny, *Ep*, V, 6, 17 and 34; Cicero, *De Leg*, III, 1.
12. Pliny, *Ep*, II, 17, 14.
13. Ciarallo, 1993, 112.
14. Moretti, 1940, fig. 48.
15. Nicene and Post-Nicene Fathers, *Gregory of Nyssa*, Letter XV.
16. Jashemski, 1993, 82–3.
17. Walters, *ARA*, 1996, 2, 13.
18. Statius, *Silvae*, III, 86–8. In this case couches only are mentioned.
19. Another example, also from Africa, is shown in Gothein, 1966, vol. 1, fig. 93.
20. Martial, *Ep*, V, 62.
21. Pliny, *Ep*, V, 6, 40.
22. Cicero, *Acad Luc*, II, 3, 9.
23. Pliny, *NH*, XIII, 29, 95.
24. Jashemski, 1993, 10.
25. Ibid., 211.
26. Martial, *Ep*, XIV, 87; Pliny, *Ep*, V, 6, 36; cf. Methodius (*Symp*) in Rossiter, 1989, 105, n. 33.
27. Pliny, *Ep*, 6, 37.
28. Vitruvius, *De Arch*, VI, 3, 10; translation by Morgan.
29. Tomei, 1992, 921, fig. 2.
30. Packer, 1967, 129.
31. Neuerburg, 1965, 258, fig. 165.

32. Tomei, 1992, figs 4–6.
33. Vetters, 1972–3, 57, fig. 60.
34. Dated to the fourth century AD (Lauter-Bufe, 1975, fig. 173).
35. Ashby, 1906, 190, fig. 33.
36. Jashemski, 1993, fig. 356.
37. Carandini & Tatton-Brown, 1980, 12, fig. 6.
38. Pliny, *Ep*, V, 6, 17.
39. Thébert, 1993, 223.
40. Ward-Perkins, 1989, 312; cf. Gleason, 1989, 255–6; Id. 1988, 33.
41. Ovid, *Ex Ponto*, I, 8, 36.
42. Ashby, 1906, 3ff.
43. Plutarch, *Luc*, 39, 2.
44. Horace, *Sat*, I, VIII, 10–15.
45. Richardson, 1992, 203.
46. For example, those of Bufalini, *c.* AD 1551 and Ligorio, *c.* AD 1553.
47. Broise & Jolivet, 1995, 191.
48. Grimal, 1969, 269.
49. Tacitus, *Ann*, XI, 1.
50. Seneca, *Ep*, LV, 6.
51. Ibid., LXXXIX, 21.
52. Pliny, *Ep*, IX, 7.
53. Statius, *Silv*, II, 2, 33ff.
54. Pliny, *NH*, XXXV, 37, 116–17.
55. Plutarch, *Luc*, XXXIX, 3.
56. Columella, *RR*, 1, 5, 5.
57. Pliny, *Ep*, II, 17, 15.
58. Van Buren, 1948, fig. 4; cf. Ricotti, 1987, figs 35–7; Castell, 1728, 17.
59. Lafon, 1981, 347, fig. 4.
60. Boethius & Ward-Perkins, 1970, fig. 125.
61. Silin (Rebuffat, 1974); Zliten & Tagiura (Rebuffat, 1969).
62. Swoboda, 1969, Abb. 32.
63. Cunliffe, 1971, 143 and fig. 31.
64. Suetonius, *Nero*, 31.
65. Hemsoll, 1990, 12.
66. *Historiae Augustae, Had*, XXVI, 5.
67. Grimal, 1969, 255. A similar portico was found at Tarracina (Lugli, 1926, 142, no. 90).
68. Plutarch, *Luc*, XLII, 1.
69. Cicero, *Ad Fam*, IX, 4, *'si hortum in bibliotheca habes, deerit nihil'*.

70. Ibid., *Ad Att*, I, 8; I, 9.
71. Hülsen, 1926, Abb. 60.
72. Hoffmann, *Das Gartenstadion in der Villa Hadriana*, 1980.
73. Pliny, *Ep*, V, 6, 32ff.
74. Such as those by Gothein, 1966, 100; Grimal, 1969, 252; Förtsch, 1993, pl. 43.
75. Pliny, *NH*, XII, 5, 10.
76. Luxorius, *Anth Lat*, 18.
77. Suetonius, *Nero*, 38.
78. Pliny, *Ep*, V, 6, 38.
79. Cicero, *Ad Fratrem*, III, 1, 1.
80. Varro, *RR*, III, 5, 11ff.
81. Van Buren & Kennedy, 1919, 61, fig. 1.
82. Broise & Jolivet, 1955, fig. 6; Lanciani, 1897, 416.
83. Statius, *Silv*, III, 1, 82f.
84. Pliny, *Ep*, IX, 39.
85. Cicero, *De Leg*, II, 3, 6.
86. Horace, *Odes*, III, 13.
87. Lavagne, 1993, 748.
88. Neuerburg, 1965, 115–16, figs 13 and 14.
89. Suetonius, *Tib*, 39 and Tacitus, *Ann*, IV, 59.
90. MacKendrick, 1962, 175.
91. Seneca, *Ep*, LV, 6.
92. Neuerburg, 1965, 156 and fig. 34.
93. Lanciani, *c.* 1924, 110.
94. Pliny, *NH*, XXXVI, 42, 154.
95. Propertius, *Eleg*, III, 3, 27–9.
96. Statius, *Silvae*, III, 1, 144.
97. Hallam, 1914, figs 8–9.
98. Wrede, 1972, 26–7, fig. 7.
99. Alarcão, 1988, fig. 73.

Chapter Four

1. Varro, *RR*, III, 3, 5; III, 17, 3.
2. Pliny, *NH*, IX, 80, 170.
3. Varro, *RR*, III, 17, 2.
4. Ibid., III, 17, 9.
5. Cassiodorus, *Variae*, 12, 15.
6. Statius, *Silv*, II, 3.
7. Cicero, *Ad Att*, II, 9.
8. Pliny, *NH*, XXXI, 57.
9. Ashby, 1906, 176.
10. Wrede, 1972, 19.
11. Sidonius, *Epist*, II, 2, 8.
12. Vitruvius, *De Arch*, X,4, 2; X, 7, 3.
13. Palladius, I, 61f.
14. Richardson, 1988, 51–4 and p. 63.
15. Jashemski, 1993, 136.
16. Musee du Luxembourg, 1983, 135–6, figs 61, 64–5; cf. Ferdière, 1988, 1, 230.
17. MacDonald & Pinto, 1995, 172.
18. Propertius, II, 32, 14–16.
19. Cunliffe, 1971, 139; also cf. Cunliffe, Down & Rudkin, 1996, 40, pl. 15.
20. Hodge, 1992, 324–6.
21. Detsicas, 1974, 77.
22. Jashemski, 1993, 227.
23. Zeepvat, 1988, 21
24. Palladius, I, 158, 1, 105–6.
25. Guillen, 1992, pls 13–16.
26. Ben Khaler & Soren, 1987, 204.
27. Zeepvat, 1988, 18.
28. Jashemski, 1993, 173, 137, 139.
29. Columella, *RR*, 8, 17, 2.
30. Pliny, *NH*, IX, 78, 167.
31. Eliades, G.S. *The House of Dionysus*, Paphos, 1984, p. 14.
32. Ricotti, 1987, 138; Jasemski, 1993, 173, 276; Laroche, 1984, 66; Thébert, 1993, 227.
33. Jashemski, 1993, 244.
34. Grew, Britannia, XI, 1980, 378.
35. Zeepvat, 1988, fig. 1.
36. Cicero, *De Legibus*, II, 1, 2; *Ad Fratrem*, III, 9, 7.
37. Seneca, *Ep*, XC, 15.
38. Martial, *Ep*, XII, 31, 2.
39. Seneca, *Ep*, LV, 6.
40. Pliny, *NH*, XXXVI, 24, 123.
41. Ovid, *Ex Ponto*, I, 8, 38.
42. Lugli, 1938, 159.
43. Laroche, 1984, 49.
44. LeGlay, 1981, 63.
45. Février, 1975, fig. 19; Gallia, XXIV, 1966, 519; Casa del Anfiteatro, Mérida (Álvarez Martínez et al, 1997, 57); and Alarcão & Etienne, 1981, fig. 5.
46. Merrifield, 1975, 56, fig. 33.
47. Sisson, 1929, pl. 21.
48. Type C is also found in the so-called Palace

of Gordian (Rebuffat, 1969, Volubilis 1) and at the villas at Cabra and Almedinilla in Spain, which have been dated to the end of the third century AD (respectively Gorges, 1979, pl. XXXIII, 2 and Gil & Diaz-Pines, 1995, fig. 8c).

49. Sidonius, *Ep*, II, 2, 19.
50. Wilson, 1990, 200.1; Ramos, 1991, 74–5; Rebuffat, 1969, Cherchel 3 & Volubilis 1, 11, 12, 16, 25.
51. Thébert, 1987, 223.
52. Alexander & Ennaïfer, 1975, pl. XI.
53. Boethius & Ward Perkins, 1970, 532.
54. Fernández-Galiano, 1994, 201, fig. 16.
55. Such as the villa of La Cocosa at Badajoz (Gorges, 1979, pl. XLIII); Torres Novas (ibid., pl. IL) and Liedena (ibid., pl. LI) in Spain. Nennig in Germany (Ferdière, 1988, 1, 215); and Wall in Britain (Webster, Wall Roman Site, London, 1994, 17).
56. George, 1997, 52.
57. Mallwitz, 1972, 254, fig. 201.
58. Rebuffat, 1969, Volubilis 7.
59. Alexander & Ennaïfer, 1975, 35 and pl. XI, 2.
60. Fremerdorf, 1956, taf. 37.
61. Balty, 1981, fig. 138.
62. Rebuffat, 1969, 662.
63. Varro, *RR*, III, 17, 6; Martial, X, 30, 21–4; Luxorius, *Poems*, 5.
64. Varro, *RR*, III, 2, 17.
65. Columella, *RR*, VIII, 16, 5; Pliny, *NH*, IX, 80, 170.
66. Pliny, *NH*, IX, 81, 171.
67. Horace, *Odes*, II, 15.
68. Gil & Diaz-Pines, 1995, 134.

Chapter Five

1. Pliny, *Ep*, VIII, 8.
2. Arlay in France (Gallia, 1966, 371) and Almedinilla in Spain (Gil & Diaz-Pines, 1995, 129).
3. Pliny, *NH*, XXVI, 184.
4. Pliny, *Ep*, V, 6, 20.
5. Hoffmann, 1980, fig. 33.

6. It is now covered by soil (Richardson, 1988, 334).
7. Sanders, 1982, 146.
8. Bellido, 1949, fig. 432.
9. Cicero, *Ad Frat*, III, 1, 3.
10. Sidonius Apollinaris, *Epist*, II, 2, 8.
11. Zeepvat, 1988, 18.
12. Erdemgil, 1989, fig. 116; Jashemski, 1993, 45.
13. Knight, 1994, 22.
14. Jashemski, 1979, fig. 531.
15. Jashemski, 1993, fig. 230
16. The serpent and three dolphins are from the same house in Pompeii (Dwer, 1982, Plate XXXVII, 139).
17. Balmelle, 1994, fig. 5.
18. Underwood, 1975, fig. 7.
19. M. Henig in Harding & Lewis, 1997, 35–6 and fig. 5.
20. Vitruvius, *De Arch*, X, 7, 4.
21. Athenaeus, *Deipn*, V, 198f.
22. Hero, *Pneumatics*, 44 and 49, trans. Woodcroft.
23. Ibid., 28.
24. Observed by Montaigne (Morton, 1970, 24).

Chapter Six

1. Cato, *De Agri*, 143, 2.
2. Pliny, *NH*, XXI, 8.
3. Virgil, *Eclog*, VII, 30 and 34; Tibullus, I, 11–18; Martial, *Ep*, III, 19, 1.
4. Vermeule, 1981, no. 121.
5. Neudecker, 1988, 234.
6. De Caro, 1987, 129.
7. Athenaeus, *Deipn*, V, 196, e.
8. Pliny, *NH*, XXXVI, 4, 23–5.
9. Aurigemma, 1971, 31.
10. Cicero, *Ad.Att*, I, 8–9; *Ad. Fam*, VII, 23.
11. Bonfante, 1990, 57.
12. Varro, *RR*, I, 1, 5.
13. Martial, *Ep*, X, 92.
14. e.g. (Pompeii, VI, ix, 6) and (Pompeii, I, xi, 12), respectively Jashemski, 1993, 139 and 152.
15. S.H.A., *Marcus Ant*. VI, 9.

16. Pliny, *NH*, XII, 2, 3.
17. Jashemski, 1979, 134.
18. Jashemski, 1979, 124.
19. Varro, *RR*, I, 16; Pliny, *NH*, XIX, 19, 50.
20. Pliny, *NH*, XXXVI, 4, 16.
21. Hill, 1981, 93, fig. 1, 16; 17–18.
22. Maiuri, 1959, 25.
23. *Per. Ven.* 28.
24. Horace, *Sat*, VIII, 6–7.
25. Virgil, *App. Priapea*, 3, 17ff.
26. Martial, *Ep*, VI, 72.
27. Clarke, 1991, 210–11.
28. Luxorius, *Anth.Lat.* 61.
29. M. Henig, 'Roman Sculpture from the Cotswold Region', *CSIRI*, 7, (1993), 3, no. 2.
30. Aurigemma, 1955, 287.
31. Cato, *De Agri*, CXLI.
32. Martial, *Ep*, X, 92.
33. Luxorius, *Anth. Lat*, 18.
34. Grimal, 1969, 55.
35. Appleton,1987,166.
36. Appleton, 1987, 146.
37. Pliny, *NH*, XXXVI, 4, 36.
38. Virgil, *Eclog*, III, 62.
39. Philostratus, *Imagines*, 2.
40. Now in the Therme Museum, Rome, Inv. no. 72274.
41. Kapossy (1969, 74) draws our attention to the symbolic meaning of water pouring from different types of fountains.
42. Virgil, *Eclog*, VI, 14f.
43. Pliny, *NH*, XIX, 19, 50.
44. Propertius, *Eleg*, II, 32, 14.
45. Jashemski, 1979, figs. 466 and 470.
46. Pliny, *NH*, XXXV, 37, 116–17.
47. Philostratus the Elder, *Imagines*, II, 17, 10–15.
48. Appelton, 1987 fig. 29.
49. Cicero, *De Oratore*, I, 7, 28.
50. Neudecker, 1988, Taf. 16. Now in the Vatican Museum.
51. Cicero, *Ad Att*, I, 8.
52. Virgil, *Georgics*, II, 388–9.
53. Circular and rectangular *oscilla* were recorded by Pailler (1969, figs. 4–10); and peltae *oscilla* noted by Espérandieu (1925, 1, 225 and 283) in France. Bellido (1949, figs. 436; 440–1) lists circular and *peltae* shaped examples in Spain. A circular *oscillum* was found at a villa at Ramla Bay in Gozo (Ashby, 1915, 74). They were also present in North Africa (Baradez, 1952, 41 and 90).
54. Pailler, 1969, 632.
55. Cicero, *Ad Att*, I, 10, 3
56. Jashemski, 1993, 163.
57. As at Pompeii, VII, iv, 57 (Jashemski, 1979, 112).
58. Vitruvius, *De Arch*, IX, 8, 1.
59. Gibbs, S.L. *Greek and Roman Sundials*, London, 1976.
60. Vitruvius, *De Arch*, IX, 8, 4.
61. Varro, *RR*, III, 5, 17.

Chapter Seven

1. Pliny, *NH*, XXI, 10, 19.
2. Ibid., XV, 39, 128.
3. Ibid., XVI, 33, 79.
4. Ibid., XXIV, 53, 90.
5. Ibid., XIX, 53, 168–9.
6. Cato, *De Agri*, CLXI.
7. Ibid., CLVI.
8. Lawson, 1950, 98.
9. Columella, *RR*, XII, 7.
10. Pliny, *NH*, XIX, 19, 58.
11. Ibid., XV, 35, 118.
12. Ibid., XX, 87, 236–40.
13. Ibid., XIV, 19, 103.
14. Ibid., 106.
15. Varro, *RR*, III, 16, 12–15.
16. Ibid., *RR*, III, 16, 15.
17. Columella, *RR*, IX, 6, 2.
18. Palladius, I, 144.
19. Ibid., I, 147.
20. Columella, *RR*, IX, 5, 6.
21. Pliny, *Ep*, II, 17, 14.
22. Pliny, *NH*, XXIV, 59, 99–100.
23. Ibid., XVII, 21, 98.
24. Ibid., XIX, 62, 187.

25. Ibid., XXI, 32, 58.
26. Ibid., XIII, 2, 5.
27. Ibid., XXI, 6, 8.
28. Pliny, *NH*, XXI, 1, 2 and XXI, 8, 11; Martial, *Ep*, IX, 40, 6.
29. Theophrastus, V, 6, 2.
30. Athenaeus, *Deipn*, XV, 677f.
31. Ibid., XV, 681b.
32. Pliny, *NH*, XXI, 3, 5.
33. Horace, *Odes*, II, 7, 24.
34. Ibid., IV, 11.
35. Pliny, *NH*, XXI, 10, 14.
36. Athenaeus, *Deipn*, XIV, 629e.
37. Pliny, *NH*, XXI, 10, 19.
38. Ibid., XXI, 10, 18.
39. Philips & Rix, 1993, 11.
40. Athenaeus, *Deipn*, XV, 678, f.
41. Pliny, *NH*, XXI, 10, 16–17.
42. Franchi, 1992, 239.
43. Pliny, *NH*, XXI, 14, 27.
44. Jashemski & Ricotti, 1992, 594, n. 36.
45. Pliny, *NH*, XXI, 18, 39.
46. Ibid., XIII, 6, 26.
47. Ibid., XXII, 34, 76.
48. Ibid., XXI, 39, 68.
49. Ibid., XXI, 34, 60.
50. Ibid., XVI, 31, 76.
51. Martial, III, 58, 2 and XII, 50, 1; Horace, *Odes*, II, 15, 5–6.
52. Pliny, *NH*, XVI, 18, 40.
53. Ibid., XVI, 60, 140.
54. Ibid., XVI, 20, 50–1.
55. Ibid., XXIII, 79, 151.
56. Ibid., XVII, 1, 5.
57. Ibid., XVI, 53, 124.
58. Horace, *Odes*, II, 15.
59. Pliny, *NH*, XVII, 1, 4–5.
60. See note 57.
61. Pliny, *NH*, XV, 14, 47.
62. Ibid., XV, 30, 102–3.
63. Horace, *Odes*, I, 38.
64. Athenaeus, *Deipn*, V, 196d.
65. Information received from C. Ryley; also cf. Cunliffe, 1981, 98.
66. Jashemski, 1979, 87.
67. Gabriel, 1955, 39–40.
68. Jashemski, 1993, 318–22.
69. Pliny, *NH*, XXI, 11, 22.
70. Balmelle, 1994, fig. 1.
71. Columella, *RR*, X, 259.
72. Id, *De Arboribus*, XXX, 1.
73. Pliny, *NH*, XXV, 41, 82.
74. Athenaeus, *Deipn*, XV, 682d.
75. Tatius, Leucippe & Clitophon, 15.
76. Cicero, *Ad Fratrem*, III, 1, 5.
77. Pliny, *NH*, XVI, 62, 149; white ivy is also mentioned by Athenaeus, *Deipn*, XV, 683c.
78. Virgil, *Georgics*, IV, 124.
79. Jashemski, 1993, 295.
80. Pliny, *Ep*, V, 6, 20.
81. Jashemski, 1993, 293–4.
82. Ciarallo, 1994, 11.
83. Jashemski, 1995, 563.
84. Unpublished. Information supplied by the excavator, E. Price.
85. Cunliffe, 1971, 138.
86. Information supplied by the excavator R. Friendship-Taylor.
87. I. Meadows, 'Wollaston', *Current Archaeology*, 150 (1996), 212–15.
88. Richardson, 1992, b, 439.
89. See note 84.
90. Cunliffe, 1981, 104–5.
91. Bond & Iles, 1991, 36; Boon, 1974, 198; Murphy & Scaife, 1991, 88.
92. Pliny, *Ep*, V, 6, 16–17; ibid., V, 6, 35–6
93. Ibid., II, 17, 14.
94. Ashby, 1915, 56.
95. Murphy & Scaife, 1991, 85–6.
96. This plant was not native to the area and is therefore assumed to be of garden origin (Moffett, 1988, 76).
97. Arnould & Thebert, 1993, 438–9.
98. Jashemski, 1987, 34.
99. Information received from C. Ryley, 1995.
100. Murphy & Scaife, 1991, 88, tbl. 8.2.
101. Bond & Iles, 1991, 36.
102. Farrar, 1996, Append. IV.
103. Martial, *Ep*, I, 7, 1; Catullus, II & III.
104. Varro, *RR*, III, 6, 6.
105. Statius, *Silv*, II, 4, 11–12.
106. Varro, *RR*, III, 5, 8.

107. Jashemski, 1979, 108; 348, n. 88.

108. Varro, *RR*, III, 5, 13.

109. Jashemski, 1993, 188.

110. Varro, *RR*, III, 7, 2.

111. Ibid., III, 7, 3; III, 8, 1–2.

112. Cato, *De Agri*, XXXVI; Varro, *RR*, III, 7, 5; Columella, *RR*, II, 15, 1.

113. Ovid, *Trista*, I, 97–8.

114. A.J. Parker, 'The birds of Roman Britain', *OJA*, 7, (1988), 197–226.

115. Jashemski (1979, 96) has found evidence for this practice at Pompeii.

116. Murphy & Scaife, 1993, 93.

117. Ferdière, 1988, 152

118. Boon, 1957, 172–3.

119. Ferdière, 1988, 151.

120. Martial, *Ep*, I, 109.

121. Jashemski, 1979, 103.

122. Petronius, *Sat*, XV, 29.

123. Jashemski, 1979, fig. 422.

124. Columella, *RR*, VII, 12, 1–9.

125. Varro, *RR*, III, 15, 2.

126. Information received from A. Ciarallo, 1992.

127. Varro, *RR*, III, 15, 1; III, 14, 1.

128. Pliny, *NH*, IX, 82, 173.

129. Varro, *RR*, III, 3, 2.

130. Ibid., III, 13, 1.

131. Columella, *RR*, IX, 1, 2.

132. Varro, *RR*, III, 12, 2.

133. Grenier, 1931, 484.

134. Columella, *RR*, IX, 1, 1.

135. Varro, *RR*, III, 13, 2–3.

Chapter Eight

1. CIL.VI, 2, 9990–1; CIL.VI, 2, 9005.

2. Pliny, *NH*, XIX, 23, 64; Columella, *RR*, X, 177 and 229.

3. CIL.VI, 2, 9457–9.

4. Columella, *RR*, XI, 1, 12.

5. Ibid., *RR*, IV, 24, 1.

6. Ovid, *Ex Ponto*, I, 8, 60.

7. CIL.VI, 2, 9473.

8. Pliny, *NH*, XII, 6, 13.

9. Cicero, *Ad Fratrem*, III, I, 5.

10. CIL.VI, 2, 8639; CIL.VI, 2, 8738.

11. CIL.X, 1, 1744; CIL.V, 2, 5316

12. Respectively CIL.VI, 2, 9947 and CIL.VI, 2, 9945. Other fragments relating to *topiarii* name: Claudius Tauriscus (CIL.VI, 4360), Dorio (CIL.VI, 4361), Cerdone (CIL.VI, 5353), Sasa (CIL.VI, 6370), Alexandri from Spain (CIL.VI, 2, 9943), Lucrio (CIL.VI, 2, 9946), Apolonis (CIL.VI, 2, 9948). Those that bear no name simply carry a message such as CIL.VI.6369 which reads 'Felix Topiarius'.

13. Ennaifer, 1973, cover illustration..

14. Columella, *RR*, X, 148; Palladius, I, 166, 1161.

15. Gracie & Price, 1979, 31, fig. 13.4. One has also been found at Chedworth.

16. Jashemski, 1979, 290.

17. Down in Cunliffe, Down & Rudkin, 1996, 148–9, fig. 6.19, pl. 26; Detsicas, 1974, 305.

18. Jashemski, 1981, 34, n. 8–11; c.f. Gleason, 1989, Appendix A.

19. Pliny, *NH*, XII, 7, 16. Theophrastus (*Enquiry into Plants*), VI, 7, 3 attests to the use of plant pots in Greece.

20. Jashemski & Ricotti, 1992, 582–3, figs 5 and 6.

21. Morel, 1993, 431.

22. Thompson, 1963, figs. 50 and 12–13.

23. Palladius, VII, 12.

24. Pliny, *NH*, XIX, 36, 121; XXI, 14, 27.

25. Cato, *De Agri*, XLVI; XLVIII; Columella, *De Arboribus*, XXV, 2.

26. Virgil, *Georgics*, II, 266.

27. Columella, *De Arboribus*, XX, 2; Virgil, *Georgics*, II, 269.

28. Cato, *De Agri*, CXXXIII; Pliny, *NH*, XVII, 21, 97.

29. Jashemski, 1992, 583, fig. 6; 1979, 293–5.

30. Pliny, *NH*, XII, 7, 15.

31. Ibid., XII, 7, 16; Palladius, IV, 64, 445; Ibid., IV, 67–9.

32. Namely the Trübner version by Lodge, therefore in this instance I have used Nisard.

33. Columella, *RR*, XI, 3, 63.

34. Pliny, *NH*, XXI, 10, 21.
35. Columella, *RR*, XI, 3, 52–3. Seneca, *Ep*, CXXII, 8; Martial, VIII, 14.
36. Pliny, *NH*, XXI, 34, 60.
37. Columella, *De Arboribus*, XX, 2.
38. Cato, *De Agri*, XL; Columella, *De Arboribus*, XXVI.
39. Pliny, *NH*, XV, 9, 35 and XV, 12, 42.
40. Calpurnius Siculus, *Eclog*, II, 40–3.
41. Palladius, XII, 24, 166; Virgil, *Georgics*, II, 70; Pliny, *NH*, XVII, 26, 121.
42. Pliny, *NH*, XVII, 26, 120.
43. Ibid., XV, 39, 132.
44. Ibid., XV, 15, 51.
45. Ibid., XV, 15, 49; XV, 16, 54; Columella, *RR*, V, 10, 18–19.
46. Pliny, *NH*, XV, 15, 50; XVII, 1, 7; XVIII, 3, 10.
47. Ibid., XII, 6, 13.
48. Ibid., XXI, 10, 21.
49. Palladius, III, 108, 750f; XII, 20, 134f.
50. Ibid., XI, 34, 232f.
51. Jashemski, 1993, 249.
52. Pliny, *NH*, XVII, 15, 78.
53. Varro, *RR*, I, 23, 5.
54. Pliny, *NH*, XIX, 20, 60.
55. Columella, *RR*, II, 10, 26.
56. Pliny, *NH*, XIX, 20, 60; XVII, 16, 81; Columella, De Arbor, XXX.
57. Pliny, *NH*, XVII, 16, 81.
58. Pliny (*NH*, XVIII, 50, 187) states that moisture from dew was collected at night in Africa, Greece and Bactris. Columella (*De Arbor*, IV, 5) appears to have used this technique for young vines. He recommends placing stones in the depression around the roots so they would 'provide moisture in the summer'. This could only refer to the process of condensation of air into dew on the stones at night-time.
59. Columella, *RR*, II, 50–6, 14.
60. Ibid., II, 15, 4.
61. Pliny, *NH*, XVII, 16, 82.
62. Jashemski, 1979, 286.
63. Jashemski & Ricotti, 1992, 588–93, figs. 9–12.
64. Pliny, *NH*, XIX, 60, 183.
65. Palladius, VI, 32.
66. Pliny, *NH*, XIX, 23, 64; XIX, 24, 69; Columella, *RR*, X, 377–8; X, 395.
67. Palladius, IV, 30.204–8; Pliny, *NH*, XIX, 24, 70.
68. Ibid.; Columella, *RR*, X, 390.
69. Columella, *RR*, II, 14, 3; Palladius, XII, 16, 111–12.
70. Pliny, *NH*, XII, 3, 8; Macrobius, *Sat*, 3, 13, 3.
71. Pliny, *NH*, XIX, 58, 179.
72. Ibid; Columella, *RR*, X, 353; Palladius, I, 122–3, 848; Columella, *RR*, XI, 3, 60–1.
73. Pliny, *NH*, XIX, 58.
74. Columella, *RR*, X, 341; Palladius, I, 120, 835.
75. Pliny, *NH*, XIX, 58, 180; Palladius, I, 124, 862.
76. Columella, *RR*, XI, 3, 64; X, 358; Palladius, I, 123, 860.
77. Columella, *RR*, X, 342–4.
78. Ovid, *Fasti*, IV, 906–42; Seyffert, 1894, 548.
79. Virgil, *Georgics*, I, 79–83.
80. Pliny, *NH*, XVIII, 65, 242.
81. Columella, *RR*, III, 8, 5.

Chapter Nine

1. Minor Poems, *Copa*, 7f and 31.
2. Varro, *RR*, I, 16, 3.
3. Johnson, 1975, 101–5.
4. Rea, 1978, 100, letter 3313.
5. e.g., CIL.XII, 1657.
6. CIL.V, 7454.
7. Petronius, *Sat*, XV, 71.
8. Johnson, 1975, 101.
9. Fraser & Nicholas, 1958, 118.
10. Cicero, *Ad Att*, XII, 23.
11. Ibid., XII, 37.
12. Jashemski, 1979, 148.
13. Virgil, *Culex*, 398–407.
14. Toynbee, 1982, 98, fig. 7.
15. Toynbee, 1982, 99, fig. 8.
16. Strabo, *Geog*, 5, 3, 8.
17. Suetonius, *Augustus*, 100.

18. Suetonius, *Caesar*, 83; Cass.Dio.XLIV, 35, 3.
19. Tacitus, *Annals*, XIV, 15.
20. Suetonius, *Augustus*, 100.
21. Cass.Dio, LIV, 29, 4.
22. Ovid, *Ex Ponto*, I, 8, 37–8.
23. Tacitus, *Ann*, XV, 37.
24. Strabo, XIII, 1, 19.
25. Martial, *Ep*, III, 19, 2.
26. Ibid., IX, 40, 1; Macrobius, *Sat*, VI, 2, 5.
27. Martial, *Ep*, III, 20, 12–13.
28. Plutarch, *Pompey*, XLII, 4.
29. Vitruvius, *De Arch*, V, 9, 1.
30. Propertius, *El*, II, 32, 11f.
31. Richardson, 1992, 318.
32. Gleason, 1994, 14.
33. Martial, *Ep*, II, 14, 10.
34. Vitruvius, *De Arch*, V, 11f.
35. Martial, *Ep*, II, 14, 15.
36. Ibid., I, 108, 3.
37. Pliny, *NH*, XIV, 3, 11.
38. Ibid., XV, 36, 120.
39. Ibid., XVI, 82, 236.
40. Ibid., XII, 2, 3.
41. *SHA, The Three Gordians*, XXXII, 6f.
42. Alarcão & Etienne, 1981, 77.
43. Sisson, 1929, Pl. 21.
44. Richardson, 1992, 88.
45. Lloyd, 1982, 92.
46. Pliny, *NH*, XXXIV, 19, 84.
47. Ibid., XXXVI, 4, 27; XXXVI, 11, 58.
48. Procopius, *Bell.Goth*, IV, 21, 11–12.
49. Pliny, *NH*, XXXVI, 24, 102.
50. Ovid, *Ars Am*, I, 75.
51. Philostratus, *Vita Apoll.Tyana*, VII, 32.
52. Lloyd, 1982, 98.
53. Details of this cult are found in Gow, 1938, 194.
54. Morel, 1993, 434, fig. 4.
55. Cato, *De Agricultura*, LII, 2.
56. Ovid, *Ars Am*, I, 72; Pliny, *NH*, XIV, 3, 11; Strabo, *Geog*, 5, 3, 8. Martial (*Ep*, III, 20, 8) mentions the *Schola Octaviae*, and is thought to allude to part of the Porticus Liviae or Octaviae.
57. Pliny, *NH*, XIV, 3, 11.
58. Vitruvius, *De Arch*, V, 9, 9.

Chapter Ten

1. Pliny, *Ep*, III, 19, 3.
2. Cicero, *De Leg*, II, 2, 1; *Acad*, II, 3, 9; *De Oratore*, I, 7, 28.
3. Ovid, *Trista*, I, 11, 37; Pliny, *Ep*, IX, 36, 3.
4. *Eleg. Maec*, I, 35–6.
5. Horace, *Odes*, II, 15.
6. Pliny, *NH*, XVIII, 7, 35.
7. Ellis, 1988, 565–9; Potter, *Towns in Late Antiquity*, 1995.
8. Dagron, 1978, 69.
9. Ellis-Rees, 1995, 10–28; cf. Lee, 1981, 171.
10. Queen Eleanor's Garden, Winchester (S. Landsberg, *The Medieval Garden*, 1995, 123).
11. Pliny, *Ep*, VIII, 18, 11.

Glossary

Aedicula (plural *aediculae*) A shrine, often a small roofed structure with a niche.

Ambulatio (pl. *ambulationes*) A walkway, pathways.

Amphora (pl. *amphorae*) A narrow-necked earthenware vessel with handles, often used for storage/transporting liquids.

Architrave Horizontal beam supported by the columns of a portico.

Atrium (pl. *atria*) The central hall in a traditional Roman house with an opening in the roof. Also the forecourt of a temple or early Christian church.

Biclinium (pl. *biclinia*) Two dining couches placed for a party of up to six (three on each *klinai*).

Cartibulum Marble or stone table placed by the *impluvium* in the *atrium* or in a peristyle.

Cepotaphia A large funerary monument, often with garden attached.

Compluvium The rectangular opening in the roof of an *atrium*.

Cryptoporticus A vaulted area or passage within the substructure of a building or beneath a terrace.

Diaeta (pl. *diaetae*) A daytime resting room or pavilion/summerhouse in the garden.

Dolium (pl. *dolia*) Large pottery jar.

Domus The Roman house or traditional home.

Exedra (pl. *exedrae*) An open-fronted room or recess.

Euripus (pl. *euripi*) A decorative water feature in the form of an elongated channel.

Fauces The entrance passage of a house.

Gestatio A drive or carriageway leading to a villa or in the grounds.

Herm A statue of pillar-like form with a sculpted head; sometimes drapery is included.

Hippodromus (in Greek *hippodromos*) A garden with a circular course that vaguely recalls a riding ground.

Hortus (pl. *horti*) The garden.

Impluvium The basin in the centre of the *atrium* into which rainwater is collected (falling through the *compluvium* above).

Insula (pl. *insulae*) A block of houses in a city or an apartment building.

Intercolumniation The space between two columns of a colonnade.

Lararium (pl. *lararia*) Shrine to the Lars, the gods of the household.

Mensa (pl. *mensae*) A table.

Museum (in Greek *museion*) A shrine or building dedicated to the muses (also a garden pavilion).

Nemus A wood or grove.

Nymphaeum (pl. *nymphaea*) A niche, shrine or building containing a spring or fountain/s to recall a grotto: the abode of a nymph.

Oecus (pl. *oecei*) A reception room, an alternative form of dining room.

Opus recticulatum A facing for concrete; of coursed brickwork or masonry laid diagonally.

Opus Signinum (abbreviated to *op. sig.*) A concrete-like mixture.

Ornithone An aviary.

Oscillum (pl. *oscilla*) A carved marble object suspended from a tree or between columns of a peristyle or *atrium*.

Paradeisos An enclosure to recall the garden or game preserve of Persian or eastern rulers.

Pelta (pl. *peltae*) The distinctive half-moon shield of the mythical Amazons.

Pergula (pl. *pergulae*) A pergola, a covered walkway of light construction, such as wood or trelliswork.

Peristylium (pl. *peristylia*) Garden or courtyard surrounded by a colonnade or porticos.

Pinax (pl. *pinakes*) A marble/stone relief panel usually mounted on a pillar.

Piscina (pl. *piscinae*) A fishpond.

Pluteus (pl. *plutei*) A low wall enclosing a garden or basin.

Porticus (pl. *portici*) A walkway under a roof supported by columns.

Puteal The marble/stone drawshaft of a cistern, which resembles a chimney pot.

Putto (pl. *putti*) Also known as *erotes* or *amorini*, small children attendants of Venus and her son Cupid.

Schola (pl. *scholae*) A curved stone bench.

Silvae Woodland or shrubbery.

Stadium A race track or elongated garden with the short sides rounded to recall such places.

Stibadium or *Sigma* A large curved (or horseshoe-shaped) dining couch where a number of guests could recline.

Tablinum Traditionally the main reception room of the house, opening on to the *atrium*.

Thiasos The mythical retinue of a god, usually Bacchus or Venus.

Tholos A circular building, usually supported by columns.

Topiarius (pl. *topiarii*) A gardener of ornamental gardens.

Triclinium (pl. *triclinia*) A dining room where three couches (*klinai*) are arranged in a 'U' formation.

Villa rustica (pl. *villae rusticae*) Rustic villa or farm.

Villa suburbana Luxurious dwelling in or near the city.

Villa urbana (pl. *villae urbanae*) Refined villa or manor house in town or country.

Viridarium An interior garden.

Xystus (pl. *xysti*) A terrace or flower bed usually near the home or other buildings.

Bibliography

Anon. *Pervigilium Veneris*, trans. F.W. Cornish, Loeb, 1988

Aksit, I. *Ancient Ephesus*, Antalya, 1994

Alarcão, J. *Roman Portugal*, Warminster, 1988

Alarcão, J & R. Etienne, 'Les Jardins à Conimbriga (Portugal)', in *Ancient Roman Gardens*, Washington (1981), 69–80

Alexander, M. & N. Ennaïfer, *Corpus des Mosaiques de Tunisie, Thuburbo Majus, 2.1*, Tunis, 1980

——. 'Quelques Precisions à Propos de la Chronologie des Mosaiques d'Utique', in *La Mosaïque Gréco Romaine II*, ed. H. Stern & M. LeGlay, Paris (1975), 31–9

Amelung, W. *The Museums and Ruins of Rome*, I, London, 1912

Appleton, G. *Animal Sculpture from Roman Gardens*, PhD thesis, University of Newcastle-upon-Tyne, 1987

Aristotle. *The Athenian Constitution*, trans. J.Warrington, London, 1961

Arnould, P. & Y. Thébert, 'Secteur D: note sur des charbons de bois provennant de la fouille 1992', in 'Chronique, Rome: le Palatin (Vigna Barberini)', *MEFRA*,105.1 (1993), 419–92

Arrian. *Anabasis of Alexander*, trans. E.I. Robson, Loeb, 1949

Ashby, T. 'Classical Topography of the Roman Campagna-II', *PBSR*, 3 (1906), 3–197

——. 'Roman Malta', *JRS*, 5, 1 (1915), 23–80

Athenaeus. *The Deipnosophists*, trans. C.B. Gulick, Loeb, 1957

Aurigemma, S. *The Baths of Diocletian and the Museo Nazionale Romano*, 3rd edn., Rome, 1955

——. *Villa Adriana (Hadrian's Villa) Near Tivoli*, 8th edn, Tivoli, 1971

Ballu, A. *Guide Illustré de Timgad*, Paris, 1910

Balmelle, C. 'Les représentations d'Arbres fruitiers sur les mosaiques tardives d'Aquitaine', in *Fifth International Colloquim on Ancient Mosaics, JRA*, supplementary series no. 9, Ann Arbor, 1994, 261–72

Balty, J.C. *Guide d'Apamée*, Bruxelles, 1981

Baradez et al, *Tipasa, Cherchel, Tebessa*, Algiers, 1952

Bieber, M. *The Sculpture of the Hellenistic Age*, New York, 1955

Bellido, A.G. *Colonia Aelia Augusta Italica*, Instituto Español de Arqueologia, Madrid, 1960

Bellido, G.Y. *Escvltvras Romanas, de España, y Portvgal*, Madrid, 1949

Ben Khader, A.& D. Soren, *Carthage: A Mosaic of Ancient Tunisia*, London, 1987

Birmingham Botanical Gardens, 'The Historic Gardens I', *Spring Newsletter* (1994), 9–11

Blamey, M. & C. Grey-Wilson, *Mediterranean Wild Flowers*, St. Helier, Jersey, 1993

Boersma, J.S. *Amoenissima Civitas, Block V, ii at Ostia: description and analysis of its visible remains*, Assen, 1985

Boëthius, A. & J. Ward-Perkins, *Etruscan and Roman Architecture*, Harmondsworth, 1970

Bond, C.J. & R. Iles, 'Early Gardens in Avon and Somerset', in *Garden Archaeology*, ed. A.E. Brown, CBA Research Report 78 (1991), 36–52

Bonfante, L. *Etruscan*, BM, London, 1990

Boon, G.C. *Roman Silchester: The Archaeology of a Romano-British Town*, London, 1957

——. *Silchester: The Roman Town of Calleva*, Newton Abbot, 1974

Börsch-Supan, E. *Garten-Landschafts-und Paradiesmotive im Inneraum*, Berlin, 1967

Broise, H.& V. Jolivet, 'Des Jardins de Lucullus au Palais des Pincii', *Bulletin de la SFAC, RA* (1994/1995), 188–98

Brulet, R. 'La Maison Urbaine en Gaule, Belgique et en Germanie Inférieure' in *La Maison Urbaine d'Époque Romaine en Gaule Narbonnaise et dans les provinces voisines*, 1, Conseil Général de Vaucluse, Avignon (1996), 72–97

Calpernius Siculus, *Eclogues*, trans. J.W. Duff, Loeb, 1961

Carandini, A. & Tatton-Brown, T. 'Excavations at the Roman Villa of "Sette Finestre" in Etruria, 1975–9, First Interim Report', in *Roman Villas in Italy*, ed. K.Painter, British Museum, London (1980), 9–43

Carrington, R.S. 'Studies in the Campanian "Villae Rusticae"', *JRS*, 21 (1931), 110–30

Carroll-Spillecke, M. *Der Garten von der Antike bis zum Mittelalter*, Mainz, 1995

——. 'The Gardens of Greece from Homeric to Roman Times', *Journal of Garden History*, 12 (1992), 84–101

Cassius Dio, *Dio's Roman History*, trans. E. Cary, Loeb, 1961

Cassiodorus, *Variae*, trans. T. Hodgkin, London, 1886

Castell, R. *The Villas of the Ancients Illustrated*, reprint of the 1728 edn, New York, 1982

Catling, H.W. 'Archaeology in Greece,1973–74', *JHS*, 94 (1974), 3–41

Cato, *De Agricultura*, trans. W.D. Hooper, Loeb, 1967

Catullus, *Opera*, trans. F.W. Cornish, Loeb, 1988

Ciarallo, A.M. 'The Garden of "Casa Dei Casti Amanti" (Pompeii, Italy)', *Garden History*, 21 (1993), 110–16

——. 'The Gardens of Pompeii', in *Garden History: Garden Plants, Species, Forms and Varieties from Pompeii to 1800, PACT*, 42 (1994), 9–13

Cicero. *Academica*, trans. H. Rackham, Loeb, 1993

——. *Ad Atticum*, trans. E.O. Winstedt, Loeb, 1919

——. *Ad Familiares*, trans. G. Williams, Loeb, 1928

——. *Ad Fratrem*, trans. G. Williams, Loeb, 1929

——. *De Legibus*, trans. C. Walker Keyes, Loeb, 1988

——. *De Oratore*, trans. H. Rackham, Loeb, 1979

——. *Laws*, trans, B. Radice, Loeb, 1969

C.I.L. *Corpus Inscriptionum Latinarum*, vols V, VI, X, Berlin (1863–1883)

Cima, M.& E. La Rocca, *Le Tranquille Dimore Degli Dei: La Residenza Imperiale Degli Horti Lamiani*, Venice, 1986

Clarke, J.R. *The Houses of Roman Italy 100 BC–AD 250 Ritual, Space, and Decoration*, Berkeley, 1991

Coffin, D.R. *Gardens and Gardening in Papal Rome*, Princeton, 1991

Columella. *De Arboribus*, trans. E.S. Forster, Loeb, 1955

——. *De Re Rustica*, trans. E.S. Forster, Loeb, 1955

Corcoran, T.H. 'Roman Fishponds', *Classical Bulletin*, 35 (1959), 34–43

Cordello. *Ostia*, Venice, 1986

Cunliffe, B. Fishbourne: A Roman Palace and its Garden, London, 1971

——. 'Excavations at Fishbourne, 1967, Seventh & Final Interim Report', *Ant.J.*, 48 (1968), 32–40

——. 'Roman Gardens in Britain: A Review of the Evidence', in *Ancient Roman Gardens*, Washington (1981), 97–108

Dagron, G. *Vie et Miracles de Sainte Thècle*, Bruxelles, 1978

Daremberg, C.H. & E.D.M. Saglio, *Dictionnaire des Antiquités, Greques et Romaines*, Paris, 1900

Daubeny, C. *Lectures on Roman Husbandry*, Oxford, 1857

——. *Essay on the Trees and Shrubs of the Ancients*, Oxford, 1865

De Caro, S. 'The Sculptures of the Villa of Poppaea at Oplontis: A Preliminary Report', in *Ancient Roman Villa Gardens*, Washington (1987), 79–133

Detsicas, A.P. 'Excavations at Eccles, 1972, 11th Interim Report', *Archaeologia Cantiana*, 88 (1973), 73–80

——. 'Exhibits at Ballots, 2. Finds from the pottery kiln(s) at Eccles, Kent', *Ant.J.*, 14 (1974), 305–6

Diodorus Siculus. *Diodorus of Sicily*, trans. C.H. Oldfather, Loeb, 1952

Down, A. 'Exhibits at Ballots', *Ant.J,* 69 (1989), 308–9

Dragotta, A.M. *Piazza Armerina*, Palermo, 1978

Dwyer, E.J. *Pompeian Domestic Sculpture*, Rome, 1982

Ellis, S.P. 'The End of the Roman House', *AJA*, 92 (1988), 565–76

Ellis-Rees, W. 'Gardening in the Age of Humanism: Petrarch's Journal', *Garden History*, 23 (1995), 10–28

Ennaïfer, M. *La Civilisation Tunisienne à Travers la Mosaïque*, Tunis, 1973

Erdemgil, S. *Ephesus {Ruins and Museum}*, Istanbul, 1989

Espérandieu, E. *Recueil Général des Bas-Relief, Statues et Bustes de la Gaule Romaine*, 9, Paris, 1925

Ferdière, A. *Les Campagnes en Gaule Romaine*, 2, Paris, 1988

Février, P.A. 'Remarques sur des Mosaiques de Frejus', in *La Mosaïque Gréco-Romaine II*, ed. H.Stern & M. LeGlay, Paris (1975), 291–300

Förtsch, R. *Archäologischer Kommentar zu den Villenbrirfen des Jüngeren Plinius*, Mainz, 1993

Fradier, G. *Roman Mosaics of Tunisia*, 5th edn, Tunis, 1994

Franchi, F. *Rediscovering Pompeii*, Rome, 1992

Fraser, P.M. & B. Nicholas, 'The Funerary Garden of Mousa', *JRS*, 48 (1958), 117–29

Fremerdorf, F. *Das Römische Haus mit dem Dionysos-Mosaik vor dem Südportal des Kölner Domes*, Berlin, 1956

Frere, S. 'Roman Britain in 1991', *Britania*, 23 (1992), 256–308

Friedlander, L. *Roman Life and Manners under the Early Empire*, 2, New York, 1968

Friendship, R.M. & Taylor, D.E. *Iron Age & Roman Piddington*, Interim Report for 1989–1993, Upper Nene Archaeological Society, 1994

Gabriel, M.M. *Livia's Garden Room at Prima Porta*, New York, 1955

Gell, W. *Pompeiana*, 2 vols., London, 1835

George, M. *The Roman Domestic Architecture of Northern Italy*, BAR 670, Oxford, 1997

Getty, J. Paul Museum, *The J. Paul Getty Museum guide to the villa and its gardens*, Malibu, 1992

Gibbs, S.L. *Greek and Roman Sundials*, London, 1976

Gleason, K.L. *Towards an Archaeology of Landscape Architecture in the Ancient Roman World*, Phd thesis, University of Oxford, 1989

——. 'Garden Excavations at the Herodian Winter Palace in Jericho, 1985–7', *AngloIsrael Archaeological Soc.* (1988), 21–39

——. 'Porticus Pompeiana: a new perspective on the first public park of Ancient Rome', *Journal of Garden History*, 14 (1994), 13–27

Godwin, H.E. *The History of the British Flora*, Cambridge, 1956

Gorges, J-G. *Les Villas Hispano-Romaines*, Paris, 1979

Gothein, M.L. *A History of Garden Art*, 1, trans. Archer-Hind, New York, 1966

Goudineau, C. & Y. Kisch, *Archeological Guide to Vaison-La-Romaine*, Vaison-La-Romaine, 1984

Gow, A.S.F. 'The Adoniazusae of Theocritus', *JRS*, 58 (1938), 180–204

Gracie, H.S. & E.G. Price, 'Frocester Court Roman Villa, Second Report 1968–77: the Courtyard', *Transactions of the Bristol and Gloucestershire Archaeological Society*, 97 (1979), 10–64

Gregory of Nyssa, *Nicene and Post-Nicene Fathers of the Christian Church*, 5, Gregory of Nyssa, trans. M. Moore & H.A. Wilson, Michigan, 1976

Grenier, A. *Manuel D'Archéologie Gallo-Romaine*, Paris, 1931

Grimal, P. *Les Jardins Romaines*, 2nd edn, Paris, 1969

Guillén, J.I.R. 'La villa tardorromana de "La Malena" en Azuara y el mosaico de las Bobas de Cadmo y Harmonia', *JRA*, 5 (1992), 148–61

Hallam, G.H. 'Horace's Villa at Tivoli', *JRS*, 4 (1914), 121–38

Harding, P.A. & C. Lewis, 'Archaeological

Investigations at Tockenham', *Wiltshire Archaeological Magazine*, 90 (1997), 26–41

Harvey, J. *Mediaeval Gardens*, London, 1981

Hawkes, J.G. *The History of the Rose*, Birmingham, 1995

Hemsoll, D. 'The Architecture of Nero's Golden House', in *Architecture and Architectural Sculpture in the Roman Empire*, ed. M. Henig, Oxford (1990), 10–38

Hero. *Herons Von Alexandria*, trans. W. Schmit, Leipzig, 1899

——. *The Pneumatics of Hero of Alexandria*, trans. B. Woodcroft, London, 1851

Heydenreich, L.H. & W. Lotz, *Architecture in Italy 1400 to 1600*, trans. M. Hottinger, Harmondsworth, 1974

Hill, D.K. 'Some Sculpture from Roman Domestic Gardens', in *Ancient Roman Gardens*, Washington (1981), 83–94

Hodge, A.T. *Roman Aqueducts & Water Supply*, London, 1992

Hoffmann, A. *Das Gartenstadion in der Villa Hadriana*, Mainz, 1980

Homer. *The Odyssey of Homer*, trans. R. Lattimore, New York, 1975

Horace. *Odes and Epodes*, trans. C.E. Bennett, Loeb, 1947

——. *Satires, Epistles & Ars Poetica*, trans. H.R. Fairclough, Loeb, 1961

Huelsen, C. 'Piante Inconografiche Encise in Marmo', *RM*, 5 (1890), 46–63

Hugonot, J.C. 'Ägyptische Gärten', in *Der Garten von der Antike bis zum Mittelalter*, ed. M. Carroll-Spillecke, Mainz (1992), 9–44

Hülsen, C. *Forum und Palatin*, Munich, 1926

Hunt, D. *Footprints in Cyprus*, London, 1990

Jashemski, W.F. *The Gardens of Pompeii, Herculaneum and the Villas destroyed by Vesuvius*, New Rochelle, 1979

——. *The Gardens of Pompeii*, 2, New Rochelle, 1993

——. 'The Campanian Peristyle Garden', in *Ancient Roman Gardens*, Washington (1981), 31–48

——. 'The Villas at Boscoreale and Oplontis', in *Ancient Roman Villa Gardens*, Washington (1987), 33–75

——. 'Roman Gardens in Tunisia: Preliminary Excavations in the House of Bacchus and Ariadne and in the East Temple at Thuburbo Maius', *AJA*, 99 (1995), 559–76

Jashemski, W.F. & S.P.R. Ricotti, 'Preliminary Excavations in the Gardens of Hadrian's Villa: The Canopus Area and the Piazza D'Oro', *AJA*, 96 (1992), 579–97

Johnson, A.C. *An Economic Survey of Ancient Rome*, 2, Roman Egypt, ed. T. Frank, Baltimore, 1975

Jordan, H. *Forma Urbis Romae*, Berlin, 1874

Juvenal. *Satires*, trans. G.G. Ramsay, Loeb, 1918

Kapossy, B. *Brunnenfiguren der hellenistischen und römischen Zeit*, Zurich, 1969

Karageorghis, V. 'Chronique des fouilles à Chypre en 1973', *BCH*, 98 (1974), 821–96

Keay, S.J. *Roman Spain*, BM, London, 1988

Knight, J.K. *Caerleon Roman Fortress*, Cardiff, 1994

Kramer, S.N. *History Begins at Sumer*, London, 1958

Lafon, X. 'A propos des villas de la zone de Sperlonga', *MEFRA*, 93, 1 (1981), 297–353

Lanciani, R. *Ancient and Modern Rome*, London (no date, *c.* 1924)

——. *The Ruins & Excavations of Ancient Rome*, London, 1897

Laroche, C. & H. Savay-Guerras, *Saint-Romain-En-Gal*, Guides Archeologiques de la France, 2, Paris, 1984

Lauter-Bufe, H. 'Zur Architektonischen Gartengestaltung in Pompeji und Herculaneum', in *Neue Forschungen in Pompeii*, Recklinghausen (1975), 169–80

Lavagne, H. 'Une Peinture Romaine Oubliée', *MEFRA*, 105, 2 (1993), 747–77

Lawson, J. 'The Roman Garden', *Greece & Rome*, 19 (1950), 97–105

Lee, C.G. 'Gardens and Gods: Jacopo Galli, Michelangelo's "Bacchus" and their art historical settings', PhD Thesis, Brown University, USA, 1981

LeGlay, M. 'Les Jardins à Vienne', in *Ancient Roman Gardens*, Washington (1981), 51–65

Lengyel, A. & G.T.B. Radan, *The Archaeology of Roman Pannonia*, Lexington, 1980

Leveau, P. 'Les maisons nobles be Caesarea de Maurétanie', *Antiques Africaines*, 18 (1982), 109–65

Levi, D. *Antioch Mosaic Pavements*, I, Rome, 1971

Ling, R. *Roman Painting*, Cambridge, 1991

Littlewood, A.R. 'Ancient Literary Evidence for the Pleasure Gardens of Roman Country Villas', in *Ancient Roman Villa Gardens*, Washington (1987), 9–30

Lloyd, R.B. 'Three Monumental Gardens on the Marble Plan, *AJA*, 86 (1982), 91–100

Lugli, G. *Forma Italiae Reg.I Latium et Campania*, Vol. I, Ager Pomptinus, pars prima Anxvr-Tarracina, Rome, 1926

———. *I Monvmenti Antichi di Roma E Svbvrbio*, 3, Rome, 1938

Luxorius. *Anthologia Latina*, trans. M. Rosenblum, New York, 1961

Macdonal, W.L. *The Architecture of the Roman Empire 2, An Urban Appraisal*, New Haven, 1986

Macdonald, W.L. & J. Pinto, *Hadrian's Villa and its Legacy*, London, 1995

McKay, A.G. *Houses, Villas and Palaces in the Roman World*, New York, 1975

Mackendrick, P. *Greek Stones Speak*, 2nd edn., London, 1981

———. *The Iberian Stones Speak*, New York, 1969

———. *The Mute Stones Speak*, London, 1962

———. *The North African Stones Speak*, London, 1980

Macrobius. *The Saturnalia*, trans. P.V. Davies, New York, 1969

Maiuri, B. *The National Museum*, Naples, Novara, 1959

Mallwitz, A. *Olympia und seine Bauten*, Munich, 1972

Martial. *Epigrams*, trans. W.C.A. Ker, Loeb, 1973

Meiggs, R. *Roman Ostia*, Oxford, 1960

Merrifield, R. *The Archaeology of London*, London, 1975

Moffett, L. Unpublished typescript, 'Gardening in Roman Alcester', Circaea vol. 5, no. 2, from Birmingham University (1988), 73–8

Morel, J-P. 'Chronique Rome: Le Palatin (Vigna Barberini)', *MEFRA*, 105, 1 (1993), 419–34

Moretti, G. *Il Museo Delle Navi Romane Di Nemi*, Libreria dello Stato, Itinerai no. 72, Rome, 1940

Morton, H.V. *The Fountains of Rome*, London, 1970

Murphy, P. & R.G. Scaife, 'The environmental archaeology of gardens', *Garden Archaeology*, ed. A.E. Brown, CBA Research Report 78 (1991), 83–99

Musée Du Luxembourg, *La Civilisation Romaine de la Moselle A la Sarre*, Mainz, 1983

Neudecker, R. *Die Skulpturen-Ausstattung Römischer Villen in Italien*, Mainz, 1988

Neuerberg, N. *L'Architettura delle Fontane e dei Ninfei nell'Italia Antica*, Naples, 1965

Nisard, M. *Les Agronomes Latins, Caton, Varron, Columelle, Palladius*, Paris, 1877

Ottewill, D. *The Edwardian Garden*, London, 1989

Overbeck, J. *Pompeji in seinen Gebäuden, Alterthümem und Kunstwerken*, Leipzig, 1866

Ovid. *Artis Amatoriae*, trans. J.H. Mozley, Loeb, 1979

———. *Ex Ponto*, trans. A.L. Wheeler, Loeb, 1988

———. *Fasti*, trans. J.G. Frazer, Loeb, 1976

———. *Tristia*, trans. A.L. Wheeler, Loeb, 1988

Packer, J.E. 'The Domus of Cupid and Psyche in Ancient Ostia', *AJA*, 71 (1967), 123–31

Pailler, J-M. 'A propos d'un nouvel oscillum de Bolsena', *MEFRA*, 81, 1 (1969), 627–58

Palladius, *Palladius on Husbandrie*, trans. B. Lodge, London, 1873

Paoli, U.E. *Rome: Its People Life and Customs*, Bristol, 1990

Percival, J. *The Roman Villa*, London, 1976

Petronius. *Satyricon*, trans. J.P. Sullivan, Harmondsworth, 1986

Phillips, R. & M. Rix, *The Quest for the Rose*, London, 1993

Philostratus, *Imagines*, trans. A. Fairbanks, Loeb, 1960

———. *Vita Apollonius Tyana*, 2, trans. F.C. Conybeare, Loeb, 1921

Platner, S.B. & T. Ashby, *A Topographical Dictionary of Ancient Rome*, Oxford, 1929

Pliny the Elder. *Naturalis Historiae*, trans. H. Rackham, Loeb, 1952

Pliny the Younger. *Epistles*, trans. B. Radice, Loeb, 1969

Plutarch. *Plutarch's Lives*, trans. B. Perrin, Loeb, 1948

Potter, T.W. *Towns in Late Antiquity: Iol Caesarea and its context*, Oxford, 1995

Presuhn, E. *Le Più Belle Parete di Pompéi*, Rome, 1879

Procopius, *Bellum Gothicum*, trans. O. Veh, Munich, 1978

Propertius. *Elegiarum*, trans. H.E. Butler, Loeb, 1912

Quintus Curtius Rufus. *The History of Alexander*, Harmondsworth, 1984

Ramos, R. 'La Casa Urbana Hispanoromana en Illici', in *La Casa Urbana Hispanoromana ponencias y comunicaciones*, Zaragoza, 1991, 69–78

Rea, J.R. *The Oxyrhynchus Papyri*, 46, British Academy, London, 1978

Rebuffat, R. 'Maisons à Péristyle d'Afrique du Nord, Répertoire de Plans Publiés', *MEFRA*, 81 (1969), 659–724

_____. 'Maisons à Péristyle d'Afrique du Nord, Répertoire de Plans Publiés, II', *MEFRA*, 86 (1974), 445–99

Reinach, S. *Répertoire de la Statuaire Greque et Romaine*, Paris, 1897

RICA, *Corpus Topographicum Pompeianum, The Insulae of Regions I–V*, 3A, Rome, 1986

Richardson, L. *New Topographical Dictionary of Ancient Rome*, Baltimore, 1992

——. *Pompeii: An Architectural History*, London, 1988

Richardson, R. 'Does Dark Earth = Black?', *Current Archaeology*, 130,11,10 (1992b), 439

Ricotti, E.S.P. 'The Importance of Water in Roman Garden Triclinia', in *Ancient Roman Villa Gardens*, Washington (1987), 137–84

Ridgway, B.S. 'Greek Antecedents of Garden Sculpture', in *Ancient Roman Gardens*, Washington (1981), 9–28

Rivet, A.L.F. *The Roman Villa in Britain*, London, 1970

Rossiter, J.J. 'Roman villas of the Greek east and the villa in Gregory of Nyssa Ep.20', *JRA*, 2 (1989), 101–10

Sanders, I.F. *Roman Crete*, Warminster, 1982

Schefold, K. *Vergessenes Pompeji*, Bern, 1962

Scriptores Historiae Augustae, trans. D. Magie, Loeb, 1960

Seneca. *Ad Lucilium Epistulae Morales*, trans. R.M. Gummere, Loeb, 1925

Seyffert, O. *A Dictionary of Classical Antiquites*, 4th edn, London, 1894

Sidonius Apollinaris. *Gai Sollii Apollinaris Sidonii Epistlularum*, trans. W.B. Anderson, Loeb, 1956

Singer, C. 'The Herbal in Antiquity', *JHS*, 47 (1929), 1–52

Siracusano, N. *La Villa Romana di Sirmione*, Firenze, 1969

Sisson, M.A. 'The Stoa of Hadrian at Athens', *PBSR*, 11 (1929), 50–72

Smith, A.H. *The Later Greek and Graeco-Roman Reliefs, Decorative and Architectural Sculpture in the British Museum*, London, 1904

Spinazzola, V. *Pompei alla luce degli Scavi Nuovi di Via dell'Abbondanza (anni 1910–1923)*, Rome, 1953

Statius. *Silvae*, trans. J.H. Mozley, Loeb, 1928

Strabo, *Geography*, trans. H.L. Jones, Loeb, 1923

Stronach, D. 'Parterres and stone watercourses at Pasargadae: notes on the Achaemenid contribution to garden design', *Journal of Garden History*, 14 (1994), 3–12

Suetonius, *The Twelve Caesars*, trans. R. Graves, London, 1991

Swoboda, K.M. *Römische und Romanische Pälaste*, Graz, 1969

Tacitus. *The Annals of Imperial Rome*, trans. M. Grant, Harmondsworth, 1966

Achilles Tatius, 'Leucippe and Clitophon', in *Collected Ancient Greek Novels*, ed. B.P. Reardon, London, 1989

Thébert, Y. 'Private and Public Spaces: The Components of the Domus', in *Roman Art in Context*, Englewood Cliffs, New Jersey (1993), 213–37

Theophrastus. *Enquiry into Plants*, trans. A. Hort, Loeb, 1961

Thompson, D.B. *Garden Lore of Ancient Athens*, Princeton, 1963

Tibullus. *Elegies*, trans. F.W. Cornish, Loeb, 1988

Tomei, M.A. 'Nota sui giardini antichi del Palatino', *MEFRA*, 104 (1992), 917–51

Toynbee, J.M.C. *Death and Burial in the Roman World*, London, 1982

———. *Animals in Roman Life and Art*, London, 1996

Underwood, P.A. *The Kariye Djami*, 4, London, 1975

Van Buren, A.W. 'Pliny's Laurentine Villa', *JRS*, 38 (1948), 35–6

Van Buren, A.W. & R.M. Kennedy, 'Varro's Aviary at Casinum', *JRS*, 9 (1919), 59–66

Varro. *Rerum Rusticarum*, trans. W.D. Hooper, Loeb, 1960

Vatin, C. 'Jardins et services de voirie', *BCH*, 100 (1976), 555–64

Vermeule, C.C. *Greek and Roman Sculpture in America*, California, 1981

Vetters, H. 'Grabungen 1971–72, Turkei', *Jahreshefte des Österreichischen Archäologischen Institutes in Wien*, 50 (1972–3), 32–62

Virgil. *The Eclogues the Georgics*, trans. C.D. Lewis, Oxford, 1983

———. *Minor Poems*, trans. H. Rushton Fairclough, Loeb, 1946

Vitruvius. *De Architectura*, trans. F. Granger, Loeb, 1962

———. *The Ten Books on Architecture*, trans. M.H. Morgan, New York, 1960

Wacher, J. *Roman Britain*, London, 1978

Wallace-Hadrill, A. 'The Social Structure of the Roman House', *PBSR*, 43 (1988), 43–97

Ward-Perkins, J. *Roman Imperial Architecture*, Harmondsworth, 1981

Ward-Perkins, J. et al. 'Town Houses at Ptolemais, Cyrenaica: A Summary Report of Survey and Excavation Work in 1971, 1978–1979', *Libyan Studies*, 17 (1986), 109–53

Warmington, E.H. *Remains of Old Latin*, Loeb, 1938

Watts, D.J. & C.M. Watts, 'A Roman Apartment Complex', *Scientific American*, Ancient Cities Special Issue (1994), 86–91

White, K.D. *Agricultural Implements of the Roman World*, Cambridge, 1967

Whitehouse, H. *The Dal Pozzo Copies of the Palestrina Mosaic*, Oxford, 1976

Wightman, E.M. *Gallia Belgica*, London, 1985

Wildrig, W.M. 'Land Use at the Via Gabina Villas', in *Ancient Roman Villa Gardens*, Washington (1987), 225–60

Willems, W.J.H. & L.I. Kooistra, 'De Romeinse villa te Voerendaal; opgraving 1987', *R.O.B., Archeologie in Limburg*, 327 (1988), 137–47

Williams, R.J. & R.J. Zeepvat, *Bancroft*, Bucks. Archaeological Society, Aylesbury, 1994

Wilson, R.J.A. *Piazza Armerina*, London, 1983

———. *Sicily under the Romans*, Warminster, 1990

Wiseman, D.J. 'Mesopotamian Gardens', *Anatolian Studies*, 33 (1983), 137–44

Wrede, H. *Die Spätantike Hermengalerie von Welschbillig*, Berlin, 1972

Wycherley, R.E. *How the Greeks Built Cities*, 2nd edn, London, 1976

Xenophon, *Oeconomics*, trans. E.C. Marchant, Loeb, 1923

Zeepvat, R.J. 'Fishponds in Roman Britain', *Medieval Fish, Fisheries and Fishponds in England*, ed.M.Aston, BAR, 182 (1988), 17–26

Index

Page numbers in *italics* refer to illustrations